70: The New 50

Retirement Management℠: Retaining
the Energy and Expertise
of Experienced Employees

William C. Byham, Ph.D.

DDI Press

Published by DDI Press, c/o Development Dimensions International, World Headquarters—Pittsburgh, 1225 Washington Pike, Bridgeville, PA 15017-2838.

Manufactured in the United States of America.

Library of Congress Cataloging in Publications Data
Byham, W.C.

70: the new 50
Retirement management^{SM}: retaining the energy and expertise of experienced employees/William C. Byham

1. Business   2. Retirement Management

ISBN 978-0-9761514-3-2

10   9   8   7   6   5   4   3   2

Dedication

To Robert Mentzer (age 95) and Helen Mentzer (age 94)
My Father-in-Law and Mother-in-Law

Bob and Helen, who have been married for 73 years, are living proof that 70 is truly the new 50. In fact, they might argue that 90 is the new 50! They remain physically and mentally active in a beautiful retirement facility in Florida, where they participate in the organization's governance. Besides their relatively good health and broad range of activities, which include playing duplicate bridge and singing in musical shows, they are marvels at making new friends and keeping up with the old ones, thus providing themselves with an extremely rich life. They have been mentors and heroes to generations of people who have come into contact with them— especially my wife, Carolyn; me; our children, Tacy and Carter; and our grandson, Spencer.

CONTENTS

Introduction

As a large percentage of its workforce nears retirement age, American business now has an opportunity to both save billions of dollars by effectively managing baby boomer retirements and, at the same time, offer many older boomers what they want in terms of a happy and fulfilled life in their 60s and 70s. This book tells how.

The oldest of the 76 million people who make up the baby boomer generation are reaching ages where retirement is an option. In many companies 50 percent of managers and key professionals will be eligible to retire by 2010, and 70 percent by 2015. If these and other members of the boomer generation choose to leave the workforce *en masse* over the next few years, organizations will be facing a severe loss of key leadership, knowledge, skills, and contacts. Talent is already scarce for many organizations, and the imminent boomer exodus will make it even more so. Companies will not be able to rely on the next generation to pick up the slack—the Generation X cohort following the baby boomers is one-quarter smaller and not nearly as experienced. With suitable replacements sparse, many open jobs will go unfilled for long periods or be outsourced. Recruiting and training costs will rise sharply because finding experienced candidates will be more difficult, and many new hires will require considerable time to ramp up and become productive.

Little known to most people is that, concurrent with the potential boomer retirements, three other scenarios are unfolding that will have a powerful impact on American businesses in the near term:

1. In terms of life expectancy and health, baby boomers at 70 will be like their parents and grandparents were in their 50s.

2. Full retirement is not in the cards for most baby boomers.

3. Many boomers will be able to collect pensions and still work for their career company (the organization paying their pension), which will provide an end-of-career bonus for those who stay on the job.

Let's take a closer look at each of these scenarios:

1. In terms of life expectancy and health, baby boomers at 70 will be like their parents and grandparents were in their 50s.

The projected life expectancy of a baby boomer who is 60 years old is 83.[1] For a married couple at 65, there is a greater than 50 percent chance that one spouse will live to be 90 or older.[2] Medical research consistently predicts that 75 to 80 percent of baby boomers will be healthy enough to continue working well into their 70s due to better health care and less physically demanding work.[3] Of course, boomers will experience the usual problems associated with aging: reduced strength and endurance, slower reflexes, and a decline in sensory functions. But they should be in substantially better physical shape than their parents were at the same age because they likely have taken better care of themselves. For example, research by the Ipsos MORI Social Research Institute (a large U.K. survey research organization) found that people in their 70s today are as active in sports and other outdoor activities as were people in their 50s, 30 years ago.[4]

And that's not all. For the last several decades, businesses have modified their work environments to become more physically accessible by replacing or supplementing stairs with walkways or ramps, improving lighting, and installing doors that open automatically. Also, today's computers and modern communication technologies afford older employees the opportunity to do some or all of their work from home. In addition, modern medicine has enabled older people to restore their bodies with new hips and knees and by medical treatments that keep arthritis and other ailments under control.

2. Full retirement is not in the cards for most baby boomers.

Forty-three percent of baby boomers don't have sufficient savings or pension income to retire at anything approaching the lifestyle they would like.[5] For almost all boomers, retirement income will be less secure as more organizations switch from defined benefit pension plans to 401(k) and other defined contribution plans. Even people with a seemingly secure retirement income will be asking themselves, "What if my company goes bankrupt and dumps my defined benefit plan onto the federal government, where the payouts won't be as much as I have planned for?" Because of these and other financial factors, many baby boomers will seek additional security simply by working longer.

The fear of rising health care costs and of the possible cancellation or downscaling of retirement health care plans also will force many older boomers to work longer to maintain and save money for health care coverage for their retirement.

Others want to continue working because they will miss the challenge and camaraderie of the work environment.[6] For all these reasons, between 60 and 80 percent of baby boomers say they plan to continue to work into their 60s and 70s, in either a full- or part-time position, in their career organization or elsewhere.[7]

3. Many boomers will be able to collect pensions and still work for their career company.

Currently, less than 14 percent of people working past 65 do so in their career company.[8] This lack of employee retention often has been the result of defined benefit pension plans that have forced people to leave their career companies in order to collect their pension benefits. But things are changing. People over 65 now can collect their Social Security pensions while they continue to work in any job, including their current one. Those in organizations with defined contribution plans, such as 401(k) plans, often can start drawing cash when they reach 59½ while staying in their current job. Retirement-eligible people in organizations that have amended their defined benefit plans (an option available January 1, 2007, under provisions of the Pension Protection Act) are able to collect their pensions upon reaching age 62 while they continue to work with their career employer.

People who collect their company's defined benefit pensions and Social Security benefits while they are still working will feel as if they've received a big pay increase, just in time to help them top off their personal retirement funds. Also, this 2006 law will allow more people to accept part-time employment with their career organization because they will suffer no loss of total income as Social Security and/or their company pension will make up the difference. People's view of staying full-time or part-time with their career company will change significantly.

Bottom Line: American businesses can survive and thrive during the deflation of the baby boomer bubble by retaining or rehiring select older individuals.

Of those who want to continue working, 43 percent would like to continue at their career company if arrangements can be made.[9] If boomers stay with their career company or return to it after formal retirement instead of giving up paid work altogether or taking a job with another organization, American businesses will reap many benefits. They will:

- Gain time for succession management programs to grow backups with the skills, knowledge, and experience to successfully assume higher-level or key contributor positions.

- Retain key people with critical knowledge, contacts, and experience until those assets can be shared with others or documented.

- Keep people in difficult-to-fill jobs, saving considerable capital by delaying recruitment, selection, on-boarding, and training costs.

- Meet the needs of the growing number of people who either don't want to or can't afford to retire.

There also would be important benefits realized by the U.S. government in the form of substantially reduced deficits in Social Security and Medicare.

However, organizations will be faced with some tough tasks. They will need to:

- Identify select older employees with unique skills, knowledge, and contacts, and then offer them special encouragement to either stay at or rejoin the organization.

- Create positions and working conditions that will be attractive to older workers and tailored to their needs and abilities. This means creating transition-to-retirement jobs that will give older workers more flexibility, different challenges, and other similar incentives.

- Foster a work environment that is conducive to the success, safety, and health of older workers.

- Ensure that leaders have the skills to meet older workers' special needs and to understand their unique situations.

- Deal with the under-performance of a small percentage of older workers who otherwise would have been allowed to coast to retirement under defined benefit plans. Because there soon will be no "normal retirement age," these older underachievers will have to be either remotivated or culled from the organization. Unquestionably, this will be quite difficult for most leaders and most organizations.

- Make themselves more attractive to older workers by providing benefits that will meet their special needs.

Organizations that can successfully manage baby boomer retirements in a cost-effective, legally acceptable way will wield a significant advantage over their competitors. The key to the success of these organizations will be *retirement management*^{SM}.

Retirement Management

For years, organizations have been concerned about *succession management* (i.e., growing their own backups for positions) and *retention management* (i.e., concentrating on keeping key employees at all ages and levels from moving on to other organizations), but they haven't spent much effort on doing anything about retirement-age workers, particularly trying to get select older workers to stay on the job longer. Historically, most companies have felt this was a waste of time, given the strong economic incentive to leave provided by defined benefit plans.

Retirement management is not about talking people out of retirement or starting their own business. It *is* about giving the large number of potential retirees who would like to continue contributing to their present organization's success the opportunity and the accommodations to do so. And, it's about organizations growing more successful through better utilization of their seasoned talent.

Admittedly, retirement management is a new concept; most organizations have never tried it. Because they've basked in a steady supply of replacement workers, they've often overlooked current and recently retired older workers as a valued resource. However, given the imminent demographic shifts, they no longer will have this luxury.

Why Now?

In 2000 Development Dimensions International, Inc., (DDI) published *Grow Your Own Leaders,* a book that examined the projected impact of baby boomer retirements at senior management levels and implored organizations to take immediate action to prepare an in-house cadre of individuals (known as an Acceleration Pool®) to assume the soon-to-be-vacant executive positions. The availability of a "ready to go" Acceleration Pool would keep organizations from trolling for senior leadership talent in an increasingly tight and expensive job market.

While "grow your own" remains a solid strategy—at all levels and at all times—most organizations won't be ready in time to meet the boomer retirement years. They'll need more time for this strategy to take root. I feel that companies can acquire this time by retaining certain people beyond their normal retirement age and, in some situations, by either rehiring individuals who have retired or hiring older workers from the open market.

Research Basis for *70: The New 50*

In addition to published research studies on issues related to older workers, *70: The New 50* is based on the following unique research done by DDI. (A description of this DDI research is presented at the end of this book.)

Chapter 7, which projects what baby boomers will be like as employees in their 60s and 70s, is based on a series of large-scale studies from a wide variety of U.S. organizations. In these studies DDI collected supervisor ratings of thousands of their direct reports and obtained test and questionnaire responses from more than 23,000 job incumbents and job applicants.

Chapters 8, 9, and 10, which deal with leading and managing older individuals, are based on questionnaire responses from more than 100,000 individuals throughout the United States as well as on DDI's experience in providing leadership training to more than 8 million leaders.

Chapter 11, which examines selection issues, is based on research over a 37-year period involving thousands of organizations and DDI's experience in training more than 5 million supervisors, managers, and executives in interviewing and selection skills.

In addition to this data, my associates at DDI and I interviewed more than 300 people over 60 about retirement and work issues, 20 managers with experience in leading older workers, and 50 HR managers with experience meeting the needs of older workers.[10]

A surprising finding of our interviews with executives and HR professionals was the reluctance of most organizations to go on the record about what they're doing for their older workers. They often were very proud of their efforts but reluctant to share their experiences in print. The Conference Board has experienced a similar reticence.[11] I believe this anxiety stems from the organizations' fearing that they might be breaking a law with their special efforts to help older employees work longer. Legal issues are discussed in several parts of this book. We were able to obtain data from more than 50 companies because most of the respondents were DDI clients, and we promised anonymity.

Who Will Benefit from Reading This Book?

70: The New 50 particularly focuses on the retirement of executives, managers, supervisors, and key contributors such as big-ticket salespeople, engineers, and scientists, although research data are presented that make a strong argument for hiring and retaining older, nonmanagement employees as well.

70: The New 50 is written for executives and professionals who don't want to sit back and do nothing when faced with a unique set of interrelated organizational challenges—people who want their organization to *manage* retirements rather than just accept an ongoing drain of valuable talent, knowledge, and contacts as a fact of work life.

How This Book Is Organized

SECTION I

Retirement Management: What It Is and Why It's Needed

The first three chapters make the case for retirement management. Chapter 1 gives a brief history of retirement and looks at its current state. Chapter 2 projects the future of retirement and shows why many people who are reaching retirement age either don't want to or can't afford to retire. Chapter 3 proposes my solution: retirement management. It also examines the general proposition of creating an organization that is friendly and supportive to older workers.

- Chapter 1—The Past and Present of Retirement

- Chapter 2—The Future of Retirement

- Chapter 3—Retirement Management

SECTION II

The Payoff of Retirement Management

After Chapter 4, which examines what attracts people to work past the age of 60, the next three chapters deal with the options organizations have for increasing their percentage of older people: retain or rehire select individuals and consider older people from outside the organization. Although I focus on retaining, as it is the strategy that has the biggest payoff for organizations and clearly illustrates the impact that retirement management can have, I offer practical advice in all three areas.

- Chapter 4—What Older Workers Want in a Job

- Chapter 5—Retaining Select People Beyond Normal Retirement Age

- Chapter 6—Rehiring People Who Have Retired

- Chapter 7—Recruiting and Hiring Older Workers

SECTION III

Managing Older Workers

The three chapters on leadership address the very real challenges of managing older workers, particularly as government regulations and retirement plans change to allow people to tap into their pensions while still working. Chapter 10 examines the difficult issues involved in forcing poorly performing individuals out of an organization—an issue that increasingly more organizations will face as baby boomers continue to work beyond normal retirement age.

- Chapter 8—Leadership Skills Needed to Manage Older Workers
- Chapter 9—Special Challenges in Leading Older Workers
- Chapter 10—Taking a Stand with Poor Performers

SECTION IV

Getting Retirement Management Started

In this section I move to implementing a retirement management system: systematically determining who to try to retain, rehire, or hire from outside the organization; helping current employees prepare for retirement; and setting up a retirement management system.

- Chapter 11—Selecting the Best
- Chapter 12—Helping with Retirement Planning
- Chapter 13—How to Implement a Retirement Management System

SECTION V

What the Government and Organizations Need to Do

I conclude by speculating on the impact of retirement management on the U.S. gross domestic product (GDP) and on the viability of the U.S. Social Security and Medicare programs. I also discuss how U.S. government laws and regulations need to be changed to allow all organizations to fully implement retirement management.

- Chapter 14—Retirement Management and the U.S. Government

- Chapter 15—Final Thoughts

Why This Book Is U.S. Centric

When starting to write this book, I intended to take a worldwide view— because the issues discussed are truly global. However, I soon discovered enough differences among countries to make worldwide coverage impossible. I point out, though, that the basic solutions presented in *70: The New 50* are applicable around the world. Every industrialized country must face up to a wave of retirements that will coincide with a relatively small cohort from which to draw replacements. Some countries, like Japan, are ahead of the wave, and other countries with younger workforces will experience the problem a little later; but all will feel the impact eventually.

SECTION I

RETIREMENT MANAGEMENT: WHAT IT IS AND WHY IT'S NEEDED

The first three chapters make the case for retirement management. Chapter 1 gives a brief history of retirement and looks at its current state. Chapter 2 projects the future of retirement and shows why many people who are reaching retirement age either don't want to retire or can't afford to retire. Chapter 3 proposes my solution: retirement management. It also examines the general proposition of creating an organization that is friendly and supportive to older workers.

- Chapter 1—The Past and Present of Retirement
- Chapter 2—The Future of Retirement
- Chapter 3—Retirement Management

Chapter 1

The Past and Present of Retirement

To decide among the options available to organizations in dealing with baby boomer retirements and to understand the implications of recent changes in how pensions may be distributed, one must understand how the current retirement system has developed and evolved over the last 50 years. This is particularly true relative to the shift from defined benefit to defined contribution retirement pension plans, the ability of many people to remain working in their career company while they collect their pensions, and the elimination or reduction of retiree health care benefits by many organizations.

Before 1935 most workers in America had no concept of retirement as we think of it today—that is, a stage in life relatively free of financial worries, where people can pursue their unique interests or hobbies or just "live the good life." Most people worked in jobs that required varying degrees of manual labor—such as steel workers or farmers—until they either were too sick or injured to work any longer or died. In 1880 the percentage of U.S. men remaining in the labor force beyond the age of 65 was 78 percent.[1] Middle-class professionals, such as doctors, managers, or company owners, might have had better-quality work lives, but they didn't retire either. Work was simply what adults did, and they kept working as long as they could. Of course, life expectancy was much shorter; the average person born in 1850 lived only 38 years, and only 3 percent of the population lived past 64. By 1900 average life expectancy had risen to 49 years; for those born in 1930, it reached 58 years for men and 62 for women.

In 1935 President Franklin D. Roosevelt signed the law establishing Social Security. It was designed to make the end of life easier for a population still reeling from the shock of the Great Depression and feeling the social strains associated with moving to larger cities and working in large manufacturing organizations. These people lacked the end-of-life social support that had been previously afforded by living with family on farms or in close-knit small towns. Social Security was not meant to be a retirement program; rather, it was designed as a minimum assistance program for older workers. When the government chose 65 as the target age to leave the workforce, the average American lived to be only 63, and those who were 60 could expect to live just 12 more years. Clearly, the plan had numbers on its side—Social Security benefits were to be paid out to retirees for a few years, and many more people were paying into the system than were receiving benefits from it (approximately 159 to 1).

Historically, the idea of setting a fixed date for retirement met the needs of both the U.S. government and American companies. Again, the numbers were right—in the 1930s millions of young people were trying to enter the workforce but had no job opportunities. Enticing older workers to retire freed up jobs for the up-and-coming youth of America. Organizations, particularly those in low-tech industries relying on manual or unskilled labor, had the same need: younger, stronger workers. With Social Security providing the retirement incentive, companies could swap out older workers for youthful, strapping replacements. Of course, it didn't hurt that many of these replacements could be hired at lower wages. Because management in these organizations saw each replacement employee as merely another "pair of hands," there were many advantages to hiring younger workers.

Over the years Social Security was extended to retirees' spouses, and the age at which people could elect to receive benefits (albeit a lower amount) was lowered to 62. Then, after years of wrangling over increases in Social Security benefits (particularly around election time), Congress finally pegged Social Security to the Consumer Price Index in 1975.

Defined Benefit Plans

The modern concept of retirement really began after World War II, led by the automobile workers' and steelworkers' unions. Until that time, only about 14 percent of the active U.S. workforce was covered by any company-provided pension.[2] Indeed, the only form of financial support within companies often came from benevolent workers' associations, which provided a pool of funds to help those in need.[3] Under the union-encouraged plans, the assumption was that individuals would start their career with a company at a relatively young age and stay there until they became eligible for retirement. Retiring employees then would receive a fixed income for the rest of their lives—a *defined benefit*. The amount of the pension payout was typically calculated on a person's salary history and years of service, with the last few years of employment weighted higher than the earlier years. Organizations of all sizes followed the lead of the larger corporations, and by the late 1970s, 62 percent of all workers were covered by a defined benefit retirement program of some type.

As pension plans proliferated and the amount of money paid out by them increased, new vistas opened for retirees. Suddenly, the concept of a new stage of life after work—the "golden years"—burst into the national consciousness. People of all income levels started to think about moving to a warmer climate, enjoying hobbies, pursuing education just for the fun of it, and "living the good life." Retirement communities, such as Sun City, Arizona, sprouted and aimed to provide an active, new way of life for retirees.

A critical historical feature of defined benefit plans is that individuals must completely leave their organization's employ before receiving any benefits. If employees continued to work after becoming eligible for retirement, they received no pension payments until they actually retired; if they continued to work, they had no way of recouping the pension funds they relinquished by not retiring. To most people in this situation, staying on the job was equivalent to taking a pay cut. For those who wanted to continue working, the obvious next steps were to retire from the company and begin receiving retirement benefits, and then find a job in another organization.

As one might imagine, people responded enthusiastically to the new opportunities provided by defined benefit plans: Participation in the workforce by men 65 and older dropped from 46 percent in 1950 to 28 percent in 1965, and continued to drop to 17 percent in 1999. For women over 65, the labor force figures were more stable during this same time period: 9.7 percent (1950), 10 percent (1965), and 9 percent (1999).[4]

Health Insurance for Retirees

In the 1960s companies started to provide lifelong health insurance for their retirees and their families. Later enhancements included vision, dental, and prescription drug coverage. It also became common to extend coverage to a worker's spouse after that worker had died. The original health care plans required no contributions from employees.

On July 30, 1965, President Lyndon B. Johnson signed the Medicare law as an amendment to the Social Security program. Medicare, the nation's largest health insurance program (currently covering more than 39 million people), has since provided health insurance to individuals age 65 and older, to qualifying persons under 65 with disabilities, and to people of any age suffering from permanent kidney failure. While the program offers payment for the most basic of eligible seniors' health care costs, many medical expenses are left uncovered as are the costs of long-term care. Many companies provided supplemental insurance to cover the additional health care costs to retirees.

From 1988 to 2004, the share of private sector employers with 200 or more workers that offered retirement health insurance plunged from 66 percent to 36 percent.[5] According to a report by the Employee Benefit Research Institute, in 2002 that figure was even lower: 13 percent.[6] Most of the remaining plans have required that retired employees shoulder part of the cost themselves through monthly charges and co-payments for doctor visits. Companies hoped that forcing retirees to use their own money would make them better consumers and result in lower company medical costs.

Defined Contribution and 401(k) Plans

After reaching a high-water mark in the late 1970s, the number of workers covered by defined benefit plans started to decline, while the number of people working under defined contribution and 401(k) plans began to increase.

In defined contribution plans, organizations chip in a certain amount of money each month (or year) to a retirement fund for each employee. The amount depends on the person's salary and other factors. The money is pooled and invested under the direction of trustees who have fiduciary responsibility. Each year, participants get a report on the profit or loss on their particular plan and any further contributions made by the organization or the participant. After a vesting period, defined contribution plans are portable; that is, participants can take their money with them if they leave the company. (This is in sharp contrast to defined benefit plans, which were designed to retain people through a long career and, thus, were not portable; if they changed jobs, individuals either lost their pensions completely if they were not vested or experienced significantly lower value on their vested benefits.)

The Revenue Act of 1978 established 401(k) plans, but they didn't become popular until 1981 when the Internal Revenue Service (IRS) clarified that employee contributions could be made on a pretax basis. In a typical 401(k) plan design, individuals contribute tax-deferred money for their retirement, and their employer matches those contributions according to some predetermined formula (e.g., dollar for dollar up to $4,000 per employee, per year). Choosing from a menu of investment options, individuals manage their own accounts—that is, the money they contributed along with the matching funds from the organization. Often, the investment opportunities are organized by the degree of perceived risk.

Figure 1.1 shows the change over time in the percentage of individuals covered by defined benefit and defined contribution plans.

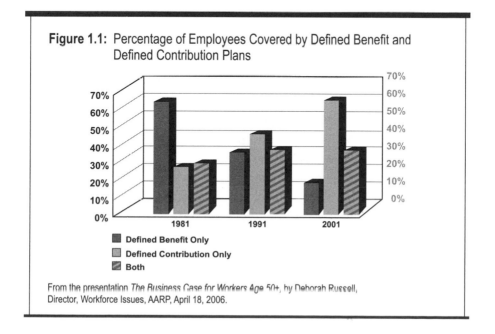

Figure 1.1: Percentage of Employees Covered by Defined Benefit and Defined Contribution Plans

■ Defined Benefit Only
□ Defined Contribution Only
▨ Both

From the presentation *The Business Case for Workers Age 50+*, by Deborah Russell, Director, Workforce Issues, AARP, April 18, 2006.

Neither 401(k) plans nor other types of defined contribution plans make any lifelong commitment to employees. Organizations contribute their share, and that's it. There are no actuarial projections of the funds required to support the retirees, no responsibility for how the investments perform, and no cost adjustments for an increase in the life span of retirees. Instead, all risks are shifted to the individuals.

> ### Retirement Risks Are Real for 401(k) Holders
>
> Enron employees lost $1 billion in their 401(k) plans, and employees at WorldCom and Kmart lost at least $100 million—all because their 401(k) plans were largely invested in their own company's stock.[7] However, even if 401(k) plans are invested in a diversified sampling of investments, those investments always are at risk of losing value, either in absolute terms or as a result of erosion caused by inflation. Not all ships ride the rising tide of stock market indices; there are always winners and losers.

Defined contribution plans, such as profit-sharing plans without 401(k) features, are substantially different in the degree of responsibility placed on the individual to participate. These types of defined contribution plans typically are provided to all covered employees without requiring them to take any action. Conversely, 401(k) plans require employees to determine their degree of participation by contributing a portion of their salary. Many organizations go to considerable lengths, including sponsoring education seminars and requiring employees to formally opt out, to encourage their employees to participate. In the end, they have a choice regarding their participation.

Upon an individual's retirement, the money in his or her 401(k) or any other type of defined contribution plan usually is dispensed to the retiree in a lump sum. Often, the amount is rolled over to an Individual Retirement Account (IRA) or to an annuity contract that will pay benefits for a stated period of time, often for the rest of the person's life. Defined contribution funds are not taxed until the retiree actually receives the money, so electing a rollover to an IRA or an annuity contract defers taxation.

There are rules restricting early withdrawals from retirement plans, including 401(k) plans, and an excise tax of 10 percent might apply. *Upon reaching 59½, the 10 percent excise tax no longer applies. Some plans permit individuals to receive a payout from their 401(k) plans at this age, even if they continue to work in the organization.* If their employment has terminated, people with retirement plans must start withdrawing their money at the age of 70½.

Legal Protection from Unfair Hiring or Dismissal Practices

Before 1967 older employees had no legal protection from age discrimination. Companies were free to dismiss them without cause or reference to performance, and it was quite common for organizations to have upper age limits for hiring. This changed with the passage of the Age Discrimination in Employment Act (ADEA) of 1967 and its associated amendments, which provide legal recourse for those 40 or older who either were not hired or were fired because of age. Related legislation, the Older Workers Benefit Protection Act of 1990, amended ADEA to prevent discrimination in employee benefits, such as health insurance.

Recent Events Affecting Retirement

A number of significant events occurred in the late 1990s and during the first decade of the 21st century that have had, and will continue to have, a profound effect on retirement:

- **Fewer workers are in the workforce to support retirees.** This fact makes some people fear for the long-term viability of Social Security and some company retirement plans. See Figure 1.2.

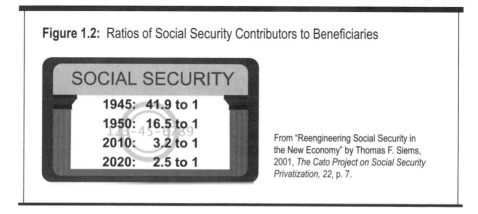

Figure 1.2: Ratios of Social Security Contributors to Beneficiaries

SOCIAL SECURITY

1945: 41.9 to 1
1950: 16.5 to 1
2010: 3.2 to 1
2020: 2.5 to 1

From "Reengineering Social Security in the New Economy" by Thomas F. Siems, 2001, *The Cato Project on Social Security Privatization*, 22, p. 7.

- **Long-term interest rates have remained historically low.** The higher the interest rates, the less an organization must contribute to meet future defined benefit plan obligations.

- **Downsizing has continued.** Organizations have viewed a fixed retirement age as an advantage in their downsizing efforts. Many have even encouraged individuals to retire earlier by giving them some type of monetary payment to fill the gap between their current age and when they would be eligible to retire under the organization's defined benefit plan.

- **The Social Security earnings test for retirees over 65 (or 67, depending on the year of birth) was eliminated.** This has allowed individuals to continue working as long and as much as they'd like while still receiving full Social Security benefits.

- **Many companies have gone bankrupt and transferred responsibility for their retirees' pensions to the federal government.** The Pension Benefit Guaranty Corporation (PBGC) is a federal corporation created by the Employee Retirement Income Security Act of 1974. It was set up to serve as an insurance plan for retirees after a few large companies, like Studebaker, went bankrupt and left their pensioners without their anticipated lifetime retirement benefits. To conserve its cash, the PBGC set limits on the amount of money a retiree of a bankrupt company can receive. In some cases this has meant that the pensions of highly paid individuals have amounted to only half as much as they would have expected to receive. Provoking even more anxiety is the prospect that, upon retirement, many workers receive only the pension benefits earned up to the time the plan folded, which can amount to a lot less than they would have received had the plan continued and the earnings and accruals increased.

When one company in an older industry, such as steel or airline, goes bankrupt and dumps its pension responsibilities on the government, it gains an advantage over its competitors. Other organizations in the same industry tend to follow suit, putting more pressure on the PBGC. In 2000 the PBGC operated with a $10 billion surplus, but that turned into a $23.3 billion deficit by 2004. It is estimated that the deficit will be much higher by the end of the decade. As Congress acts to fund the PBGC's deficit, there may be an attempt to limit the outflow of money by further restricting the benefits guaranteed. See Figure 1.3.

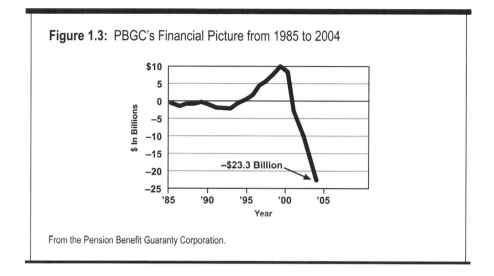

Figure 1.3: PBGC's Financial Picture from 1985 to 2004

From the Pension Benefit Guaranty Corporation.

- **It gets "colder" for retirees, as many companies freeze their defined benefit pension plans.** Employees' defined retirement benefits normally grow with each year of their service, but a pension freeze stops that growth. They are eligible to receive only the benefits they accrued before the freeze. Until 2003 most of the plans that were frozen were in small companies. After that, large organizations started doing it too—at least for their nonunion workers. Other organizations, such as DuPont, have "cooled" their defined benefit retirement plans, cutting by as much as two-thirds the rate at which current employees accrue benefits. Organizations have generally replaced their defined benefit plans with a 401(k) or other defined contribution plan (e.g., Sears, Roebuck & Company; FleetBoston Financial; Halliburton; AON; Motorola; IBM; Verizon; Lockheed Martin).

A Change of Perspective at Verizon

Nonunion employees at Verizon had their pensions frozen in June 2006 while being told that anyone with fewer than 15 years of Verizon service would not be eligible for retiree health benefits.[8] Previously, Verizon had paid 50–80 percent of health care premiums for its retired workers. This dual change will have a significant impact on the retirement planning of Verizon employees under 50.

• **In most organizations new employees have no defined benefit retirement coverage at all.** Most organizations that are freezing their defined benefit plans are eliminating them totally for their new hires—starting a long-term transition to 100 percent defined contribution benefits. Virtually all new pension plans implemented in the United States in the last 10 years have been some sort of defined contribution plan. This trend will not be unpopular with job applicants, who tend to prefer 401(k) plans over conventional defined benefit plans anyway. Because 401(k) plans are portable after a brief vesting period and can be tapped before retirement in certain special situations, they appear more tangible to applicants and are therefore more appealing. Watson Wyatt found that only 16 percent of employees under 35 said a traditional pension plan was of high importance in choosing an employer; while 64 percent said it was of little or no importance.[9] Recruiters report that applicants ask more questions about the extent of the organization's 401(k) match than about its defined benefit program.[10] I know of companies in highly competitive industries that have had 401(k) match wars with their rivals—with one company meeting or beating what the others have offered, but often by taking away benefits from other retirement programs.

- **Organizations are starting to buy out employees who have earned defined benefits.** Harbingers of the future are the few companies that are paying employees to switch to defined contribution plans. In 10 to 15 years, companies will find that less than half of their employees will have a defined benefit plan and that the value of these plans will have only a marginal effect on their retirement decisions (see sidebar below). At that point, these organizations will feel a great deal of temptation to abandon their defined benefit plans to save money in administration, accounting, and reporting costs. They are likely to decide that their greatest economic benefit could come from buying out the remaining frozen plans.

The Tipping Point for Frozen Plans

For people working in companies offering either no retirement plans or only defined contribution plans, the future is here—or almost here. For those with frozen defined benefit plans (e.g., IBM, Verizon, and the salaried employees of General Motors), the future will arrive when their frozen benefits are too small to affect their employees' work/retirement decisions. A person earning $60,000 a year who will receive only $1,000 a month from the organization's frozen defined benefit plan will be forced to make a retirement/work decision based on other factors, such as how well his or her 401(k) or other defined contribution plan is performing.

Organizations with frozen plans will soon find that employees won't consider their eligibility date for collecting retirement benefits as a major driver of their decision to continue working for their career employer or to leave it. Instead, it will be only one of several considerations to ponder.

Because most defined benefit plans emphasize the final years of employment in calculating yearly pensions, the tipping point relative to the importance of defined benefit plans in making a retirement decision will come sooner than organizations might expect—somewhere between 5 and 10 years after a benefit freeze. In other words, people retiring 5 to 10 years after a freeze will start to act like individuals with defined contribution plans.

- **Organizations must fully account for pension liabilities in financial statements.** New regulations of the Financial Accounting Standards Board require companies to include the funding status of pension plans on their balance sheets. These new accounting rules make defined benefit plans much less attractive to organizations.

- **The Pension Protection Act of 2006 has attempted to slow or even stop the trend of companies' freezing or eliminating defined benefit plans.** The stated objective of the Pension Protection Act (PPA) was to encourage organizations to retain their defined benefit plans while securing the financial viability of their existing plans. Throughout the Act's 900+ pages, Congress tried to do both but may have inadvertently pushed more organizations toward abandoning those plans (e.g., by increasing the cost of payments to the Pension Benefit Guaranty Corporation and other costs of maintaining a defined benefit plan). Increasingly, organizations with sound plans will find themselves assuming more of the costs of other organizations' poorly funded plans. In reviewing the long-term implications of the PPA on the PBGC, Jonathan Rose and Ryan Liebl, who authored an article in the *Employee Benefit Plan Review*, say, "Industry analysts seem to share the view that the new measures will only hasten the decline of the system (defined benefit plans)." They quote the President of the American Benefits Council and others who agree with them.[11]

- **Employers have attempted to reduce their health care costs by either cutting or ending coverage for their employees and retirees.** In 2006 GM, saddled with health care costs for current workers and retirees of nearly $5.6 billion a year (which works out to $1,100 to $1,500 per manufactured car), persuaded the United Automobile Workers (UAW) to have union employees and retirees start paying part of their health costs.[12] GM's action reflects what more and more companies have been doing to keep their escalating health care costs in check—decreasing expenses by increasing how much their employees must contribute or co-pay into their benefit plans. Many organizations have completely eliminated their retiree health care coverage for newly hired and younger employees. According to a 2005 Mercer Human Resource Consulting study, only 21 percent of organizations offer retiree health benefits—down from 40 percent in 1993.[13] In July 2006 *BusinessWeek* reported that the Accounting Standards Board is likely to require companies to put their retiree health care liabilities on their balance sheet, a step that could shrink shareholders' equity by as much as 9 percent.[14] This may well force more organizations to give up retiree health care plans.

Factors That Lead Older Workers to Continue Working or Retire

Various laws and programs have been put into place that also have had an impact on people's decisions to retire or keep working.

Table 1.1 summarizes the factors that currently encourage individuals to continue working into their 60s and 70s and the factors that discourage such actions.

Table 1.1: How U.S. Laws and Company Programs Encourage and Discourage People to Continue Working in Their 60s and 70s	
Encourage Continued Work	**Discourage Continued Work**
• Social Security payments can be collected at age 65½ whether or not the person is working. The age rises to 67 for people born after 1959.	• Reduced Social Security benefits are available at age 62, but only if a person stays under established earning limits. In 2002, 56.1 percent of eligible individuals elected to start benefits early.
• Medicare Part A (hospital insurance) starts at 65 without regard to work status.	• Medicare Part B (medical insurance) and Part D (prescription drug coverage) are secondary to the health insurance plan offered by the employer or union or under COBRA (unless benefits are less). Working people don't get extra benefits from their tax dollars going to these areas. It seems like a takeaway to them. • Medicare Parts A and D encourage retirement because they provide medical help for those who don't take their health plans with them when they retire.

Table 1.1 (cont'd): How U.S. Laws and Company Programs Encourage and Discourage People to Continue Working in Their 60s and 70s	
Encourage Continued Work	**Discourage Continued Work**
• As the age of eligibility for full retirement rises under Social Security, many people may refrain from retiring because they want to work until they can collect their full benefits. Also, the new age targets (e.g., 67) automatically create a target retirement date for many people.	
• Fear that Medicare, Medicaid, and company retirement health care plans will not adequately cover medical expenses.	• Expectation that Medicare and the company plan will cover health care costs. • Expectation that Medicare will be enriched (e.g., addition of prescription drug coverage).
• Fear that medical expenses not covered by insurance will have a negative effect on a person's lifestyle during retirement.	• Availability of Medicaid as a last resort. Medicaid is a state-administered program whose guidelines regarding eligibility are set by each state. It is available to certain low-income individuals and families who fit into an eligibility group that is recognized by federal and state law. Payment is directly to the health care provider. Some states require the individual to pay a small part of the cost for some services.
• 401(k) and other types of defined contribution plans allow employees who are 59½ to start withdrawing funds without incurring a penalty or having to retire from the organization.	

It must be noted that less than 50 percent of the U.S. labor force (private and public) has *any* type of employer-provided retirement plan.[15] For those individuals, government programs are critically important.

The End of the Golden Era of Retirement

Future historians undoubtedly will look back on the last 40 years of the 20th century and the first 10 years of the 21st century as the "golden era of retirement." To them, it will be clear that more people from all walks of life were able to retire comfortably—with livable incomes and adequate health care coverage—than ever before (and ever after). Young baby boomers and Generation Xers will view this period—particularly their parents' retirement lives—and think about what they missed out on. And they'll take a hard look at what they had to pay for—*directly*, in taxes and retirement plan contributions, and *indirectly*, in lower salaries because of their organization's obligations to support its pensioners' retirements. The post-baby boomers will be very envious—perhaps even a little resentful—and most importantly, very discouraged about their own retirement prospects.

Chapter 2

The Future
of Retirement

Baby boomers are not going to retire *en masse* at age 55, 60, or 65. As discussed in the Introduction, most boomers will be healthy enough to continue working if they want to, and many will want to keep working well into their 70s in full- or part-time positions, either with their career company or with other organizations. There are three very valid reasons for this:

- Companies need baby boomers to continue working.

- Most baby boomers don't want to—or can't afford to—stop working in their 50s or 60s.

- Many more employees in their 60s will be able to collect their pension while working for their career employer and thus move more easily—and on their own timetable—toward retirement.

This chapter examines each reason in detail.

Companies Need Baby Boomers to Continue Working

U.S. organizations need their baby boomers to stay at their jobs into their older years because:

- **An impending labor shortage will fuel the competition for talent.** As more and more baby boomers retire, the United States will experience a workforce shortage. As Figure 2.1 depicts, the Generation X cohort that is following the baby boomers is substantially smaller than the retiring boomer generation. In addition, downsizing in some companies has hit Generation X disproportionately hard. Having fewer skilled and experienced workers to support baby boomer retirements is bound to have a serious impact on organizations' staffing activities. Most organizations will be challenged to fill a large number of technical, professional, and managerial positions in a relatively short period of time; most are not prepared for the task.[1]

Likely, there will be competition among companies for skilled older workers as organizations attempt to replace what they've lost from their workforces in terms of skills, experience, industry knowledge, and contacts. Executive recruiters will lure increasing numbers of select older individuals away from their career companies to fill talent gaps in other companies, thus exacerbating the personnel shortages of the organizations already losing people.

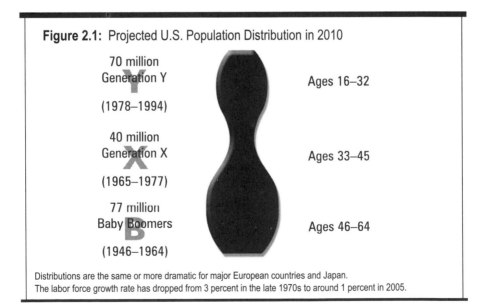

Figure 2.1: Projected U.S. Population Distribution in 2010

70 million
Generation Y
(1978–1994)

Ages 16–32

40 million
Generation X
(1965–1977)

Ages 33–45

77 million
Baby Boomers
(1946–1964)

Ages 46–64

Distributions are the same or more dramatic for major European countries and Japan.
The labor force growth rate has dropped from 3 percent in the late 1970s to around 1 percent in 2005.

- **Many organizations don't have backups for retiring executives and key professionals.** Numerous surveys have pointed out the perilous situation many organizations will face as baby boomers retire.[2] It will be quite common for companies to find that 50 percent or more of their senior executives and key performers will have retired by 2012. Most organizations simply are not ready for a leadership exodus of that scope; they haven't groomed replacements yet. In my 2002 book *Grow Your Own Leaders* (co-authored with Audrey Smith and Matthew Paese), I gave advice about how to rectify that situation by developing backups for senior leadership positions. However, I also acknowledged that it will take time for people to accumulate the range of experience necessary to prepare them for a move into senior management. Often, that time can be gained only by persuading certain executives and professionals to stay longer in their jobs.

- **Most organizations don't have systems to capture important organizational knowledge and contacts that might walk out the door.** If organizations don't take preventive action, their impending boomer retirements will drain important skills, contacts, and even vital organizational knowledge (e.g., why and how things were built or decisions were made, how systems operate). This is already happening at some organizations as a consequence of past downsizing and other circumstances. Unfortunately, two-thirds of companies don't have a system in place to capture their vital knowledge before it is lost.[3] Keeping individuals with such knowledge or contacts on the job for a few more years would afford organizations time to systematically tap what they know and to transfer their contacts.

The postponement of retirement by select individuals will go a long way toward alleviating workforce shortages. This will give organizations a few more years to grow people into jobs and allow them to cast a wider net for outside talent. It also will be a means of keeping valuable contacts and product knowledge away from competitors.

Most Baby Boomers Don't Want to—or Can't Afford to—Stop Working in Their 50s or 60s

As mentioned in the Introduction, a variety of research studies have shown that between 60 and 80 percent of people reaching retirement age (55–65) prefer to continue working, although often with reduced hours, a more flexible schedule, less travel, and changed responsibilities.[4] (See Figure 2.2 below.)

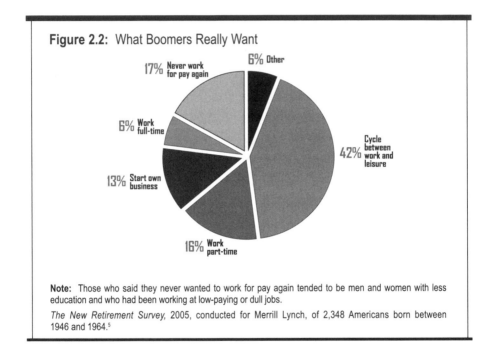

Figure 2.2: What Boomers Really Want

17% Never work for pay again

6% Other

6% Work full-time

Cycle between work and leisure 42%

13% Start own business

16% Work part-time

Note: Those who said they never wanted to work for pay again tended to be men and women with less education and who had been working at low-paying or dull jobs.

The New Retirement Survey, 2005, conducted for Merrill Lynch, of 2,348 Americans born between 1946 and 1964.[5]

According to surveys, people want to continue working because they:

- **Like the camaraderie and structure of the workplace and their business contacts.** In a 2002 Conference Board survey of exempt and nonexempt employees age 50 and above, 54 percent of the 1,645 respondents said they wanted to keep active and thought they would, upon retirement, miss the structure and focus of their daily routine.[6] They felt that being with younger people helps keep them young. Others cite their contact with clients, customers, and vendors as a reason for staying on the job.

- **Like working.** A 2002 AARP survey found that 84 percent of respondents (ages 45–74) said they would work even if they were financially set for life,[7] while a 2007 DDI study of 50- to 65-year-olds found that 35 percent said that enjoying their job is their top motivation not to retire.[8]

- **Enjoy the status and the lifestyle provided by an interesting, prestigious job and job success.** Many managers and professionals don't look forward to answering the question, "What do you do?" with "I'm retired." They wonder what they will talk about in social situations.[9]

- **Need money to finance their retirement.** About half of the baby boomers will approach retirement with no company-sponsored pension plan. They will have to rely on Social Security and their personal savings. Unfortunately, boomers are generally not very good savers, so they won't bring much in personal savings to their retirement. According to former Secretary of the Treasury Pete Peterson, in 1992 Americans were saving about 8 percent of their disposable income; by 2006, the savings rate had dropped to –1 percent. In addition, the average family has 13 credit cards and more than $9,000 in credit card debt. Contrast those figures with the personal savings rate in China, which is 32 percent.[10]

Survey Results of Middle-Income Americans for *PARADE* Magazine[11]

> 66% say they tend to live from paycheck to paycheck.

> 47% say that no matter how hard they work, they cannot get ahead.

> Nearly 83% say that there is not much money left to save after they have paid the bills.

A 2005 ABC News/*USA Today* poll surveying people's retirement anxieties found that 69 percent of older workers responding cited "running out of money" as a top concern.[12] Naturally, this was more of a concern for lower-earning people (under $35,000 a year), who worry more about survival, than of people with higher incomes (earning $100,000 or more), who tend to worry about having enough money to sustain the quality of life they would like in their retirement. Regarding their preparation for retirement, 64 percent of respondents said they would like to put a few more years of personal and organizational contributions into their retirement account. According to the 2005 Retirement Confidence Survey by the Employee Benefit Research Institute, more than 50 percent of workers feel they are behind schedule in saving for retirement, and 32 percent rated themselves as "a lot behind schedule."[13]

The need to meet family obligations is another reason people require more money for retirement. A surprising number of people in their 60s have second or third families with young children they need to put through college. They want to give their young children the same advantages (e.g., graduate school) that they provided their older children. Others are supporting grandchildren after the marriage breakup of one or more of their children. Also, many boomers are supporting their aging parents or helping with their high health care costs.

- **Are concerned about health care costs.** Employer-subsidized retirement medical coverage is a deciding factor in encouraging or dissuading people from continuing to work.[14]

  - Even people who expect to enjoy a relatively rich retirement income still worry about medical coverage. They worry about how long their health coverage will last. Organizations that are dropping their defined benefit programs also are dropping their retiree medical coverage costs. Although the federal government, under the auspices of the Pension Benefit Guaranty Corporation (PBGC), provides a continuation of pension plans (albeit usually at a somewhat lower amount), it does not guarantee the continuation of medical plans. This can be a shock to people who already have high medical costs or who just worry about them. People considering retirement know that after age 65 they will be supported by Medicare and, if they have severe financial problems, by Medicaid, but most think that won't be enough protection. They want supplemental coverage. A 2004 study estimated that by 2030 the percentage of after-tax income spent on health care will approximately double for older married couples and singles.[15]

— The social contract that many potential retirees felt they had with their employer is being broken in many cases by unexpected changes in retiree medical plans. As potential retirees see these changes, their anxiety about retirement rises. This pushes them to either consider working for a few more years to retain full medical insurance or to take another job that will provide medical coverage after their formal retirement from their career employer. Ongoing health insurance coverage—even at an increased deductible—from a current employer is usually easier to obtain than coverage from a new employer. Many part-time jobs that are open to retirees do not offer medical coverage; thus, the need for health coverage is a strong motivator to continue working for their current organization.

The "High Anxiety" Era of Retirement

Based on the factors noted above, one can anticipate a dramatic rise in the anxiety levels of baby boomers who are thinking about retirement or who are in retirement as:

- Individuals must decide for themselves when to retire. No longer will a defined benefit plan give them a date. A 2005 study cited by *The New York Times* found that 23 percent of older respondents don't expect to retire until they are at least 70, if at all. This is up from 15 percent just five years before.[16]

- The responsibility for financing retirement shifts to individuals. People have to decide how much to contribute to their 401(k) plans and how to invest that money as well as their funds in Individual Retirement Accounts (IRAs). There will be a great deal of uncertainty caused by the vagaries of the stock market, inflation, and other shifting economic factors. Individuals with defined benefits must worry about their company dumping or freezing their retirement plan.

- Life insurance options are proliferating and becoming more complex. Many are sold as a savings tool for retirement. People approaching retirement are finding it very difficult to know what to do.

- Health care costs continue to rise. People will have growing concerns about how much personal health insurance coverage will be enough. For most people, 65 will become the minimum target retirement age because it is the age they can look to Medicare for help with health care costs. Personal responsibility also will increase as organizations start to offer health savings accounts—sort of a 401(k) plan for medical bills. As medical costs rise, potential retirees' concerns about medical insurance coverage increase in kind.

- There will be a broad range of job opportunities for individuals in their 60s and 70s inside their career organization as well as in other organizations, including starting one's own company. Individuals might have to make two or three career moves after age 60 to obtain their desired combination of work and lifestyle. These are highly stressful decisions that most people didn't think they would have to make.

- They face potentially large expenditures to support their aging parents and their children who either never left the nest or are pursuing extended, advanced educations.

Baby boomers at all organizational levels and at all income levels will be very concerned about their future—particularly relative to health care costs. Average people will worry about eking out a living. Well-to-do people will worry about maintaining their lifestyle and having enough wealth for their children. But, almost everyone will worry! And this anxiety will make the option of continuing to work much more appealing.

Many More Employees in Their 60s Will Be Able to Collect Their Pension While Working for Their Career Employer and Thus Move More Easily—and on Their Own Timetable— Toward Retirement

While the U.S. federal government has been slowly moving toward encouraging people to work past 60 (e.g., allowing individuals who have reached full retirement age to collect Social Security benefits regardless of the amount of money they've earned, and permitting workers to tap their 401[k] savings at 59½ while continuing to work for their career or any employer), the big obstacle has been a government-mandated feature of almost all defined benefit plans that has forced eligible individuals who want to collect their pension to quit their career employer. Originally, the IRS regulations were designed to move older people out of jobs to make room for younger people coming up behind them. These rules were introduced at a time when the generation following the retirees was much larger than the retiree population—a situation that is contrary to what we have today. If older employees continued to work beyond their company's defined retirement eligibility age, they were not permitted to receive any pension payments until they retired. Continued work, then, amounted to lost pension funds that could never be recouped. Since January 1, 2007, it's been possible for companies to amend their plans so that employees who continue working past their retirement eligibility (and who are 62 or older) will get what will seem like a big bonus: They can collect their regular work pay while also receiving their pension funds. This extra money will be particularly appreciated by individuals who have calculated their retirement expenses and found that they don't have enough money to support themselves in the way they would like. Because of the amendment to company plans, people can continue working and bank the money from their pension for later use, while also retaining the benefits of the organization's health plan.

In addition, the freedom to receive retirement benefits and continue working for a career employer will make part-time, transition-to-retirement positions much more attractive. Older employees will be able to work 50 percent of the time with no loss in monthly income because their pension payout will compensate for their salary loss. This opportunity, coupled with the chance to stay on the organization's health plan, will be a very desirable alternative to many people.

Given this opportunity, it's a good bet that many people working for organizations with defined benefit plans will jump at the chance to stay with their current company. It won't take many people to make a big difference; in 2005 only 2 or 3 percent of people retiring under defined benefit plans remained with their career company. With the new government rules, that number may, in the next 10 years, rise to as high as 10 or 15 percent.

No one knows how quickly companies with defined benefit plans will amend their plans to allow their employees to work and receive pension benefits at the same time. (See the discussion in Chapter 3.)

Two Kinds of Defined Benefit Plans

To differentiate traditional defined benefit plans from those that have been amended to allow people to collect pension payments at age 62 while they continue working, the following definitions will be used in this book:

> *Conventional plans* are those defined benefit plans that have not been amended; that is, they contain no provisions for people to receive their pension while working.

> *Amended plans* are those defined benefit plans that allow an option for a pension payment at 62 while the employee continues to work for the company paying the pension.

Staying with a Career Company Makes Good Sense for Many Boomers

Many boomers are neither economically nor psychologically ready for retirement, and most are physically able to continue working. These realities, coupled with expected shortages of skilled and experienced people in the workforce, all but guarantee that a sizeable contingent of baby boomers will work well into their 60s and even their 70s. For many, their career company will offer the best deal they can get for such continued employment. They know the organization, its products and services, the management, their coworkers, and their probable responsibilities. They have a much better feel for what's ahead of them for the next 5 to 10 years than they would at another organization. But most of all, it will be hard for boomers to find jobs that pay more and have equal or better health care benefits.

A Sharp Rise in Anxiety Among Employers

- Many of the old certainties about retirement are vanishing. People once retired when they reached a fixed age determined by their organization's defined benefit plan, and managers would base their business planning on that. In the future, retirement dates will be more flexible and largely determined by the potential retiree. Some people will leave in their 50s; others, in their 70s. Organizations will be challenged to keep pace and will operate with some uncertainty regarding their employees' retirement plans.

- Organizations will be forced to compete to keep their best people, and to do so, they will need to be much more flexible and creative. To compete successfully, they will need to create transition-to-retirement jobs that are unique to individuals and thus are outside the organization's traditional list of job titles and responsibilities. These jobs will allow people to progressively downscale their duties and work conditions to fit changes in their needs and responsibilities (see Chapter 4).

- Companies will no longer be able to think of retirement as the end of their relationship with their employees. It will be quite common for people to retire—go off to travel or indulge in their hobbies—then, after a year or two, come back to work. And some might repeat this cycle several times.

- Leadership skills will be tested as companies strive to keep their best people and deal with other older workers displaying performance or work habit problems on the job.

Summary

Along with the increased anxiety on the part of both employees and employers will come new opportunities to change how people in their 60s and 70s do their work. No longer will retirement be a fixed event; rather, people will move into a period where they make a transition into retirement at their own pace and according to their own needs. People working for organizations with defined benefit plans will have the possibility of staying with their career company if they wish to, thus opening up a whole variety of flexible work options.

This book is intended to help organizations through this period of anxiety and opportunity by detailing a sound program for dealing with older workers—a program we call retirement management[SM].

In the Government Sector, It's Out the Retirement Door

From many points of view, city, state, and federal government retirees are in much better shape than those in the private sector. Most have retained their defined benefit plans, and many have excellent health plans that often include dental and eye care. Thus, there is very little incentive for government employees to stay on the job beyond the age of their retirement eligibility.

The downside of generous government plans is the issue of how these benefits will be funded in the future, with many such plans now being deeply in debt. Just as businesses must accurately account for the long-term costs of their pension and health care liabilities, the city, state, and federal governments soon will have to do the same. Taxpayers should expect quite a shock.[17]

Chapter 3

Retirement Management

When organizations intentionally attempt to do something about retirements (rather than passively accept them as inevitable), they are practicing retirement management. For the purposes of this book, I define retirement management[SM] as "a proactive business strategy aimed at retaining, rehiring, or hiring from the general population a select group of older individuals who have been identified as needed for organizational success and who want to continue working." Retirement management is the optimization of human resource efforts to encourage select older individuals to continue working in an organization instead of retiring or leaving to join another company. It is *not* about talking people out of retirement; rather, its goal is to provide the job and leadership characteristics desired by people who want to continue working or who want to return to work.

To better understand the concept, consider its outcomes. An effective retirement management program:

- Retains important knowledge and contacts within the organization.

- Keeps positions filled until backups are prepared to step into them.

- Staffs hard-to-fill positions with capable older workers.

- Reduces the costs of recruitment, selection, and training by delaying the need to hire replacements.

- Meets older workers' personal and financial needs.

- Helps preserve the financial viability of Social Security and Medicare.

Retirement Management Is Part of a Talent Management Initiative

Retirement management is part of a bigger system that can best be labeled *talent management.* As depicted in Figure 3.1, talent management, in its broadest sense, comprises seven subsystems:

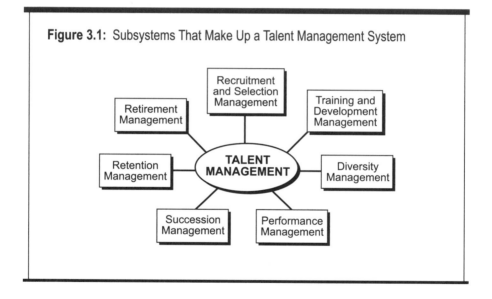

Figure 3.1: Subsystems That Make Up a Talent Management System

All these subsystems work together in an effective talent management system built to support the organization's business strategy. Organizations attempt to manage employee turnover through *retention management.* They enact procedures to identify people at risk of leaving the company, and then follow through with appropriate actions to minimize the number of high-quality people who go out the door. Increasing compensation, giving special attention from higher management, assigning a new job or responsibility, changing bosses, and allowing people to work from home all are possible strategies designed to encourage key talent to stay. Retention management is comparable to retirement management, except that the focus in the latter is on older people who might be ready to leave through the retirement door.

Retirement Management Is Largely Overlooked

All the talent management subsystems shown in Figure 3.1 are widely recognized as legitimate strategies, except for retirement management. Very few organizations have an explicit retirement management program, and most are not even thinking about the possibility. In a 2003 survey aimed at issues regarding older workers, the Society for Human Resource Management (SHRM) asked respondents if their particular organization had made any special provisions specifically designed to address the needs of older workers; 71 percent answered no.[1] This lack of concern about retirement management is very different from typical organizations' concerns about the difficulties they will have filling open management positions when the baby boomers retire. In response, they are implementing programs to identify and rapidly accelerate the development of people to fill these vacancies. This interest in succession management holds true in organizations throughout the world. A major purpose of this book is to raise the level of concern about retirement management to the same level as succession management. Then, by using succession management, retention management, and retirement management together, organizations will be able to handle the challenges stemming from the impending baby boomer retirements.

Retirement Management Decision Making

Retirement management should operate at two levels in an organization: at the senior management level for the overall organization and at the individual leader level for each direct report.

Top Management's Role

Top management's role in retirement management decisions is similar to its role in succession and retention management. In fact, tasks associated with all three roles can be carried out during the same talent review committee meeting. (There are many other names for these meetings, including pipeline review meetings, bench strength reviews, high-potential reviews, succession planning meetings, people planning, leadership bench reviews, succession reviews, and strategic talent review meetings.) There might be one talent review committee for the entire organization, or in bigger companies, committees might be in place for large units or divisions. The CEO and/or the COO and their immediate reports usually make up the main committee.

To fulfill its retirement management responsibilities, the talent review committee examines collected information on possible candidates and decides on appropriate actions. The time spent on retirement management decisions depends on the size of the organization, how many potential retirees are considered especially important to the organization's success, and the competition for talent in the employment sector in which the organization operates. (More on these meetings in Chapter 13.)

The Leader's Role

For potential retirees who don't fall under the purview of top management in its talent review committee meetings, retirement management responsibility usually falls on the immediate leader who: 1) ascertains people's retirement plans, 2) decides whom to keep, and 3) develops a strategy to retain those individuals. However, sometimes it's more appropriate for the manager above the immediate leader to handle these responsibilities. The higher-level manager is more able to see the bigger picture of the organization's direction and therefore knows what knowledge, skills, and contacts will be needed. Sometimes, lower-level leaders who are pressured by budget cuts can make short-term decisions that could have a highly detrimental effect in the long run. For example, the immediate leader might decide to let certain people retire for a small, short-term impact on the budget, but this decision might have a potentially large long-run impact in terms of lost knowledge or contacts. (The role of immediate and second-level leaders is covered in Chapter 9.)

The role of a human resource department in dealing with individuals deemed to be a retirement risk is discussed in Chapter 13.

Employment Options Open to People Considering Retirement

Having no job:

> Pursuing hobbies (e.g., fishing, gardening, golfing, traveling), enjoying family, spending time with grandchildren, or helping others through volunteer work.

Retaining the same job in the organization (need the money, love the job):

> Full-time—perhaps with less pressure (e.g., not as many committees, less travel).

> Part-time—better balance of life and work; more work and time flexibility.

> Sometime—short-duration projects (e.g., meeting seasonal needs for a tax accountant).

Finding a new job in the organization:

> Full-time—something new; using different strengths or taking on fresh challenges.

> Part-time—special projects (e.g., installing a new computer system).

> Sometime—project assignment; gaining more control over time; more time for other activities.

Finding a new job in a different organization:

> Full-time—something new; use different strengths.

> Part-time—something new; use different strengths; better work options or benefits.

> Sometime—special project (e.g., running an organization until a replacement is found).

Is Retirement Management Legal?

Concern about the legality of retirement management prescriptions to meet individuals' specific needs (e.g., part-time employment, job sharing, unique working hours, new job assignments) is the single biggest obstacle preventing organizations from adopting a retirement management strategy. It also accounts for the reluctance of many companies to talk on the record about what they're doing for their older workers.

Let's look at the pertinent laws and regulations that are causing this organizational heartburn:

Employee Retirement Income Security Act

The Employee Retirement Income Security Act (ERISA) states that organizations must treat employees uniformly relative to pension benefits. These rules seem to make it difficult to selectively retain some individuals and not others. The legality of customizing transition-to-retirement positions rests on this argument: Organizations are creating new jobs (transition-to-retirement jobs), so they have the right to decide how many jobs to create and who gets them. This is covered in Chapter 5.

The ERISA, the Age Discrimination in Employment Act (ADEA), and their applicable regulations were written when there was great interest in shielding older workers from inadvertent or planned discrimination. Lawmakers didn't give much thought to situations in which an organization would turn the tables and offer special, highly attractive benefits to older workers but not to their younger colleagues.

Age Discrimination in Employment Act

The ADEA requires either that employee benefits be uniform or that the cost of benefits be uniform. This comes into play particularly when organizations want to employ people in transition-to-retirement jobs but ask them to assume a higher percentage of their health care costs than they had paid when they were full-time employees. There also are state mandates to be considered. The rationale presented in Chapter 5 is that the organization is getting less work for its investment in health care coverage.

Equal Employment Opportunity Act

Age discrimination cases account for roughly 20 percent of all cases filed with the Equal Employment Opportunity Commission.[2] The law promotes equal employment opportunities for American workers over 40. There also are state laws that deal with age discrimination. Many organizations fear that, if they offer unique jobs to older workers, they will be charged with reverse discrimination under the Equal Employment Opportunity Act. I believe this anxiety is the overriding obstacle blocking their implementation of retirement management.

Supreme Court: No Such Thing as Reverse Age Discrimination

According to the U.S. Supreme Court, there's no such thing as reverse discrimination in age cases. In a 2004 ruling (General Dynamics Land Systems, Inc., v. Cline, 540US581), the Supreme Court found that the idea of reverse discrimination under the ADEA was "clearly wrong," stating that, "if Congress had been worrying about protecting the younger against the older, it would not likely have ignored everyone under 40."[3]

However, companies should consult their attorneys regarding whether their state's age discrimination laws prohibit reverse age discrimination.

Pension Protection Act of 2006

The Pension Protection Act (PPA), passed in August 2006, attempted to correct outdated pension rules to:

- Ensure that employers properly and adequately fund their worker pension plans.

- Ensure that employers and unions don't make promises to workers they know cannot be kept regarding pensions.

- Adjust premiums paid by employers to the Pension Benefit Guaranty Corporation (PBGC) to ensure its viability.

- Allow cash-balance pension plans.

- Improve the transparency in pension systems' funding.

- Provide workers with meaningful disclosures about the status of their pension plans.

- Modernize the defined contribution laws to encourage greater personal and retirement savings.

- Encourage automatic enrollment in defined contribution plans, such as 401(k) plans.

- Enhance retirement savings in individual retirement accounts (IRAs) and pension plans.

- Encourage savings for health care and long-term care.

A minor portion of the Pension Protection Act's 900+ pages, but a very important one for retirement management, was an amendment to the Employee Retirement Income Security Act of 1974 and the Internal Revenue Code of 1986. It states that defined benefit pension plans *can provide* in-service distribution for retirement-eligible participants who are 62 or older. In other words, the amendment enables older workers in companies with amended plans to take part-time jobs and receive pension benefits to maintain their current earning level, and it allows full-time older employees to increase their savings to prepare for their later retirement.

Many issues under the Pension Protection Act have yet to be clarified, particularly whether some organizations are permitted to offer retirement payments earlier then 62 (e.g., under an organization's defined benefit plan, an individual might be eligible for retirement at age 60). The IRS is expected to promulgate regulations that will clarify what organizations must do to amend their plans and to provide further guidance on implementing the intent of this act.

Why Organizations Should Amend Their Defined Benefit Plans to Allow Payments to Their Employees Who Continue Working

If organizations with defined benefit plans buy into the idea of retaining select people in their 60s and 70s, then the benefits of amending their plans to allow pension payments while these employees are still working for them should be obvious. Just look at the math: The cost of a person's retirement pension is the same if he or she leaves or stays with the organization. If the company has a retirement health care plan, then those costs would be eliminated because the individual would be on its health care plan as an employee (if the person was not retained, then someone else in the position would be covered by the health care plan). The only real costs are the increased health care, salary, and benefits related to employing older workers (see Chapter 7). But these should be outweighed by the higher productivity and better work habits of the older workers. Remember, those people who are retained were selected because of their ability to make a unique contribution that most other people couldn't make.

In talking with executives about the opportunity to amend their defined benefit plans, the only downside I've heard is the concern that underperforming individuals will want to continue their employment as well. In other words, because organizations are afraid to face up to and deal with their poor performers, they are willing to miss the opportunity to tap into this rich source of experience, ideas, and wisdom.

Two Cautions

Throughout this book I offer my suggestions and rationale about implementing various aspects of retirement management as well as point out gray legal areas. Note, however, that I provide two cautions:

- The fact that large, prestigious companies are taking the actions I describe here to retain and rehire older workers is no guarantee that their practices are legal.

- I am not providing legal advice or intending to create an attorney-client relationship in this book. I am merely providing information about the existence of and general nature of certain laws that should be considered in implementing a retirement management process. I strongly recommend that an organization check with its own legal counsel before taking action relative to implementing retirement management practices.

Is Retirement Management Right for Your Organization?

Before an organization's management team considers implementing a retirement management system, they first must understand that there is something to manage—that people have many unique needs and desires relative to their final working years and that the organization has options relative to how older workers are handled. The next chapter describes what organizations must provide to attract or retain older workers. Chapters 5, 6, and 7 examine the three options open to management relative to an aging workforce: retaining workers, rehiring workers who have left, and hiring new, older workers.

Once organizations realize that retirement management is possible, legal, and what their employees want and that it will benefit both the company and its employees, then they will be ready to start implementing the process. Chapter 13 deals with starting a retirement management system.

Section II

The Payoff of Retirement Management

After Chapter 4, which examines what attracts people to work past the age of 60, the next three chapters deal with the options organizations have for increasing their percentage of older people: retain or rehire select individuals and consider older people from outside the organization. Although I focus on retaining, as it is the strategy that has the biggest payoff for organizations and clearly illustrates the impact that retirement management can have, I offer practical advice in all three areas.

- Chapter 4—What Older Workers Want in a Job
- Chapter 5—Retaining Select People Beyond Normal Retirement Age
- Chapter 6—Rehiring People Who Have Retired
- Chapter 7—Recruiting and Hiring Older Workers

Chapter 4

What Older Workers Want in a Job

Older workers who are thinking about extending their work life have distinct needs they are looking to fulfill. More than anything else, they want to work fewer hours per week and/or have increased flexibility in the hours they work.[1] Secondly, many want new responsibilities or challenges to make their final working years more interesting or personally rewarding.[2] Very few individuals who anticipate working into their 60s and 70s *don't* want any changes in their work situation. Faced with these needs, organizations sometimes can make certain accommodations easily and informally (e.g., a change in job assignments or an agreement for less overtime work); but often, a new position must be created—a *transition-to-retirement* position. Other names for transition-to-retirement jobs include bridge employment, partial retirement, phased retirement, or simply a part-time or temporary job preceding retirement. This chapter examines in depth the two major inducements for continued work that organizations can offer and briefly describes several others that are attractive to certain older employees. Chapter 8 delves into what older workers want from their leaders.

Fewer Working Hours with More Flexibility

Surveys have shown that 13 percent of older workers who found jobs after leaving their career jobs would have stayed on with their career employer if they had been given the option to work fewer hours.[3] Older employees want shorter, more flexible work schedules for several reasons:

- **They want to ease into retirement.** Many people (particularly managers and professionals) don't like the idea of abruptly ending their work career on a specified, predetermined date. Rather, they prefer to make an orderly transition from work to retirement, spending progressively less time working. Some might want to try new lifestyles, hobbies, or even other jobs while maintaining a relationship with their career employer. Others want to have the opportunity to relax, but are not sure that they should leave work "cold turkey." In short, they want to keep their options open.

  A survey of senior Fortune 500 male executives revealed that 84 percent would like job options that let them realize their professional aspirations while giving them more time for things outside work. More than half (55 percent) said they were willing to sacrifice income to achieve this.[4]

- **They want or need to spend more time with grandchildren or dependent parents or in situations where they are important caregivers.** An article in the *Pfizer Journal* found that 52 percent of primary caregivers shoulder their responsibilities while holding down full-time jobs.[5] They frequently must leave work early, arrive late, or take time off to provide care.

- **They want to help others.** As they grow older, many people get more involved in volunteer activities, such as working in a community food bank, helping people with their income taxes, or providing Meals on Wheels or similar activities.[6]

- **They'd rather not work so hard and work fewer hours.** Many people in their 60s and 70s have quite a bit of energy and can hold their own in 40 hours of office work each week. Many professionals and executives, however, typically log more than 40 hours. It's simply not realistic to assume that, on average, people in their 70s would still be as energetic as people in their 30s. Typically, as people grow older and their energy levels decline, they have a natural desire to reduce their workweek. People in positions requiring more physical exertion, such as machine operators or laborers, might need shorter hours for health and safety reasons.

In a 2005 study done by the AARP, 53 percent of people who reported an interest in reducing their work hours said they wanted to trim their weekly schedules by at least 12 hours; 39 percent wanted to cut them by 10 or fewer hours.[7] And many are achieving this goal. A 2006 MetLife survey of more than 2,700 mature workers (ages 55–70) found that 56 percent wanted jobs that required fewer than 20 hours of work per week and 39 percent of still-employed 66- to 70-year-olds were, in fact, working fewer than 20 hours per week.[8]

To the extent possible, organizations must be flexible and creative in setting reduced work hours and trying to accommodate older workers who want this option while meeting the organization's overall needs and maintaining fairness to all age groups. The following are the work preferences I heard most in my interviews with older workers:

— Three 7-hour days per week

— Four 7-hour days per week

— Three 10-hour days per week

• **They want more vacation time.** Interest in cultural or travel opportunities frequently increases with age. During the earlier stages of a person's career, these interests often get sacrificed to ambition or family commitments. It's not uncommon to hear a younger worker dismiss an opportunity to travel by saying something like, "I'll do that when I'm older." Later, when the career begins to wind down, that person realizes what he or she has missed; and then, traveling, attending cultural events, or pursuing other unfulfilled special interests becomes a priority.

Almost all organizations adhere to a fixed vacation schedule, determined by tenure. For example, people who have been with a company up to five years might get three weeks of vacation, while employees of four to seven years get four weeks, and so on. Work group morale can erode quickly if one person having the same tenure and doing the same job as another gets more vacation. Usually, the most appropriate way to address the more vacation issue with older workers is to provide an option for nonpaid vacation time for those over a certain age. Just as most vacation schedules are based on employee tenure, it seems very appropriate to tie the availability of nonpaid vacation to tenure as well.

Interestingly, most of the people I talked with indicated that the aggregate amount of vacation is not an issue. Four to five weeks' vacation seems to be plenty for most people. It's the frequency and flexibility of the time off that counts most. People said they would rather have a number of short breaks—long weekends, half-weeks off—rather than more extended periods of time. One reason for the popularity of these frequent, shorter breaks is that families are often located all over the United States; for many older workers who want to visit their grandchildren in another state, it's definitely not a weekend jaunt. Also, people want the flexibility to be able to help out when family members become ill or need them for some other reason.

Most people don't expect to take a vacation anytime they want; they understand time off must be approved well in advance and not be disruptive to the work group.

- **They want more personal time.** Older people want more time to take care of their personal affairs. This might mean taking an extended lunch break for a doctor's appointment or leaving early to pick up a grandchild from school.

- **They want the option of cycling in and out of work.** Many older professionals describe their ideal work situation as having the opportunity to work for 3 to 12 months and then take off 6 to 12 months to do whatever strikes their fancy. For example, I know an optometrist who fills in at an ophthalmology practice in Alaska for three months during the summers, but for the rest of the year, he plays golf in Florida. However, he reports that some years he just "skips the time in Alaska." I also know a 75-year-old engineer/manager who, since "retiring" at age 60, has completed three projects for his former company—each lasting a year or two and each in a different country; in between, he collected seashells from beaches around the world.

There is evidence that flexibility in work hours yields its own rewards. A Michigan State and McGill University study revealed that organizations agreeing to reduced workloads for employees of all ages are repaid with increased productivity, greater retention, and more effective teamwork.[9]

> **Flexible Working and Telecommuting Options at John Deere**
>
> For many years John Deere, a company named by the AARP as one of its "best places to work," has retained a small workforce of individuals into their 70s by offering them flexible hours (to slow their work pace or to allow them to care for elderly parents or grandchildren), telecommuting, and ergonomically adapted workplaces to accommodate their needs. John Deere offers all of these accommodations on a case-by-case basis.[10]

New Job Responsibilities and Challenges

About half of the people approaching retirement want a more radical change—make that a challenge—in their work life, according to a 2003 AARP survey.[11] These people can handle their current duties with their eyes shut and are bored with their particular job, not with working. Some I talked with said that they want a bigger or different stage on which to show what they've learned and what they can accomplish. That stage can be within or outside their career organization. As they approach retirement, many want to move toward the work activities they enjoy and away from tasks they don't like.

For a surprising number of people in leadership positions, the responsibility of leading and managing has lost its appeal. Being a leader can be tough, grueling work, so a lot of older leaders find themselves saying, "I've done it. I was good at it. And now I don't want to do it anymore." Instead, they'd like to get back to what attracted them to a field in the first place, whether it be sales, engineering, or a particular scientific pursuit. Thus, these people are often only too glad to give up their leadership responsibilities.

Are people too hooked on power to take on a vastly different role, particularly in their own organization? (One could hypothesize that doing the new task in another organization would be slightly easier because there's no organizational memory about the person's previous position.)

Most people I've talked with who have gone through this transition have claimed that they have no problem with experiencing a loss in power, that they were ready to step away from day-to-day operations, and that they were more interested in leaving a legacy at their organization—often through working with key people. People in their 50s report being more concerned about a loss of organizational power than people in their 60s or 70s, perhaps because they obtained their clout more recently and find it difficult to relinquish. Older individuals have long since worked through the "novelty" of exercising organizational power and can more objectively see its plusses and minuses. Also, older people might see a job change as simply a natural transition that happens at a certain age.

Hierarchical Advancement

An opportunity to maintain baby boomers' knowledge and contacts—and yet change their daily work—would be to increase their leadership responsibility. Certainly, many individuals would be eager to raise their level of responsibility by adding on a supervisory or managerial element. But research has generally found that the desire for hierarchical advancement diminishes with age.[12] Consequently, people's feelings regarding these opportunities vary greatly.

This decline in interest relative to leadership jobs might be attributed to rationalization. People who didn't make supervisory or management levels when their colleagues were achieving such positions often cope with the disappointment by deciding they never wanted that kind of work anyway. Some may want to reconsider this view in their later years, but most likely would not. In making decisions about promoting an individual, a leader must be careful to check the person's motivation and not just assume that people would jump at the chance for these additional responsibilities.

Job Switching

Sometimes two individuals at the same general level of responsibility can change jobs in a way that imbues in both a sense of a new challenge and additional responsibilities. There's no real advancement—just different challenges. For example, two supervisors might exchange their areas of responsibility, or two individuals in the accounting department might swap duties relative to certain reports that have to be compiled each month.

Special Assignments

A popular way to accommodate older individuals' needing more challenging work is to give them special responsibilities, such as leading a team, investigating whether a facility should be relocated, preparing for the introduction of a new technology, or studying why employee turnover is particularly high in an area. If carefully chosen, a special assignment can be an excellent way of sharing an older worker's basic wisdom, knowledge, and contacts with a larger portion of the organization.

Coach and Internal Consultant Transition-to-Retirement Positions

A popular full-time or transition-to-retirement job for older employees is internal consultant or coach. In these positions, incumbents are directly responsible for passing on their accumulated knowledge and the lessons they've learned through hard experience. Areas where a company fears losing significant organizational knowledge or experience are ripe for creating coaching or internal consultant positions, through which important knowledge can be captured and passed on before it is lost. Older incumbents can impart what they know or be available for others to tap into their knowledge. They also can be assigned to develop training programs that incorporate their key knowledge.

A Model of Acquired Wisdom

In November 2006 I spent an entire day watching Jack Welch handle the questions of business leaders in Brazil—all of whom spent a great deal of money for the opportunity to hear his views. As I listened to the questions and answers, it struck me that what I was really observing was the passing on of wisdom accumulated over years of handling problems and people at General Electric. In no way was Jack giving a "how-to" lecture; he was giving a "what-to" lecture.

Few older people have had the opportunities that Jack Welch has had in learning from his good and poor decisions, but many have been in similar situations on a smaller scale. It's unfortunate that we don't have more occasions for older managers to pass on their wisdom.

Outside Work Options: The Principal Financial Group

The Principal Financial Group of Des Moines, Iowa, provides temporary transfer opportunities for its managers and other senior-level employees so they can take on international assignments, which can last from two to three years. Unlike management training programs, which aim to cycle newer employees through a broad range of positions, these opportunities target more experienced—and, often times, older—workers.[13]

Other Inducements for Older Workers to Stay with an Organization

While offering fewer, more flexible hours and providing new job responsibilities and challenges are the two primary incentives that organizations can use to help retain their older workers, they are by no means the only inducements that will do the trick. Here are a few more.

More Time with Spouse or Significant Other

As people age, they are more likely to be empty nesters. Stay-at-home wives and husbands have more free time than they once had and thus are more available and interested in travel and other activities they can share with their spouse or significant other.

Some organizations are changing their travel policy to encourage spouses or significant others to travel with employees. While they are taking care of business, it seems less like work and more like a vacation when their spouse or significant other is with them. It also allows the spouse or significant other to spend this time in exotic, or at least interesting, places when normally he or she would be back at home alone.

Most organizations allow a spouse or significant other to share the hotel room. Some pay for the person's plane fare—particularly if it means that the couple stays over a Saturday night, thus reducing the plane fare for both, or if having the spouse or significant other with the employee saves the company the cost of a weekend trip home.

I know of one senior executive who had been traveling internationally for years and was growing tired of it—so tired, in fact, that he was considering retirement. His company wanted him to stay on for a few more years while a replacement was being groomed and some major organizational changes were taking place. Part of his agreement to stay on included the company paying for all of his wife's expenses while she accompanied him on trips. He reports that this situation has truly changed his life. He once flew into cities, conducted his business, and flew out again, never taking advantage of the local culture or historical offerings. Now, with his wife at his side, he is able to spend time in all kinds of interesting places, and he says he's more efficient than he ever was because his wife takes care of all the travel and meal arrangements. And to cap it all off, he feels that his "international acumen" has increased significantly because he's meeting more people on his travels than he used to. He and his wife are very fond of staying in small bed-and-breakfast inns, where they get to meet the "real people, not the kind of people one meets in grand hotels over a business breakfast."

Elder-Care Assistance

As more baby boomers find themselves caring for aging parents, family benefits oriented to older workers are becoming more common in organizations, although they are still rare. These benefits include long-term care insurance for older dependents and company-sponsored backup care for emergency situations so employees don't have to miss work (e.g., when an elderly parent's paid caregiver doesn't show up one morning). According to a 2006 survey conducted by the Society for Human Resource Management (SHRM), only 3 percent of companies provide elder-care benefits, and only 5 percent offer emergency backup services—subsidized or not.[14]

Advice on Decisions Regarding Older Parents and Other Dependents

One of the most welcome benefits that organizations can offer is to help employees who are taking care of aging parents—some of whom might live hundreds or thousands of miles away—as they navigate through the available medical and legal options. I know of a Pennsylvania woman who was so worried over what she should do about her mother that she became ill herself and started to miss work. She was responsible for her 83-year-old mother, who was the only caregiver for her 105-year-old aunt. Both were in California, thousands of miles away. It was a huge chore to find a location where the two women could be together and still get the individual attention they needed, let alone figure out the finances. The Pennsylvania woman had to travel to California numerous times and spend hours each week on the phone. She would have loved receiving some help from her organization, and having this assistance likely would have paid off in her improved job productivity.

A few companies offer counselors to help employees of all ages understand and decide on options for their dependents, get in touch with people who can provide needed services, and evaluate medical caregivers.

Retirement Planning

Because they will be living in an era of high retirement anxiety, younger baby boomers as well as the Generation X cohort that follows them will greatly value receiving help in retirement planning. People will need to understand the options they have—including transition-to-retirement employment—and they'll need help in next-life-phase planning (discussed in Chapter 12). Organizations that provide access to guidance and/or support in retirement planning will become more attractive to older workers in the future.

The next three chapters show how meeting the two basic needs of potential retirees (i.e., fewer working hours with more flexibility and new job responsibilities and challenges) can pay off for organizations that want to retain or rehire their older employees or to seek to hire older workers from outside the company.

Chapter 5

Retaining Select People Beyond Normal Retirement Age

Where an organization's options regarding retirement are not constrained by a traditional defined benefit pension plan, I believe retaining people, rather than rehiring them after their formal retirement, is the preferred course of action. By employing this strategy, a company decreases the chance that it will lose talented individuals to another company or to full-time retirement, and reduces the disruption to a work group if the person's new job requires working with the same people.

Does Retaining Older People Make Good Economic Sense?

Maybe organizations shouldn't even consider keeping older workers. They cost more than younger people because they earn higher salaries due to seniority raises, are eligible for more vacation time, and carry higher health care costs for themselves and their families. However, a 2005 Towers Perrin study conducted for AARP found that the average per-employee total compensation costs associated with retaining workers over age 50 is very small: 1 percent of total compensation for sales managers, 2 percent for nurses and store managers, and 3 percent for engineers. Further, Towers Perrin found that the probable benefits of a more stable workforce combined with reduced turnover costs (e.g., recruitment, training, on-boarding, getting people up to speed) often exceeded the incremental compensation and benefits costs associated with keeping older workers. I feel this is particularly true for managers and professionals, whose jobs require specialized skills, advanced training, extensive experience, and unique knowledge.[1]

The economic return from retaining older workers depends on the quality of those individuals. If the organization is truly selective and asks only its high-caliber individuals to stay on, its additional costs around their health care and other benefits should be relatively small compared to the large positive impact they would make. Chapter 11 discusses selecting people for transition-to-retirement jobs.

What Will It Take to Retain People?

Many of the people we interviewed who were approaching retirement would be very happy to stay a little longer in their present position with only some minor changes in their responsibilities, hours worked, or some other aspect of the job. Of the 60 to 80 percent of people who say they want to continue working upon reaching retirement age, I believe about a third of them would feel this way. They might be trying to top off their retirement nest egg by putting more funds into their 401(k) and health care accounts, or wanting to stay to finish a large project (e.g., seeing a 10-year worldwide research project to its conclusion). To keep them on board past their retirement eligibility date, all these people need is a clear path to the finish line (e.g., no loss in pay or benefits, and management's encouragement to stay).

The remaining two-thirds of the people who want to continue working are looking for more major adjustments in their work situation; that is, they want to start making the transition into retirement.

Chapter 4 discussed inducements that management needs to offer to key, high-performing older employees who want to continue working past normal retirement age. Some ideas would be relatively easy to implement, while others would involve alterations to long-established HR policies as well as the acceptance of individualized offerings in many cases. These alterations are the same policy changes that an organization must make to become more attractive to older people seeking work, both those who are returning to their career organization (discussed in Chapter 6) and those from outside (discussed in Chapter 7). This chapter examines what organizations can offer to retain their older workers and looks at legal gray areas, such as how extra perks or considerations can be given to some individuals and not to others.

Changes in Working Hours and Job Schedules

Shorter or More Flexible Work Hours

As noted in Chapter 4, older workers' desires relative to shorter or more flexible work hours are very idiosyncratic and sometimes change as their life situations change (e.g., the arrival of grandchildren). An organization needs to be as flexible as possible in responding to these changing desires. Each situation needs to be considered on its own merits: How important is it to retain the individual? What is the nature of the person's work? What will be the impact on others of making special accommodations (e.g., will others have to work less-attractive hours)? In many cases, all that's required is a simple loosening of work rules to allow people more leeway in how they put in their time, with no change in total time worked.

More Telecommuting

Many older workers who want more control over their time so they can reset the balance between their work, leisure, and family are content just being able to do more work at home, free from the hassle of commuting to the office or plant. They aren't looking to cut back their hours; instead, they want more flexibility around where they spend their time. While at home, they still would be available through e-mail, voice mail, web cam, or conference calls, and they don't mind coming to the office periodically— even two or three days each week.

Many organizations are accustomed to making these kinds of accommodations for people with disabilities or who have special family situations. Depending on the job, there's no reason such accommodations can't be made for older workers who wish to continue contributing to their organization. Doing so might require some adjustments by the organization, such as establishing set hours for meetings (e.g., between 9 a.m. and 4 p.m.), equipping conference rooms with high-quality teleconferencing equipment so that everyone in the room can be heard or seen by the virtual attendees outside the workplace, or equipping key colleagues' laptops for high-speed conferencing and work sharing. Because teleconferencing is so common today, making the necessary accommodations for older workers would not be difficult for most organizations.

> **Organizations Making Accommodations for More Flexible Hours**
>
> Here are two real-life examples of how well-known organizations have established policies to accommodate their older workers.
>
> > At **Aerospace Corporation** older workers can downscale to either part-time or self-employed consultant positions, or they can remain full-time employees, eligible for an unpaid leave of absence of three months each year.[2]
>
> > At **Deloitte Consulting,** senior partners can customize their jobs, choosing how many hours they want to work, where they want to work, and which projects they want to work on.[3]

Job Site Mobility

At least two companies, Borders and Home Depot, regularly offer "snowbird" specials that let their employees in the north move south in the winter and maintain their employment with the company. Other organizations make special individual arrangements with people who want to be in a specific region for part of the year or with people who want to move around the United States.

Job Sharing (Work 50 Percent of Time—Any Combination of Hours)

Job sharing, when two people work together to cover the responsibilities of a single position, is a very attractive option to many older workers because it offers them the flexibility to trade off their time. It also can provide significant benefits to an organization. In almost all the job-sharing situations I've observed, the organization gets more output from the two people than it would have from one person working the job full-time.

And the practice of job sharing seems to be moving up the organizational ladder. I know of two women who together share a $200,000/year financial job and two others who share a highly paid marketing position. Job sharing offers many advantages, but it's rarely initiated by the organization; more often, two people work out the details themselves and then present their idea to management.

On the downside, the costs to the company are often higher because, even though the salary for the position is divided in half, both people typically get benefits, including health care.

Pay Issues Relative to Working Less Time

It might be necessary to change someone's job title and responsibilities to provide the lifestyle changes he or she desires. For example, a salesperson who has been on the road extensively for years might want to travel less and live in a warmer climate even though he or she would make less money. If people want to continue working, albeit with significant reductions in their work responsibilities and hours (e.g., working four 7-hour days each week instead of five), should their pay be cut proportionately? I would answer yes. Compensation should be adjusted appropriately, assuming the person is making a smaller contribution to the organization. Most older workers realize this and expect lower pay for less work. They recognize that the organization is making an exception for them, and they appreciate it, especially when they are receiving supplemental money from the organization's retirement plan or Social Security.

What about professionals and managers who once worked 70 hours a week but then curb their work to only 40 hours in a scheduled three-day week? Should they be paid less? Again, I think the answer is yes, on the grounds that they're available to the organization fewer days; however, their incentive pay structure should stay the same. In such a setup, an experienced salesperson with an extensive portfolio of long-time customer contacts should be able to meet or exceed sales quotas while working fewer days a week.

In general, people should be paid relative to their contributions to the organization and the market-driven price point for the nature of their work. If a salesperson changes his or her work schedule by working only as a coach to other salespeople, carrying no sales quota, and traveling less, then the job is different, and it would be appropriate to pay this person less.

Many leaders are hesitant to ask potential retirees to take a pay cut, even if a move to a transition-to-retirement job would substantially change their job or reduce their output. Apparently, they fear that bringing up the subject would be a sign that the organization neither respects nor appreciates the individual's past contributions. In some organizations this reluctance to talk about lower pay restricts how older workers can be used; the leader would choose to lose the person altogether rather than broach the subject of a pay cut. Given the choice of not working or working for lower pay with different job expectations, many older people gladly would accept less money, particularly when their economic situation has changed (e.g., their children are out of college, their home is paid for, or they have started to collect their pension). Some organizations would never think to ask people to work for less money, but many that do are quite successful at getting these people to accept a situation that is a win for both sides.

Asking someone to work for less can be complicated because of how a company's defined benefit retirement plan is set up. Retirement payouts often are related to the last two to five years of a person's salary. Having this kind of plan in place usually negates the possibility of asking people to work for less money in their later years. However, I know of organizations that have changed their retirement plans so that the person's two highest-earning years become the basis on which a pension is calculated, thus allowing their employees to ease into retirement. There also are increasingly fewer defined benefit plans. Plans that are frozen are no longer tied to end-of-work pay levels.

I definitely *am not* recommending that an organization make a policy or practice of routinely paying older employees less, which is a situation prevalent in some companies in Japan. I *am* recommending that organizations be flexible about the issue and consider the possibility of paying someone less—if appropriate to their contribution—rather than encouraging the employee to leave the company.

Importance of Health Care Coverage in Short Workweek Situations

In many cases the social contract that many potential retirees felt they had with their employer is being broken by the unexpected elimination or downsizing of retiree medical plans. As changes are announced, potential retirees' anxiety about their own retirement rises. Also, their fears increase as medical costs rise. This growing uneasiness will drive many people to consider either working for a few more years to retain full medical insurance or taking a job with another company that will provide medical coverage after their formal retirement from their career employer. For most people, ongoing health insurance coverage—even at an increased deductible—from a current employer is usually easier to obtain than coverage from a new employer. Many part-time, nonexempt jobs open to retirees do not offer medical coverage. Thus, the need for health coverage is a strong motivator for an older person to continue working for his or her career organization.

It's possible for an organization to calculate the financial risk involved relative to the hours a person works and require the appropriate increases in that employee's contributions. For example, if an individual working four days a week puts in 80 percent of the time that a full-time employee devotes, then the organization should contribute 80 percent of the amount toward that person's health care that it contributes for a full-time worker. Similarly, for a classic job-sharing arrangement with two people, each working 50 percent of full-time, the organization's health care contribution to each person would be half of what it contributes for a full-time employee. Practical considerations might require real-world adjustments to these numbers; for example, the employee's share might be so large as to be burdensome for someone working at half-time. Also, many health plan insurers have minimum weekly requirements (often 30 hours per week) for an individual to be eligible for group health coverage. Such plans would have to be renegotiated by the organization to accommodate the needs of its part-time workers.

A small but increasing number of companies are offering "bridge health care coverage" until individuals reach 65, and then are letting Medicare assume responsibility for health care costs for part-time older workers.

Different Job Responsibilities and Challenges

Organizations should consider creating positions where older workers who desire new or different challenges can make meaningful contributions on a full- or part-time basis. Some possibilities for injecting a sense of challenge include:

- Putting a veteran salesperson into the marketing department to be the "voice of sales."

- Asking a seasoned employee to create an on-boarding program for new hires.

- Giving someone a knowledge-conservation assignment (e.g., recording how a major project was handled).

- Asking a highly skilled planner to teach planning skills to new recruits as a way of filling hard-to-staff positions.

- Letting an engineer try working at a sales job.

- Having two managers switch their job responsibilities.

- Letting a person do the same job in another district or country.

- Transferring technology to other offices or units around the world.

- Allowing an employee to fill in for another who is on special assignment or who has unexpectedly left the organization.

Remember, the goal is not to make unnecessary or meaningless work available for a person; rather, it's to get meaningful, necessary work accomplished by someone who knows the organization and has unique skills or contacts.

Employees Must Earn Special Consideration

Individuals who want or need special consideration from their organization relative to retention options (e.g., transition-to-retirement jobs) will need to show that they deserve that consideration. They will have to show they are motivated to work at their highest level and that they have any special skills (e.g., coaching) that might be required. This will prompt some older employees to take a dramatically different view of their 50s and 60s: Instead of gradually coasting to an easy stop, they will exhibit sustained—or even increased—effort, output, and engagement in order to earn the opportunity to work longer in jobs designed to fit their particular needs.

Coach or Internal Consultant Positions

As described in Chapter 4, a popular full-time or transition-to-retirement job for older employees is an internal consultant or coach. In these positions, incumbents are directly responsible for passing on their accumulated knowledge and the lessons they've learned through their experience. Chapter 9 lists reasons that older workers make good coaches, internal consultants, or trainers.

I know many people in their 50s and 60s who have a strong urge to give back to their organization before they retire. They want to leave a mark. An easy way to do that is to pass on what they know to the next generation, so they jump at the chance to be a coach or internal consultant. However, having the desire to pass on information is not the same as actually having the ability to do it. For some people, the role of an internal consultant or coach comes easily; for the majority, however, it does not, and considerable training is required to build the interpersonal and coaching skills needed for them to effectively pass on what they know. An inexperienced coach can easily be fooled by his or her charges' nodding their heads in agreement while they aren't really accepting the person's advice. This passive lack of acceptance of ideas or advice causes many internal consultants to leave their jobs after a year or two once they realize that they're not really having much of an impact. The coaches and consultants who are fulfilled are those who work through projects with colleagues, constantly listening and responding to their personal and practical needs, checking for understanding, and maintaining the self-esteem of the people they counsel. All these skills are trainable.

In many companies coach, internal consultant, and trainer positions tend to be short-term, "going-out-the-door" assignments. An organization should not restrict its consideration of potential transition-to-retirement jobs to these types of positions. Many older people are seeking jobs with more bottom-line impact, such as leading a new unit, helping the organization go in a new direction, or taking on a new, difficult assignment.

Dr. M.E. Szinovacz, of the University of Massachusetts, Boston, discovered that the following types of people are more likely to work beyond their normal retirement age:[4]

> Workers whose current job entails high substantive complexity.

> People who are attached to their jobs.

> Married individuals in troubled relationships.

> Women who delayed child bearing.

> People who see their jobs as empowered.

> High-performing, successful workers.

> People whose spouses continue to work.

Szinovacz found that these types of people are more likely to leave at the normal retirement age:

> Childless women.

> Individuals who experience job interruptions and unemployment spells.

> Underperforming (less productive) workers.

> People whose spouses have already retired.

Are the Inducements of Different Work Schedules and/or New Work Challenges Effective?

If a person has decided to retire, there are almost no reasonable incentives an organization can offer to change his or her mind. The inducements described in this chapter apply to individuals who are undecided relative to retirement or to those who have decided not to retire. Of course, these must be people the organization wants to retain.

The AARP was interested in how people 50 and older felt about phased retirement (which includes the activities discussed in this chapter). According to a 2005 survey, 38 percent of the 2,167 respondents said that they would be interested in participating in a phased-retirement program, and 78 percent said that the availability of such a plan would encourage them to work beyond their expected retirement age. About half (46 percent) of the people who were interested in phased retirement said they would like to start it between the ages of 60 and 64.[5]

It might take a combination of incentives to persuade a valued older worker to stay on. For example, I know of an excellent sales manager who had become bored with her position. To get her to stay a few more years with her company, she was assigned to help salespeople move to more consultative sales roles (a new challenge), was asked to be the model in a sales training film the organization was making (a recognition need), and was assigned responsibility to recruit new graduates at the university her daughter was attending (personal need). She reports that everything worked out wonderfully. The company was very pleased with her achievements.

Are These Incentives Legal?

Management and professional benefits in today's organizations are far from consistent. Many people negotiate "deals" when they are hired—some on paper, some as off-the-record agreements. According to a 2000 survey by William M. Mercer consultants, organizations are becoming more flexible:[6]

- 47 percent allow older workers to reduce their hours.

- 17 percent allow job sharing for older workers.

- 45 percent have special positions for older workers, including job training and mentoring.

- More than 50 percent are willing to negotiate special arrangements for older workers.

It doesn't seem that a little additional flexibility in meeting the unique needs of older workers should get an organization into legal trouble. However, your organization should check with its own legal counsel prior to implementing any of these, or any similar, practices for its older workers.

Relative to the creation of new positions to appeal to older managers and professionals, the best course of action seems to be recognition of the situation in which organizations actually find themselves. When trying to remake managerial and professional jobs to allow people to ease into retirement, most organizations actually create new jobs with different titles, responsibilities, working hours, and pay scales. In some organizations a person might go from being a manager, to a practicing professional, to an internal consultant in the span of three or four years—all very different roles requiring different pay and work schedules. To the extent that these individuals are in truly new jobs, they can then be managed and compensated differently.

At nonexempt and unionized levels of an organization, proving job uniqueness in order to be flexible is more difficult—but still possible for newly created jobs (e.g., a trainer).

Some organizations fear opening the door too wide to special assignments and thereby getting a large number of people asking for special treatment. They can skirt the issue by establishing a unique job with a different title, responsibilities, compensation, and working hours. Then, if others ask for the same accommodations, management can respond that it doesn't need more jobs in that category.

Once again, be advised that I am not giving legal advice and that you should consult your own legal counsel about these issues.

Working Past Retirement Might Be Good for People's Health

There's considerable evidence that work keeps older people healthier and even helps them live longer. Several studies have noted that cognitive function seems to decline when older workers are removed from challenging environments. In addition, James House, commenting on his own research, said, "Across the full age range we observe the greatest physical and psychological well-being in those who were doing as much paid work as they would like to do."[7]

In her book, *My Time,* Abigail Trafford provides the alarming statistic that white men over 65 have the highest suicide rate of any age group.[8] She says the immediate explanation for this is often untreated depression, triggered by the lack of purpose that comes with retirement. According to Trafford, older men often feel trapped in a "biological purgatory"—too old to live and too young to die.

The retired fathers of baby boomers often spent their free time in social clubs named after animals (e.g., Moose, Elks), in veteran's organizations (e.g., VFW), or in volunteer organizations (e.g., volunteer fire departments). For the most part, such diversions are not as attractive to baby boomers, thus eliminating a place for them to get away from their house or spouse. More attractive work options provided by their career organization might help them meet their social and financial needs.

Impact of Being Able to Collect Social Security and a Pension While Still Working for Career Employer

As discussed earlier, the attractiveness of extended work years for career employees will greatly increase as companies amend their defined benefit plans to allow people to collect a pension while they continue to draw a salary (they already can get Social Security at 65 or 67, depending on their year of birth). People in these situations will be able to take part-time jobs with no actual loss in income, or they will get what will feel like a big bonus for continuing to work full-time.

How Will Younger Workers Feel About Special Working Assignments for Older Workers?

DDI asked 1,200 workers how they felt about their organization letting older workers work part-time or have flexible hours. Overall, two-thirds thought it was a good idea, but as one would expect, there were age differences. Respondents over 40 thought it was a better idea than did individuals under 40, only 50 percent of whom liked the idea.[9] This research shows that organizations will have to do some selling of the purpose and importance of retirement management if it is implemented on a large scale. The occasional use of retirement management may not even be noticed.

Chapter 6

Rehiring People
Who Have Retired

When people retire from an organization, they usually have high expectations for life in retirement or in other employment. But sometimes those expectations don't work out. After six months or a year, conventional retirement activities, such as travel, golf, or gardening, can get boring. The five stages of retirement, proposed by Ken Dychtwald, are described in Appendix 6A. His research suggests that after sampling retirement, many people change their minds and are ready to reestablish ties with their former employer.

The urge to return to work is particularly strong for people accustomed to running their own unit or operation or whose self-image had been defined by their job and the company they worked for. Also, many retirees quickly learn that post-retirement expenses are higher than they had planned. A 2006 McKinsey survey found that 43 percent of retirees at all income levels reported that they had seriously underestimated their retirement expenses. The McKinsey study also found that 36 percent of respondents with a shortfall sought work, but that only 10 percent found it.[1] These individuals are prime candidates to be rehired, usually on a part-time basis.

I don't recommend rehiring *all* the people who want to come back—just those select individuals who can make meaningful contributions to the organization on a full- or part-time basis.

Some common assignments for rehired retirees include:

- Filling periodic peak employment needs, such as during the Christmas season for retail stores or during tax time for accountants. A part-time retiree also might be brought in when an organization gets a large contract or when an emergency situation suddenly occurs.

- Serving as a temporary replacement for someone who becomes ill, goes on sabbatical, or is otherwise unavailable for a finite period of time.

- Filling hard-to-staff slots in a work schedule, such as the peak time at a call center.

- Assuming responsibility for a project or joining a project-based team. Many people jump at opportunities for project-based work in which they take on a company assignment and stay on through its completion. The project might be something they can handle by themselves or as part of a team. Project work often means long hours, a lot of travel, and seemingly endless meetings. But when the project is done, it's done; the individual can, with a free mind, take a few months off or do whatever he or she wants to do. Most projects are not overstaffed, so people involved with them feel they're making a significant contribution to their organization.

As noted in Chapter 4, many managerial and professional retirees are very attracted to the idea of alternating between retirement and work, rather than mixing the two by working part-time. These individuals are prime prospects for rehiring.

Organizations with Defined Contribution, 401(k), and Amended Defined Benefit Plans

Organizations whose retirement plans allow monetary retirement plan distributions to older employees while they continue to work tend to do little rehiring of their retirees. Instead, they focus on retaining their people full-time or placing them in part-time, transition-to-retirement positions. These organizations, in which continuous employment is an option, feel that it's a waste of money and time to formally sever their relationships with retired individuals only to then have to reestablish the ties, especially if they don't have to. During their period of unemployment, the retirees might take a job with a competitor or lose interest in working. Because reemployment of retirees occurs so infrequently in these organizations, it is usually handled on an *ad hoc* basis as part of the normal hiring process.

As the war for talent intensifies, firms with defined contribution, 401(k), or amended defined benefit plans probably will need to broaden their recruitment efforts to encompass more rehiring of retired employees. Some of those individuals would like to come back to work—and where better than to a place they know and with whom they are comfortable. Due to the nature of 401(k) and other types of defined contribution plans, there are only minor impediments for returning employees who want to maintain their retirement income and their organization-provided retirement health care coverage while working.

> ### Extended Time Off to Try Out Retirement
>
> If an organization really wants to keep someone who has valuable knowledge and contacts and who is committed to retirement, one solution is to give that person an extended, unpaid leave of absence to try out retirement. After the absence some will say that they love retirement or that they've found a new direction for their life and are going for it. But many will come back to their company and say, "Now I'm refreshed. I know what I want to do, and I want to do it in this organization." Of course, the company must be sure that it can meet the person's work requirements (e.g., days worked per week).
>
> What does the organization have to lose by granting a six-month or year-long unpaid leave? The retiring person would be gone anyway. The only risks of an extended time off from work are perhaps some health care benefits that the organization would not have had to cover otherwise. These would be small if the company has a retiree health plan.
>
> I know individuals who have come back from their extended time off with fresh insights into business opportunities for their organization, particularly in countries they've visited while traveling.

Organizations with Conventional Defined Benefit Plans

The selective rehiring of former employees is much more important to organizations that have conventional defined benefit plans. The vast majority of their retirees leave the company's payroll upon becoming eligible for retirement in order to receive their pension benefits. Many organizations would like to keep some of these retirees because of their unique skills, knowledge, and experience, or just because it's a tight labor market in a particular area. Yet, conventional defined benefit pension plans were written in such a way that makes retaining these workers very difficult. Their best option is rehiring select people for part-time jobs after they have retired.

Get People to Commit to Part-Time Employment Before They Formally Leave the Company

If an organization really needs to retain certain people, the time between their retirement and subsequent rehiring can be an anxious period. Some retirees might have a change of heart and decide not to return after they've tasted the fruits of retirement. Others might be attracted to jobs in other organizations after they've officially retired from their career company.

I know of no reason a "continuation of employment" contract can't be entered into by the individual and the organization before the person retires. Even if it's not enforceable, it would have a positive psychological benefit on the relationship between the individual and the organization. The agreement would be seen as a positive symbol of the organization's gratitude for past work and faith in possible future contributions. Such a contract assures the individual that a meaningful part-time job would be available when he or she is ready, perhaps after a four-month leave. It also gives some assurance to the organization that key talent is not totally lost.

Passing the IRS "Test"

The following IRS "tests" must be met, or a retiree can lose pension benefits for the period of his or her employment.

> There must be a clear break in employment. A person can't quit one day and start working for the organization in the same job the next day. (Many organizations set a standard time period, such as one month, before permitting reemployment.)

> The employee is permitted to work no more than 1,000 hours a year (approximately half-time).

Fear of "Double-Dipping"

In many organizations there is an irrational fear of "double-dipping." To many, the idea that a person can be paid a salary while also receiving a company pension just doesn't seem right. Thus, many organizations won't even consider the idea of retaining or rehiring extremely capable people despite the fact that, in some circumstances, double-dipping can save them money. (The organization is going to pay the person's pension and perhaps retirement health care benefits if he or she is working or not.) Whether there are actual cost savings depends on an individual's salary level, type of health care plan offered to rehired people in part-time jobs, and other factors.[2]

What About the "Boomerang" Factor?

An old but quickly disappearing concern of some management is the notion that rehiring individuals will encourage other people to leave the organization to try out risky job alternatives because they feel they can always come back. I don't know of any evidence indicating that a company that forbids boomerang rehiring has less turnover than one in which the selective rehiring of former employees is a company policy. On the other hand, I know of organizations that have greatly benefited from rehiring workers who have tried out other jobs and not found the grass to be greener. Indeed, many have come back stronger in their commitment to the original organization.

Managing the Rehiring of Retired Former Employees for Part-Time Assignments

Organizations that have made rehiring a major element in their retirement management system usually have formalized and centralized the selection and management of the rehires. Centralized hiring provides an opportunity for the entire organization to tap into the total population of potential rehires. However, the vast majority of people rehired seem to end up back in their original departments or units.

Deciding Whom to Rehire

Rehiring decisions can be more difficult than they initially seem, especially if the job for which a retiree is being considered is substantially different from his or her previous job (e.g., moving from individual contributor to consultant) or the initiative for rehiring is the employee's. The organizations with formal rehiring programs that I have visited are quite careful in deciding whom to rehire (see Chapter 11). They often find it effective to have people who don't know the potential rehire conduct the interviews, rather than the person's previous boss or coworkers. Such a practice minimizes the chances that an interviewer will make unwarranted assumptions or hold unintended biases, pro or con—which are very real considerations for former leaders or colleagues.

Of course, it also would be appropriate to interview the person's former leader to understand how the candidate exhibited the target competencies for the new position in his or her previous job.

Planning to Rehire Select Retirees

There's nothing stopping a company from making a special effort to maintain contact with select retirees whom they might want to rehire. For example, by:

> Retaining their names on company address lists to keep in touch with them through general communications, newsletters, etc.

> Inviting them to company activities (e.g., holiday parties, new product unveilings, company picnics).

> Calling them 3, 6, and 12 months after they retire to ask how they are doing.

> Supporting an "alumni association." This is done at The Mitre Corporation; members (retired employees) meet quarterly at the organization's facilities.

Such talent practices might not be well suited to implement on a large-scale basis, but for certain situations, they offer a very legitimate means for career employers to avoid losing valued retired employees to another organization if and when those people desire to go back to work. Too often, people start a second career elsewhere when they would much rather have returned to their original organization, where they know the people, products, and culture.

Compensation

The compensation for rehired individuals should be set relative to the work they will be doing (the market rate for the job), not relative to their previous salary. They should not be paid less just because they also are receiving retirement payments from the organization.

Medical Benefits

For many people, the primary attraction of full- or part-time post-retirement work is medical coverage—even if part-time workers have to contribute more. (See the discussion of medical coverage for part-time employees in Chapter 5.) Of course, for people who return with a rich retiree medical plan, medical benefits are probably not an important issue, but for people who don't have retiree health coverage, medical benefits are of the utmost importance—even for highly paid individuals.

Currently, there is considerable interest in so-called "bridge plans," which provide coverage until an individual is eligible for Medicare. In these plans, long-term health care (after Medicare eligibility) is not covered, so the financial risk to the organization is much less, but the psychological benefits to those covered are disproportionately positive.

Two Types of Bridge Plans

> Coverage is offered to employees who have retired before age 65 after meeting certain age or service requirements—regardless of their coming back to work.

> Coverage is offered only to those retired employees younger than 65 who want to be rehired, but who might not qualify for their organization's existing part-time medical coverage because of age or service requirements.

Using Third-Party Organizations to Rehire Talent

Quite a few organizations, such as the Principal Financial Group, rehire their retirees as independent contractors or as employees of an employment agency. By doing this, they are not on the company's payroll and thus don't get benefits. Procter & Gamble, Eli Lilly, and Boeing are founding members of a company called YourEncore™, Inc., which allows them to circumvent the many issues associated with rehiring people in a traditional defined benefit environment. This independent, unrelated organization hires retirees and places them in part-time, short-term projects with member organizations. Hiring organizations can obtain the services of their own retirees or any of the retirees in the YourEncore database without putting them on the payroll. The rates charged for people by YourEncore are similar to those at which the individual worked before retiring.[3]

Another strategy is to have a retired individual form a "personal services corporation" and work as an independent consultant. Then, the organization can hire that person back on consulting assignments, which must be very well defined in terms of both output and time requirements.

How Much Publicity Should Rehiring Opportunities Be Given?

Up to this point, I've tended to speak about rehiring as an initiative of the *organization*. Management identifies people who would be good rehiring prospects before or after they retire and then approaches them about the possibility of returning to their former organization.

Another rehiring strategy would be for the organization to simply provide information about rehiring opportunities to all its retirees and then let them take the initiative. (Of course, this doesn't mean that leaders couldn't suggest to certain retirees that they volunteer or that everyone who signs up for an opportunity gets rehired.) Monsanto has such a policy. Its Retiree Resource Corps (RRC) celebrated its 15th anniversary in May 2006. When an employee retires or voluntarily leaves Monsanto or an affiliate, that person is eligible to apply for the RRC program after six months. RRC candidates must complete an application to fill temporary, part-time employee positions. Then their names are entered into the RRC database, and a recruiter tries to place them. The length of assignments varies greatly from very short to very long. Positions involve all skill sets—auditors, receptionists, scientists, technical people, administrative assistants, etc. Some former employees come back in the same role, while others try something entirely different. Deb Lebryk, head of the RRC, says, "I wonder why there aren't more programs like this. It gives a former employee the opportunity to give back to the company, and it benefits the company. Sometimes the RRC person will work on a project, but because he or she is not needed all of the time, he or she has the flexibility to float in and out of the project. We call them our *Frequent Flyers.*"[4]

Another company where employees can nominate themselves for part-time employment is the Aerospace Corporation, which has several programs that appeal to older workers, including the "Retiree Casual" program, which is their most popular offering for older workers contemplating retirement. Its employees can retire with full pension and medical benefits, and then be rehired for up to 1,000 hours per year. Retiree casuals are most often used during peak times during midyear to fiscal year end. According to Aerospace Benefits Representative Judy Gonser, "The Retiree Casual program has become part of the Aerospace Corporation's culture. When employees start to think about retirement, they also think about how they might continue to contribute to the company and discuss it with their manager."[5]

Turner Broadcasting System (TBS) has created Turner Temps, an in-house agency for supplying temporary help that enables retirees to return to work for short-term projects or administrative support. The agency provides short-term staffing for all TBS divisions in Atlanta.

The Principal Financial Group uses its web site to tell former employees about its employment opportunities. Their Happy Returns Program™ allows individuals to work on a full-time, part-time, or temporary basis, without any adverse impact to their retiree benefits.

What Are the Legal Issues?

For those who retire and are then rehired into part-time jobs, an organization should not encounter a problem about offering differentiated benefits. However, there is one caution regarding medical benefits offered on a pre-tax basis under Section 125 of the Internal Revenue Code (IRC): Employers may not discriminate in offering benefits.

Structuring differentiated benefits for rehires as a group must be done carefully and in compliance with IRS rules. When rehiring is done on an ad hoc basis, the people being rehired are free agents who can negotiate any kind of deal they want. (Exceptions are unionized situations and organizations that have one or more unique job classifications for returnees.)

Most organizations feel that the best way of staying out of legal trouble in this matter is to define the returning retirees' jobs in a way that makes them markedly different from both the company's other jobs *and* the particular individual's previous job. Fortunately, this often happens automatically because the jobs envisioned for returning older workers are, indeed, unique.

Probably the biggest potential legal problem in traditional defined benefit organizations is getting people to restrict their work to 1,000 hours a year. An advantage of centralized control (by total organization or by large units) is that it enables an organization to ensure that the deployment of retirees meets government regulations, particularly regarding the number of hours worked. People returning to their career organization tend to quickly resume full-time work—as opposed to part-time duty—because there is always a lot of work for highly qualified people to do. Extremely proficient individuals become hot commodities. When their availability becomes known, they frequently get overbooked and then find themselves working harder than before they had retired.

I recommend that you check with your organization's legal counsel regarding how returning retirees' jobs should be defined and managed.

Appendix 6A
Five Stages of Retirement

Ken Dychtwald, Ph.D., author of several books on retirement and president of Age Wave, a firm he established to guide Fortune 500 companies and government groups in product/service development for boomers and mature adults, has posited five stages leading up to and following retirement.

The five stages can be found in the report titled *The New Retirement Mindscape*[SM] compiled for Ameriprise Financial in conjunction with Age Wave, Dychtwald, and Harris Interactive. The 2006 report was based on 2,000 interviews with Americans ages 40 to 75.[6]

His description of each stage follows:

Stage 1: Imagination (15–6 years before retirement)—Even though retirement is still years away, during the Imagination stage people have very positive views about it, although only 44 percent say they are "on track" in terms of preparation. In this stage people have high expectations of adventure (65 percent) and empowerment (53 percent) for retirement.

Stage 2: Anticipation (5 years and less before retirement)—As retirement draws closer, positive emotions are on the rise, with 80 percent of potential retirees saying they "will be able to achieve their dreams in retirement." However, in the two years before retirement, worries and anxiety mount, with 22 percent saying they will feel a sense of loss after their working years are over. The most commonly cited triggers for retirement readiness were achieving "financial freedom" (18 percent) or a significant birthday (16 percent).

Stage 3: Liberation (retirement day and 1 year following)—This is a time of great excitement, relief, and enthusiasm, as 78 percent of people say they are "enjoying retirement a great deal." But, similar to a honeymoon, the feeling of liberation is short-lived, as a new reality soon begins to set in.

Stage 4: Reorientation (2–15 years after retirement)—During the Reorientation stage many say the joy of retirement has passed, giving way to feelings of emptiness (49 percent), worry (38 percent), and boredom (34 percent). This is the point in the progression where an emotional letdown might occur to varying degrees.

Stage 5: Reconciliation (16 or more years after retirement)—This stage is marked by increased contentment, acceptance, and personal reflection. People have come to terms with all that retirement has to offer. While there are lower levels of depression (5 percent), some people (22 percent) report feelings of sadness as they confront end-of-life issues.

Three of Dychtwald's stages are particularly important to organizations that are thinking about retaining older employees or rehiring retirees:

Stage 2: Anticipation (5 years and less before retirement)

This is the period when retirement management intersects with the individual's feelings. Dychtwald's findings help explain why people's views about their retirement frequently shift in the years leading up to their retirement date. Some writers have called this anticipation period a "second adolescence." Adolescents have a world of opportunities in front of them, as do older workers approaching retirement. Adolescents also find it difficult to accept guidance from others because they feel that their own situation is different from everyone else's—an assumption also shared by many older adults. A big difference is that older people know through real experience what they don't like.

Without any real data to confirm it, I estimate that about 20 percent of working adults feel they have ended up in the wrong job. They took on a career before fully realizing what that career meant. They accepted responsibilities, such as leadership, without completely understanding the corresponding responsibilities. The Anticipation Stage, in particular, is a time for these individuals to look broadly over the horizon to see what's available and how they might better spend the next part of their work and non-work life. Many will have the courage to "break out of the box" and experiment.

Stage 3: Liberation (retirement day and 1 year following)

At least initially, most retirees are quite satisfied. This is particularly true of males, who often experience a "honeymoon" period just after retirement.[7] However, this time is then often followed by one of disillusionment or discontentment with retirement. This could explain why some people who had said that they weren't interested in doing any part-time work might reconsider and become quite interested. This might be a good time for organizations to contact their retirees to gauge their interest in coming back to work.

Stage 4: Reorientation (2–15 years after retirement)

Dychtwald found four types of people at this stage:

- *"Empowered Reinventors* (19%) who have entered a time of adventure, new challenges, and fulfillment and most likely to say that they feel adventurous and empowered. For the Empowered Reinventor, doing more meaningful or satisfying work is very important to them, engaging in hobbies, traveling, and enjoying their newfound freedom are all priorities. Over one-third say they are now working full-time, part-time, or cycling between periods of work and leisure.

- *"Uncertain Searchers* (22%) are still trying to figure out what to make of this time in their lives. They report mixed feelings about this stage— neither very positive nor very negative. They are still trying to discover the goals and activities that will give them purpose, meaning, and fulfillment in retirement.

- *"Worried Strugglers* (10%) have the most difficult time in the Reorientation Stage. They are more likely to admit being worried, bored, or sad. They have fewer aspirations in this stage and are more likely to feel a sense of emptiness resulting from a lower work capacity. Worried Strugglers gave little thought to what they wanted to do in their retirement years.

- *"Carefree Contents* (19%) are reorienting successfully to this new time in their lives, but in a very different way. Almost all tell us that they feel optimistic about their current retirement lifestyle but, unlike the Empowered Reinventors, this is not really a time of adventure or new challenges. This group is quite content adjusting to a less frantic lifestyle without the stresses of work and multiple responsibilities. Few say that continuing their education, doing meaningful or satisfying work, or pursuing hobbies is very important to them. In addition, eight out of ten say they are not working at all."

The picture Dychtwald paints of the period 2 to 15 years after retirement is not a pretty one. There are a lot of unhappy, unfulfilled people (Uncertain Searchers and Worried Strugglers). The Empowered Reinventors represent the prototype of older people most organizations would want to keep, rehire, or hire, but, according to Dychtwald, there are relatively few (only 19 percent) of those individuals in the retirement ranks. An organization's task is to help the Uncertain Searchers and the Worried Strugglers understand the alternatives open to them and take advantage of what they think they need and what it can offer to fit their particular situation.

Chapter 7

Recruiting and Hiring Older Workers

Up to this point, I've focused on the importance to organizations of retaining or rehiring select older employees—usually the preferred methods of retirement management. I've also targeted people with difficult-to-replace knowledge, experience, or contacts—often people in management and professional positions. In this chapter I'll explore a third alternative: recruiting and hiring individuals from the general population of older people. Also, I'll provide evidence that hiring older workers to fill entry-level positions can be a good investment.

Will Baby Boomers in Their 60s Be Worth Hiring?

This question can best be answered by extrapolating from what managers say about current workers in their late 50s and early 60s. The following pages summarize DDI's research involving thousands of individuals in organizations throughout the United States.

Most Will Have Good Work Habits

Managers rate their employees age 56 or older who work in non-management, entry-level jobs (e.g., bank tellers and retail sales employees) higher than any other age group—especially the under-26 bracket—in work habits, such as safety awareness, attendance, punctuality, and reliability (i.e., follow-through) (see Figure 7.1).

Figure 7.1: Standardized Manager Ratings of Work Habits by Age Group (n=2,699 nonmanagement job holders in 39 organizations)[1]

WORK HABITS	AGE GROUP				
	< 26	26–35	36–45	46–55	56+
Work Standards	▼	...	...	...	...
Safety Awareness	▼	...	...	...	▲
Reliability/Follow-Through	▼	...	...	▲	▲
Attendance	▼	...	...	▲	▲
Punctuality	▼	...	...	▲	▲
Avoidance of Disciplinary Actions	▼	...	...	▲	▲

Note: Symbols indicate distance from the average performance level within each organization in our sample for that performance factor. (▲ = .1 standard deviation [sd] above the average for the factor; ▲ = .2 + sd above the average for the factor; ▼ = .1 sd below the average for the factor; ▼ = .2 sd below the average for the factor; ... = within .1 of an sd from the average for the factor)

For more information see "DDI Research Design and Methodology" at the end of this book (pp. 261–266).

Confirmatory findings about the good work habits of older workers in nonmanagement positions were reported in 2004 by Shore and Goldberg.[2]

It seems that the positive relationship between good work habits and age continues past age 65. Although the sample size of the DDI data for individuals over 65 who are still working is smaller, as would be expected, the general trends in the data are quite clear. The positive trend lines are maintained in supervisory ratings of safety awareness, attendance, punctuality, and avoidance of disciplinary action. These are trend lines, not statistically significant differences.

Work habit ratings of supervisors and professionals generally show a similar pattern to the nonmanagement employees, but the differences among age groups are not statistically significant because of the smaller sample size in the DDI research. Older supervisors and professionals tend to maintain their age group superiority in ratings of attendance, but appear to be lower in punctuality than people ages 26 to 55.

Most Will Stay in the Organization Longer

Older individuals in nonmanagement positions tend to stay in their jobs longer. When asked about their intention to continue working for their current employer, people over 56 reported much longer time frames as contrasted with the relatively short time frames of those under 26. The differences in self-reports of retention plans shown in Figure 7.2 are particularly meaningful when the alternative to hiring older people is to hire people under 26.

Figure 7.2: Anonymous Self-Reports of Retention Likelihood by Age Group (n=1,178 corrected for tenure)[3]

RETENTION	AGE GROUP				
	< 26	26–35	36–45	46–55	56+
Retention Likelihood	▽	▪▪▪	▪▪▪	△	▲

Note: Symbols indicate distance from the average performance level within each organization in our sample for that performance factor. (△ = .1 standard deviation [sd] above the average for the factor; ▲ = .2 + sd above the average for the factor; ▽ = .1 sd below the average for the factor; ▼ = .2 sd below the average for the factor; ▪▪▪ = within .1 of an sd from the average for the factor)

Similar results surfaced in three other DDI studies totaling 4,702 individuals.[4] Other research[5] and a Harris Interactive survey of HR managers also found high retention to be an advantage of hiring older workers.[6]

The retention advantage of older workers seems to evaporate at supervisory, managerial, and professional levels[7] probably because these positions have a higher average retention expectation for all age groups and the relative number of people under 26 is much smaller.

Most Will Be Engaged in Their Work

DDI's definition of employee engagement is "the extent to which people enjoy and believe in what they do and feel valued for doing it. Engagement goes beyond job compliance to a genuine commitment to the organization in the form of job ownership/pride, contributing more discretionary effort, and job passion and excitement." Between 2004 and 2006 DDI administered an engagement survey to 1,322 nonmanagement workers and found that older workers were slightly more engaged than other age groups, but the differences were not statistically significant. A number of other researchers who have relied on ratings by supervisors and HR managers have reported a more positive relationship between engagement and age.[8] In a study by the AARP and the Society of Human Resource Management (SHRM), 77 percent of HR managers felt that older workers were more engaged; only 5 percent disagreed.[9]

Most Will Be Good at Some Types of Problem Solving but Not at Others

Figure 7.3 reflects the test scores by age group of 5,002 workers who were applying for supervisory jobs. Older workers performed better than younger colleagues on a situational judgment test that evaluates problem solving regarding people and work situations. Younger workers, however, did better than their older counterparts in an applied problem-solving test that involved understanding charts and diagrams and applying mathematics and statistics to job situations.

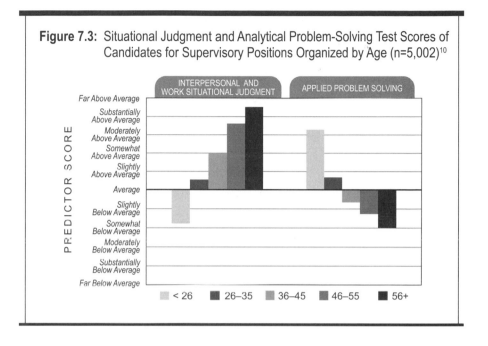

Figure 7.3: Situational Judgment and Analytical Problem-Solving Test Scores of Candidates for Supervisory Positions Organized by Age (n=5,002)[10]

The situational judgment scores represent the wisdom that is acquired through experience. As long as people continue to work, they make better work judgments. The problem-solving skills are learned in school, so they are fresher in the minds of younger workers.

A parallel DDI study of 5,136 managerial candidates shows a similar pattern of score trends by age group in situational problem solving and applied problem solving, although the differences between the youngest group (<26) and oldest group (56+) were generally smaller for the managerial subset, as compared to the supervisory sample.

Other research has shown that practical intelligence and verbal skills do not decline until very late in life. For instance, the verbal skills of 74-year-olds are almost identical to those of 40-year-olds and are actually higher than those of 32-year-olds.[11] Some other intellectual abilities, such as those that depend on specific knowledge bases, show a slight decline with age.[12]

"Use it or lose it" seems to be the key to maintaining intellectual functioning as we grow older. People in intellectually challenging jobs such as physicians, attorneys, and architects are known for working well into their 70s and even 80s, probably because they remain intellectually active.

Most Will Perform as Well as Other Age Groups in Initiative, Communication, and Planning and Organizing

When compared to younger employees, no substantial differences were found in the ratings of older nonmanagement workers in important performance areas such as initiative, communication, and planning and organizing. However, there seems to be a slight downward trend in the ratings of older workers relative to planning and organizing and communication.

Research Summary

The research data in this section make a strong argument for hiring older job applicants—especially when contrasted with young (under 26) applicants. Compared with young employees, older workers come to work on time more frequently, have fewer absences, follow procedures (such as safety rules) better, follow through on their commitments, and stay in their jobs longer. Older workers have the perfect profile for many entry-level jobs, such as clerking in retail stores, staffing call centers, and working in light manufacturing. Many organizations with these job classifications experience very high employee turnover—as high as 70 to 100 percent a year! Hiring a greater number of older workers might solve part of this problem. Progressive organizations, like Toyota, have already done this, adapting their manufacturing workstations to allow them to hire more older workers.[13]

DDI research on people age 56 and older in supervisory and professional positions has found the same positive work habits and job performance. However, the differences are not statistically significant. It certainly can be said that older supervisors and professionals perform no worse than other age groups and tend to do slightly better.

Big Differences Within Age Groups

Baby boomers in their 60s and 70s will be looking for jobs at all organizational levels, and they will bring with them a wide assortment of skills and abilities.

The range of talent differences among individuals in the over-60 group will be far greater than the mean differences between older workers and other age groups. For instance, some older people will find it difficult just to leave their homes, let alone hold down a job; meanwhile, others who are more physically fit than an average 50-year-old will want to work forever. Some will embrace change; others will shrink from it. Some will want to retreat in life, while others will want to move forward and seek new and expanding opportunities.

This diversity means that there are appropriate people in their 60s and 70s out there for most positions in organizations. With a good recruitment and selection system, they can be found.

The Pros and Cons of Hiring Older Workers

The value brought by older workers to many positions is apparent, but what about the costs of hiring them?

Value vs. Health Care Costs

The biggest inhibitor to organizations' hiring more older workers is a concern over increased health care costs. There's no question that health care expenditures rise with a person's age; but for most working people, these costs really don't increase that much. If people are well enough to work, they're probably in fairly good health—but of course, they might have family members in poor health. Figure 7.4 shows annual medical claims costs for employed individuals of different ages and their dependents.

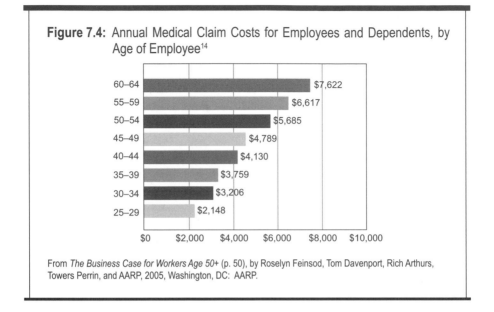

Figure 7.4: Annual Medical Claim Costs for Employees and Dependents, by Age of Employee[14]

From *The Business Case for Workers Age 50+* (p. 50), by Roselyn Feinsod, Tom Davenport, Rich Arthurs, Towers Perrin, and AARP, 2005, Washington, DC: AARP.

An analysis by Towers Perrin and others found that company-paid medical claim costs for employees age 50 to 65 averaged 1.4 to 2.2 times the costs of workers in their 30s and 40s.[15] Of course, there were large individual differences in costs depending on factors such as high blood pressure, obesity, and smoking.

The increased health care costs associated with older workers must be weighed against the increased value they bring to an organization—particularly when compared to the young workers they are competing against for many entry-level positions (see Figures 7.1, 7.2, and 7.3). The value of older workers rises with compensation level, where the added benefits of their experience and practical decision making come into play (see Figure 11.2).

Each organization will have to weigh the added costs and value of hiring older workers and make its own decision. Clearly, the major positive factor for hiring older workers is the reduced costs of turnover. The following scenarios illustrate this. If a job can be learned in a few hours (e.g., a fast-food restaurant crew member) and there are a lot of job applicants, then the cost of turnover is relatively low. But in the more common situation—where training and on-boarding costs are significant and finding good replacements is difficult, which can cause positions to be open for some time and result in loss of business—the advantage of bringing in older, more experienced workers who will stay longer is much more significant.

Both Borders and Days Inn cite the higher attendance and retention rates of older people as important reasons why they make special efforts to hire them. These organizations have concluded that the higher retention and attendance outweigh the additional health care costs associated with older workers.[16]

Can an Organization Cut a Full-Time Employee's Health Care Coverage When the Person Becomes Eligible for Medicare?

With respect to health coverage, an organization's options are limited when employees reach 65 and become Medicare eligible. Although a company may decide not to offer health coverage to its retirees, an active employee who reaches 65 cannot be forced out of the health care plan just because of his or her age. Employers also are not allowed to provide incentives to induce an older, active employee to opt out of the employer plan, nor charge this person more for health care coverage than it charges younger employees who work the same hours.

These restrictions arise from the federal government shrewdly making Medicare coverage secondary to company health care plans for individuals who are working and covered by their employer's plan.

One of the few planning options available to employers is to inform active employees who are eligible for Medicare that the cost of Medicare and supplemental coverage might be less than the employee's required contribution to participate in the employer's health plan. As noted above, the employer may not provide incentives or other inducements for an active employee to opt out of the employer plan, but I currently know of no restrictions that would preclude an employer from sharing the comparative costs of the employer's plan and Medicare.

Value vs. Salary and Non-Health Care Benefit Costs

In retention and unique rehiring situations in which a person is coming back full-time to his or her old job or an equivalent position, older employees carry additional costs: They are paid more to do the same job because of the annual raises they've received during their career, and they will have more vacation time because it's tied to their tenure. These additional costs usually don't apply to older workers employed from outside the organization. Thus, older outside applicants can be less expensive than people who have remained with the company; but of course, they won't have the skills, knowledge, or organizational experience and would be more expensive to recruit and hire.

Value vs. Leadership Challenges

As you have seen, compared to young workers, older workers excel in many of the most commonly sought work habit areas: attendance, punctuality, reliability, and safety awareness. These are by far the most frequent situations that require a supervisor to hold a coaching-for-improvement session with a direct report. Their relative lack of work habit problems often makes older workers easier to manage than their younger counterparts. On the other hand, Chapters 9 and 10 discuss how older workers are in some ways more difficult to manage than their younger colleagues. However, the leadership challenges they bring to the job are slight compared to those brought by people under 26. If that is the tradeoff that organizations face, then the balance clearly favors the older worker.

Hiring Older Workers

If I have convinced you that older workers are a "good buy" for the organization, then your next question would likely be "How do I find these good people?"

Recruiting Passive Potential Hires

As baby boomers retire and the competition intensifies for those with the needed skills, organizations will need to markedly improve their recruitment and selection systems. Most organizations interested in recruiting older applicants will not have trouble reaching *active* applicants; they can advertise or post jobs on the Web and in newspapers. Rather, the major challenge for them will be finding *passive* applicants—people who are not overtly looking for jobs, who have unique skills or knowledge or good aptitude and motivation. Although passive potential hires might be living quite comfortably, often they aren't really happy with their lives. They'd like to do something different but haven't thought very much about getting another job. For example, they might be seeking the companionship that comes from work more than the money they can make from it.

Here are some ideas for recruiting passive potential older workers:

- Ask incumbent older employees for referrals as well as for suggestions about how to attract workers their age. Not only will this bring in new talent, but it also will demonstrate to current employees the company's commitment to age neutrality and the value it places on older employees.

- Give recruitment talks and presentations at retirement homes, church groups, or other locations where older people might gather.

- Hang posters in places frequented by older adults, such as health centers, senior centers, condominium common areas, grocery stores, laundromats, community centers, golf courses, and bingo halls.

- If in a retail organization, assign older employees to work in the front of the store where customers can see them and realize that there are jobs available for older workers.

EEOC Amendment Would Legalize Targeting Older Workers for Open Positions

On March 5, 2007, the U.S. Equal Employment Opportunity Commission (EEOC) approved an amendment to its Age Discrimination in Employment Act (ADEA) regulations to clarify that it is permissible for employers to encourage relatively older people to apply for available jobs. Under the amendment, "Employers may post help wanted notices or advertisements expressing a preference for older individuals with terms such as, over 60, retirees, or supplement your pension."[17]

However, the EEOC cautions that any organization seeking to hire older workers must indicate that it's looking for people of all age groups but is particularly interested in older workers. Companies focusing on finding older applicants are not permitted to automatically screen out younger workers.

Note: While this amendment has been approved, as of this printing it has yet to be formally ratified by the federal Office of Management and Budget (OMB) and published in the *Federal Register*. Until the amendment has been formally enacted, readers who are interested can check its status by visiting this OMB web site:
http://www.reginfo.gov/public/do/eoViewRule?ruleID=271535

Selecting Older Workers

Among older workers (more than all other age groups), there will be a range of abilities in key areas.[18] Organizations will be challenged to maintain a selection system that will ensure that individuals who are particularly proficient in the target job requirements will be selected. One certainly cannot conclude that all people at a certain age are proficient or deficient in any given competency.

Strategies for selecting older candidates from within or outside the organization are covered in Chapter 11.

Who's Hiring Older Workers?

According to SHRM, only 41 percent of members surveyed recruit older workers.[19] Many of these are in the retail field (e.g., Borders, Wal-Mart, Home Depot, CVS). Older workers are attractive to retailers because they mirror one of the main demographics of the organization's customer base. Also, older people want part-time—as opposed to full-time—work, and they are available to staff hard-to-fill time slots.

The war for talent will compel increasingly more organizations in other industries to turn to older workers as well. They offer skills, job flexibility, and a positive work attitude. Older workers are a great (for the most part), untapped, willing resource that is difficult to ignore.

SECTION III

MANAGING OLDER WORKERS

The three chapters on leadership address the very real challenges of managing older workers, particularly as government regulations and retirement plans change to allow people to tap into their pensions while still working. Chapter 10 examines the difficult issues involved in forcing poorly performing individuals out of an organization—an issue that increasingly more organizations will face as baby boomers continue to work beyond normal retirement age.

- Chapter 8—Leadership Skills Needed to Manage Older Workers
- Chapter 9—Special Challenges in Leading Older Workers
- Chapter 10—Taking a Stand with Poor Performers

Chapter 8

Leadership Skills Needed to Manage Older Workers

Top management can define organizational values and policies and HR can promulgate organizational rules and systems, but leaders (direct supervisors) at every level are the key to a successful retirement management effort. They are the ones who must implement adopted policies and systems on a daily basis. Leaders are "the organization" in the eyes of their direct reports; for top management, they represent a key line of communication for conveying the organization's policies and business strategies and for keeping apprised of what's going on in the company.

I start this discussion of leadership in a retirement management environment by summarizing 35 years of DDI research into what people need from their leaders and what leadership behaviors meet these needs. According to DDI's research, the needs and responses are common for all age groups, but there are important, unique nuances for dealing with older workers. Chapter 9 discusses the unique leadership challenges presented by an aging employee population and the skills leaders need to respond. Leaders need these skills to enhance the commitment and satisfaction of their older workers and thus make staying with an organization more attractive. Chapter 10 reviews one of the most difficult challenges facing leaders of older workers: taking a stand with poor performers.

Six Things Older Workers Want from Leaders

DDI's research involving more than 100,000 individuals has consistently found six personal needs that must be addressed by effective leaders.[1] These are presented in reported order of importance for the general population, but the order varies by organizational level. For instance, the opportunity to learn and grow is the number one need at higher organizational levels—perhaps because higher-level jobs are naturally highly empowered. The six needs, also known as Leadership Constants because they are what effective leaders must continually work on, are:

1. Empowerment—interesting/challenging work, control of outcomes

2. Opportunity to learn and grow—develop new skills and knowledge

3. Recognition

4. Consistency/Fairness of leadership

5. Cooperation/Support

6. Sense of organization's direction—complete and timely communication

1. Empowerment—Interesting/Challenging Work, Control of Outcomes

Feelings of empowerment have been shown to be closely related to all kinds of organizationally positive indices, such as profits, competitive quality, productivity, and customer service.[2] These positive relationships are a function of the psychological ownership people bring to empowered jobs—that is, their degree of engagement in their work. The more they're allowed to make meaningful decisions and be responsible, the more they psychologically own their particular job. And the more they own their job, the more energy they put into making it a success. For empowered people, job success equals personal success. Thus, when something goes wrong, they work harder—without being asked—to remedy the situation; when things go right, they take pride in the achievement.

It's natural that individuals seek empowerment. People at all organizational levels have a strong desire for interesting and challenging work, and they want an opportunity to use their skills, be involved in meaningful decisions about their work, be responsible for their actions, and be able to measure their own effectiveness. They *don't* want to wait until their boss taps them on the shoulder and says, "Here's what I need you to do next." However, although empowerment is a basic desire of all people, unfortunately it has been acculturated out of some people over a lifetime of exposure to poor leadership and energy-sapping job design.

As people mature, their tolerance for micromanaged, mind-numbing work decreases. If older people weren't very empowered during their earlier work life, then they often feel that the later stage of their career is when they should be respected for what they know and can do. People at higher levels in an organization, who already have considerable freedom to do their jobs, expect even more freedom as they mature.

Baby boomers who continue to work in their 60s and 70s will want an opportunity to prove their value to their organization. They'll want to be needed and trusted—a sign of their leaders' and coworkers' respect. This theme came up time and again in my interviews with older individuals who had left their jobs. A common reason for their leaving a company was "I was just not important to the organization anymore." A Conference Board study of people over age 50 in eight organizations found that 25 percent of the people who expressed interest in retirement cited "not respected in my current job" as a reason. This was the respondents' most common job-related reason for looking into retirement.[3]

What the Leader Can Do

Empowerment is created by job design (extent of decision making, responsibility, and authority) and leadership actions.

Job Design—Every job can be empowered, but often it takes some creativity. In higher-level positions, responsibilities can be added or the positive consequences of success can be ratcheted up in terms of personal recognition (e.g., being mentioned at a large company meeting). At lower organizational levels, empowerment is just as important, but it takes on very different forms. For example, a supervisor might stop checking an older employee's work, or an older employee might be given responsibility for training new people. Empowerment is particularly important for the retention of older people because it directly affects two of the main reasons older people give for leaving jobs: boredom and stress. Empowered jobs are far less boring because workers can vary their work activities or job tasks as long as the work gets done. They are encouraged to think of better ways to do their jobs. Empowered jobs are less stressful because people in them have more control over what they do. The reason that hyper-busy executives have fewer heart attacks and live longer than employees in highly demanding, but boring, clerical or manufacturing work is that the executives control their jobs, how they're done, and when they're done.[4] Stress-related illness often occurs when people don't have control over crucial elements of their job. A person under such stress seeks relief, usually by leaving; thus, the lack of empowerment is a prime cause of turnover.

Leadership Actions—Leaders are the main determiners of empowerment. They can make people feel adept, needed, and important, or they can demoralize individuals and sap their self-esteem. Leaders largely control rewards and recognition for their employees' accomplishments. They set the tone for the work area through their actions.

Effective leaders help people solve their own problems; they don't step in to solve them. This is the kind of leadership support older employees want— perhaps even more so than younger employees. A DDI study of job seekers over age 58 found that 80.5 percent were looking for interesting work and 70 percent were seeking opportunities for accomplishment—20 percentage points higher than job seekers under age 20.[5] Older employees who have not experienced much empowerment in their work lives will be just as unsure when facing new challenges as younger people who are experiencing a new work situation. A leader must be sympathetic to their needs, empathetic to their feelings and concerns, and encouraging without embarrassing them by doing the work for them or withdrawing an assignment.

Although everyone wants empowerment, there is a wide disparity in what energizes each of us. A leader can't assume empowerment opportunities will be perceived in the same way by everyone and must realize that people's needs change over time. As much as is possible, a leader is responsible for tailoring jobs to each person's empowerment needs. A good example is the need to accomplish something meaningful and lasting—to leave a legacy in an organization. That legacy might take the form of products or services a person helped to develop or, more often, people whom an individual has helped to grow and achieve success. Leaving a legacy is not a typical accomplishment need of young people, but it is quite common as people approach retirement.

> ## Challenging Work Keeps Workers Sharp
>
> A leader who "goes easy" on older individuals and doesn't push them too hard to continually learn new things might actually cause their intellectual decline. As noted in Chapter 7, older workers who are challenged intellectually in their jobs and who are forced to learn new things maintain their intellectual abilities longer than people who have not been so stimulated.

2. Opportunity to Learn and Grow—Develop New Skills and Knowledge

Research by DDI and other organizations has shown that the other major determiner of job satisfaction—along with meaningful, empowered work—is the opportunity to learn and grow (i.e., develop new skills and knowledge). People want to be up to date with the most current technology, and they want to know what's going on in their field of interest. For people in professional, technical, or leadership positions, there seems to be no age cap on the need to learn, although older workers might have less need than people in their 30s and 40s. A 2000 Conference Board study of people over age 50 found that two-thirds desire more training and leadership development.[6] Yet, it's easy for leaders to fall into the trap of assuming that training or updating older workers on new technology or products would be a poor investment. Leaders often reason that an older person might be with the organization for only another year or two, so the return on investment of training that person is low compared to that of a younger employee going through the same training.

One of the quickest ways to lose a more senior employee is to deny that person the opportunity to grow and learn on the job to at least the same extent of other employees. When leaders deprive older workers of critical skill or knowledge development, they can start those workers on a downward spiral. Knowledge is king in an organization; the person with the most knowledge ranks among the most respected, trusted, and indispensable people in a company. Want a sure-fire, easy way to send a negative message? Just make it clear that someone is out of the knowledge loop. People who are kept "on the outside" don't know what's happening in the organization. They frequently are unaware of new services or products that are being offered or new policies that are being implemented, and they must rely on coworkers to answer questions, confirm facts, or inform them. Older workers are not oblivious to these slights; in fact, they're often hypersensitive to them. When older employees start feeling cut out of the communications loop, they start thinking about leaving the organization.

Developmental assignments also have another function. Older workers consistently report that a main attraction of work is the stimulation that it brings. DDI's *Selection Forecast 2006–2007* found that 72 percent of job seekers over age 50 said that the opportunity to learn and grow was important to their selection of a company to work for.[7] People are energized by taking on new tasks that often result from putting training they received into practice. Conversely, repetitive work is not very stimulating and can encourage older workers to entertain thoughts of working elsewhere.

Learning Speed Declines with Age, but Many Older Workers Don't Have to Learn as Much

Apart from the positive motivational values that most older people attach to taking on new tasks and learning new things is the issue of learning speed. DDI has several large-scale research studies that clearly show an age-related downward trend in the learning speed for people in non-management positions. According to their supervisors, older workers on average take longer to learn new tasks.[8] The trend is most evident in new hires who staff customer service positions (e.g., bank tellers, store clerks).

An important issue to consider when thinking about older workers' learning speed is their need to learn new skills. Well-performing older workers who are staying in their current job or who are moving to a similar job in their organization already have all or most of the knowledge and skills they need to do the job (e.g., customer service skills that would have to be taught to young, new workers). In other words, their total learning time might be shorter because they already know most of what they need. In addition, they possess survival skills and knowledge—such as knowing who to see to resolve issues or an understanding of the organization's vision and values—and have a social network that will allow them to access any information they need quickly.

Actually, speed of learning is relatively unimportant in most jobs. A few extra hours or even days for a newly hired older worker to reach acceptable performance levels are often more than offset by that person's long-term good job performance, low turnover, and generally solid work habits once the skills are learned. If speed of learning is important, then it should become a selection issue for the organization (see Chapter 11).

Issues with learning agility seem to decrease as individuals mount the organizational ladder. In fact, almost all the managers I interviewed commented that older supervisors, managers, or professionals were as good as or better than their younger compatriots with regard to learning agility.

What the Leader Can Do

There are vast differences in people's learning needs and wants, and leaders must be attuned to them and act accordingly. Leaders should avoid stereotyping older individuals in regard to their particular learning style or preferences. For example, I've observed big differences, by organizational level, in people's desire to learn and grow; I've found it much more important to people at higher organizational levels. An individual's background also plays a major role. People who have, throughout life, taken on new assignments or who have stretched their capabilities want to continue doing so. Conversely, people who have been in stagnant jobs, haven't pushed themselves to learn new things, or haven't been pushed by others are, as they grow older, less willing to seize learning opportunities and enjoy the accomplishment of mastering a new task, although they still may enjoy the accomplishment when they succeed.

Leaders can make sure individuals nearing normal retirement age get the same opportunities for training and development to improve their job skills as everyone else in the organization. And they'll have to carefully set up the learning by:

- Clearly communicating its purpose and importance. If an older worker doesn't understand the benefits of the learning experience, he or she might be less willing to participate or might ask so many questions that the training activity is disrupted.

- Discussing how the learning can be used immediately on the job and offering coaching and other help during early applications of the new skill or knowledge. In other words, assume that learning will take place and that it will need to be applied.

Setting up people for learning is important for workers of all ages and organizational levels. It's particularly critical with older workers. At least in frontline jobs, older workers seem to have a low tolerance for theory;[9] instead, they want practical information and skills they can use.

Providing the development opportunities that older workers (along with everyone else) crave might be more of a problem for leaders than one would think. In studies of hundreds of thousands of supervisors and managers, DDI has continually found that Developing Others is the competency most lacking in supervisors and managers; that is, when workers evaluate their leaders, Developing Others is consistently the lowest-rated competency. Thus, it's not enough just to remind supervisors and managers that they need to develop their direct reports; an organization's management must provide training and considerable encouragement to make that happen.

Do Older People Benefit from a Mentor?

Yes, according to research,[10] but on average they experience less career-related mentoring and have shorter relationships. The same study found that organizations don't necessarily need to have an older person mentor another older person, but most organizations still establish such relationships.

3. Recognition

While people at all organizational levels want personal recognition for their contributions, it might be even more important to recognize older workers. Inevitably, many older employees have doubts about their ongoing contribution to the organization. They might begin asking themselves, "Am I still as good as I used to be?" The organization's recognition of their contributions is a way of reaffirming that they are, indeed, important.

Because many older employees are working with a very strong safety net beneath them (i.e., they can retire at any time), leaders must remain acutely aware of their need to have their contributions recognized.

What the Leader Can Do

Good leaders at all levels understand the importance of maintaining and boosting their charges' self-esteem in day-to-day contact, at meetings, and during organizational events. They should tell people frequently how much they appreciate their contributions and how important they are to their group's success. Strong leaders also can help older workers set up some kind of system to measure their own success so that every day or week they can see a record of their own accomplishments.

Most important, leaders can recognize individuals through their actions: who gets the interesting new assignments, who gets trained in new technology, who gets the tough jobs, and so on. When older workers are excluded from these opportunities, they interpret it as a definite sign of their diminished importance. If an organization is looking to retain its older workers, its leaders must be prepared to provide a balance among age groups in distributing developmental or high-profile opportunities. A good alternative is to pair a younger worker with an older employee to accomplish a task, thereby recognizing their dual capabilities and allowing the older individual to be an informal coach to the younger person.

Future-Oriented Assignments Are Attractive

A special attraction for older individuals might be the opportunity to lead or serve on a committee charged with planning for the future (e.g., visualizing new products or new directions for the organization, making useful products or services based on insights from the organization's research unit, or planning a meeting where new ideas are shared and discussed). An older individual would see leading or serving on a committee dealing with the organization's future as a vote of confidence and recognition of his or her accumulated wisdom.

Some organizations give awards for "lifetime achievement" or "ongoing contributions to the company." While these types of recognition are fine and should be given, their impact is short-lived. Other, longer-lasting actions that leaders can take include:

- Having the older person represent the organization in community activities or at technical or industry conferences.

- Asking the individual to serve as the organization's spokesperson to the press.

- Having the older person become involved as a government liaison.

- Giving the individual a prestigious job title such as "senior consultant" or "chief scientist."

All these kinds of recognition help older employees feel important and appreciated over a period of time—every time they attend a meeting or see their name in print. Of course, leaders must be wary of the frequency with which they hand out plum assignments or titles to older employees. They don't want to create the perception among their younger reports that there are fewer (or no) opportunities in the organization for them. Often, leaders can finesse this by handing out responsibilities that might be quite appealing to older individuals yet not overly attractive to younger people (e.g., responsibilities requiring night meetings or weekend travel).

Showing Appropriate Respect Is an Important Form of Recognition for Older Workers

Countries such as India and Japan have a strong culture of respect for older people. Respect is shown in subtle and overt ways such as deeply bowing or asking for an older person's opinions first in meetings. The United States doesn't have such a strong culture of respect for older workers, but good manners require a degree of deference and consideration. Here are some ways that leaders can convey both disrespect and respect.

Disrespect	Respect
> Calling older workers by names such as "Mom" or "Pops."	> Publicly asking older workers for advice.
> Telling jokes about older people.	> Sending people to older workers for advice.

Disrespect (cont'd)	Respect (cont'd)
> Assuming that older people can't do every task.	> Asking older workers for ideas in meetings.
> Assuming that older people are hard of hearing.	> Sharing assignments equally— not giving all difficult assignments to younger workers.
> Providing physical help when it's not needed.	
> Centering communication around current recording artists or other celebrities who are probably unfamiliar to older workers.	> Seating older workers at a prominent place in meetings.
	> Mentioning the importance of experience in asking for Ideas. For example, "You've had a lot of experience in this area. What do you think?"

Leaders who show appropriate respect for older workers are modeling the respect that would be appropriate from their coworkers. It creates a climate that makes older workers feel wanted and appreciated.

4. Consistency/Fairness of Leadership

When it comes to what people want from their leaders, DDI surveys show that consistency and fairness rank near the top of most lists.

Consistency—A moody leader who reacts in very different ways to the same situation depending on how he or she feels that day causes much consternation in the workplace. In such situations, people often try to gauge the mood of their leader each morning and then adapt their behavior to it. If the leader is particularly irritable, employees quickly hear about it and try to avoid contact with the person that day. Many people report that they would rather have a leader who is consistently in a bad mood than one whose moods change without warning. According to various DDI research, there is no difference by age in the importance of consistency.

Fairness—To survey respondents, fairness does not mean that everyone is treated the same; rather, it means people are treated as appropriate to their contributions—or lack thereof—to the organization. As noted earlier in this chapter, people want to be recognized and rewarded when they do well, but that recognition falls flat when they see others getting rewarded similarly for lesser, or even poor, performance. Remarks such as this one are not uncommon in such situations: "It's just not fair. I get my weekly report in on time, and Charlie is late most of time. Yet, we both get paid exactly the same, and no one seems to care about Charlie's lateness."

Why Leaders Don't Confront Performance Problems[11]

> The organizational culture doesn't support such action.

> Performance measures and the definition of minimum performance are unclear.

> Leaders lack the confidence to confront the situation without making it worse and perhaps alienating an entire team.

> Leaders lack the skills to set performance goals, periodically review them, and evaluate success (performance management).

> Higher management fails to provide coaching, reinforcement, and support.

What the Leader Can Do

While consistency and fairness are equally important to people of all ages, older workers might be even more sensitive to a leader's behavior. The antennae of many older workers are able to pick up the slightest hints that they're not being treated fairly compared to younger people doing similar work. In addition to empowerment, recognition, and growth opportunities, issues of concern might involve timing of vacations, overtime assignments, project deadlines, or staffing allocations. Cognizant of this, effective leaders spend a little more time with older workers to explain the rationale for their decisions so their charges understand that the decisions were correct and fair. For example, a leader might plan to spread high-visibility assignments among team members, but the plan would only become evident over time after several people had received the highly coveted assignments. When the first person gets that first plum assignment, the leader's actions might seem quite unfair unless he or she shares the broader plan with the group so they understand that everyone meeting certain criteria will get their chance.

Of course, fairness cuts both ways. Young workers don't like older workers coasting along, not pulling their weight. The next chapter addresses appropriate responses to this situation.

5. Cooperation/Support

Cooperation/Support is *always* important—whether individuals are placed in formal or informal teams. When there's a large project or a high-priority job with a tight deadline, people prefer to work in settings in which coworkers help one another. And, they want the people who volunteer help to be competent so they really do add value and finish their tasks with high quality, on time, and without exception. According to DDI surveys, people want their organization to prize and reward cooperation and mutual support. This is a common need across all age groups.

DDI research indicates that older workers receive the highest manager ratings of all age groups in their cooperation and willingness to support others in getting assignments done on time, every time, with high quality.

What the Leader Can Do

Many older workers seek a sense of community at work, where they can support others and receive support in return. The leader's task in instilling a cooperative/supportive spirit is to ensure that people are cross-trained and have the skills and knowledge they need to help one another, to communicate the importance of cooperation and support, and to take appropriate action when people aren't pulling their weight. And leaders must be a positive role model of cooperation in their dealings with other units or departments.

A major issue with older workers seems to be the communication gaps across age groups. As shown in the personality data collected by DDI on thousands of nonmanagement employees, older workers are likely to be reluctant to ask other workers for help, even though they get along fine with one another on the job.[12] Also, younger workers might be hesitant to offer help to older workers. If asked, both groups are happy to do whatever is necessary. A leader's role is to foster a climate of cooperation by spotting situations in which help is needed and then line up the needed support across age and other demographic groups. After a few positive examples of mutual support, cooperation becomes standard operating procedure for the unit.

Empowered, Semiautonomous Work Teams

Cooperation (teamwork) is particularly important in formal work teams that have been set up to give decision-making responsibility to a group of people working together with a common, measurable output. In an empowered team, members make decisions, set the team's goals, and measure progress toward those goals. Team members have psychological ownership in the team's progress, which in turn translates into powerful motivation for on-the-job success.[13]

The more psychologically committed individuals are to the team, the more they identify with it and, thus, the more motivated they are for success. Feelings of team commitment have been shown to be related to turnover and productivity.[14]

Integrating older workers into a formal, semiautonomous work team can pose a challenge for leaders. Most won't jump into team situations with blazing enthusiasm; rather, they tend to be more hesitant, exhibiting a "show me" attitude. They won't be uncooperative; they just won't be as enthusiastic as younger workers—at least initially. A leader's best course of action in such a situation is to have patience. Often, older workers will begin turning around their interest in working on an empowered team through mere experience. Chances are they've seen many past organizational initiatives come and go, and it will take a little longer for them to believe that the organization is really changing how it plans to operate. Also, it's important to let older workers test the waters of team participation at their own pace, rather than throwing them in and hoping they'll swim. Such an approach will boost their confidence in their ability to survive and thrive on the team. With good leadership, older workers can evolve into highly enthusiastic team members and become extremely motivated by participating on an empowered team.

6. Sense of Organization's Direction—Complete and Timely Communication

The final leadership behavior revealed consistently in DDI's surveys is the ability to clearly tie each direct report's activities to the organization's vision (strategy) and values. People want to know how their work fits into the bigger organizational picture and how what they do makes a difference in organizational success. In other words, they need to understand why their work is important. If unusually high quality is demanded from them, they will be much more motivated to meet this standard if they understand the impact of lower quality on the company's customers. Because organizations frequently change their direction and strategy, older individuals often have developed a heightened need for the latest information. As noted earlier, they don't want to be locked out of the communication loop. They often can recount anecdotes of wasted time, effort, and money on a project that was redundant or not coordinated with other organizational efforts.

Also, important to many older workers is a sense that they are making a difference for the people their organization services. Civic Ventures and MetLife Foundation have found that half of older workers want jobs that contribute directly or indirectly to the betterment of society.[15]

What the Leader Can Do

Constancy and clarity in providing organizational, unit, and job information is a hallmark of a good leader. Everybody wants information relevant to their work. Good leaders provide it—often several times in several different ways to make sure that everyone understands the message. Just tacking a notice on a bulletin board is often quite ineffective. A leader needs to make the message personal. Sometimes this means talking to each person individually to be sure that he or she understands what's happening and the ramifications of what he or she is doing. After communicating information, effective leaders check for understanding by asking questions about how the individual will use it.

Sometimes leaders don't provide the necessary communication about a strategy, initiatives, or new products simply because they don't receive the information themselves. While this puts them in a very difficult situation, they retain responsibility to proactively get the information that their people need to do their jobs. When important events are occurring, good leaders help their people get up to speed and in position to make the greatest contribution. This means the entire unit, including the older workers.

Summary

The Leadership Constants—responses to the six common needs discussed in this chapter—are vital to leading workers of all ages. The good news is that the Leadership Constants are trainable (see Chapter 13). Effective leaders of older workers probably must work a little harder to apply the Constants. These leaders also face an interesting conundrum: Older workers want to be treated just like everyone else, but they also expect unique treatment and considerations appropriate to their age and past contributions to the organization. As one leader commented, "I treat everyone the same, but I spend more time with my senior people—not checking up on them, but making sure they're on board with what's going on and that they're OK."

Chapter 9

Special Challenges in Leading Older Workers

The importance of effective leadership will grow as baby boomers reach their 60s, because the boomers will have more work and nonwork options. For instance, many older employees will be working for the intellectual stimulation and the social aspects of the workplace, rather than just for the money or benefits. Some will have employment agency "head hunters" calling them every day with job offers because of their experience. And the lure of warmer (or colder) climates or the desire to be near family will make some individuals more mobile. These and other options will lead boomers to hold their leaders to a higher standard relative to their personal needs and situations.

In addition to using the six Leadership Constants described in Chapter 8, leaders of older individuals face some unique challenges. They need to:

- Make accommodations, where possible, for the special physical needs of older workers.

- Understand the retirement intentions of people age 50 and older.

- Determine who should be encouraged to stay with the organization (if they want to).

- Find the optimum position for each person.

- Be honest about future job prospects for marginal performers.

- Encourage people to plan for retirement.

- Regularly check in with older workers regarding their job performance and job satisfaction as well as any changes in their retirement intentions.

- Help people implement their transition-to-retirement plans (if they have them).

All these challenges are covered in this chapter. Another particularly difficult task—taking a stand with poor performers—is examined in Chapter 10.

Make Accommodations, Where Possible, for the Special Physical Needs of Older Workers

Older workers want two kinds of accommodation. The first relates to their work schedule—such as the number of days worked in a week, the number of hours worked in a day, and their daily start and end times. These needs, and possible organizational responses to them, are discussed in Chapter 5. Sometimes leaders can adjust employees' work schedules or make other small accommodations to meet their needs, but if an older person wants to move to a three-day workweek, the manager must collect more information, involve others in the decision, and then take careful action (see the remaining challenges).

The second area of accommodation relates to the work itself. There are many subtle actions a leader can take to make life easier for an older worker. For example, if the employee works at a computer all day, the leader might show the person how to increase the font size displayed on the monitor. This would take just a few minutes, but many people don't realize this option is available. Or, the leader might reposition the monitor according to the user's height so that an older worker wearing bifocals or trifocals can see it without straining. Another possible—albeit more costly—accommodation would be to provide this person with a large-screen monitor.

Here are some other real-life examples of accommodations that have been made for older workers:

- An older forklift driver in a large warehouse had a chronic stiff neck that hurt when he turned his head, so he was having trouble seeing what was in his path when he backed up his vehicle. The driver's leader helped him mount a rearview mirror on his forklift. With this accommodation, the driver was able to work successfully for five more years.

- An older college professor had her classes scheduled in one building near her office to reduce the amount of walking she had to do around campus.

- Older nurses were assigned people to help them lift and turn patients.

- An older worker with a slight hearing problem was given a phone with volume control.

- An older individual in a manufacturing facility who had trouble standing up for long periods of time (a job requirement) was given a special standing desk, which helped him record data and allowed him to use the desk as a support.

I talked with several managers of older white-collar workers who mentioned that the only accommodation they made was to encourage their older employees to take a nap in the afternoon at their desk if they felt like they needed it. One advertising manager shared that he had arranged for a comfortable chair to be placed in an older worker's office so that person could take a brief nap after lunch. Other managers surmised that many of their younger workers also took quick naps, but just didn't admit it. All the leaders I spoke with said that they didn't mind people napping and even wished they could do it themselves.

How Older Baby Boomers in Managerial and Professional Positions Will Cope with the Rigors of Growing Old

Like current managers and professionals who have chosen to work into their 70s and 80s, baby boomers will need to compensate for common problems brought on by old age (e.g., less energy, poorer memory) by developing new work strategies.

Here's some advice for boomers from some current older professionals and managers:

> **Focus your efforts**—Narrow your goals; don't take on more goals. This might mean scaling back your duties to the most important tasks or the ones you're good at, giving up parts of your job so that you can develop other key skills more fully, dropping out of some committees, not trying to keep up to date on all professional areas, delegating more.

> **Pace yourself**—Put less stress on yourself (e.g., don't try to squeeze as many meetings into one week or make a presentation at night after a full day's work). When traveling, give yourself some time to recuperate after a long flight, get to the airport earlier, or start working on reports earlier.

> **Capitalize on your skills, insights, and connections**—Allow your years of experience to help you be more efficient or effective. For instance, an older surgeon might organize operating instruments more carefully so he or she knows exactly where everything is. Noted concert pianist Arthur Rubenstein, who continued to perform into his 80s, would perform a bit of stage magic by slowing his pace immediately before a particularly up-tempo segment, thereby accentuating the faster section. Stay attuned to the company grapevine so that you can anticipate and prepare for changes in work. Make greater use of organizational support systems and people (e.g., delegate more to IT professionals).

> **Don't try to remember everything**—Write more notes to yourself. Use your personal digital assistant (PDA) to record ideas, meetings, etc. Depend more on others to keep your schedule for you. Insist that follow-up actions be documented after meetings. Keep an organization chart handy to make name recall easier. Write and store directions for seldom-used operations. One interviewee quoted Mark Twain: "If you tell the truth, you don't have to remember as much."

> **Depend more on others**—Listen more intently to others to get their ideas. Become more dependent on your team (e.g., show more faith that they will do things right).

Understand the Retirement Intentions of People Age 50 and Older

Chapter 3 discussed the roles of senior leadership in a retirement management system. I've emphasized the importance of their review of anticipated retirements and the actions they must take to retain select people. However, such organized retirement management efforts are, at the time of this writing, extremely rare (although I expect they will become much more prevalent in the next few years). In the meantime, the bulk of the responsibility for both anticipating people's retirements and taking appropriate actions relative to retaining select individuals rests with the leaders who are one and two levels above the potential retirees. These leaders will feel the greatest impact of their retirees' departures.

Anticipating retirement means not waiting for people to stop by and announce they're ready to retire. At that point, they've already decided. They've been thinking about retiring for some time and perhaps have even told their family and friends already, so it's difficult to get them to consider alternatives to retirement. The situation is analogous to someone who approaches his or her boss and announces that he or she has accepted a job in another company; while it's sometimes possible to change the person's mind, most often it's not. People in these situations have invested too much psychologically in deciding to retire or take a new job. To avoid being blindsided by the loss of a key worker, leaders who are good practitioners of retention management will make a special effort to identify well in advance the people who are most at risk of leaving the company. Then they take appropriate actions to meet those individuals' needs to remove any temptation to follow the next opportunity out the door. The same approach needs to be taken for older workers who are considering retirement—it's the essence of retirement management. The issue is not whether leaders need to find out about their people's retirement plans— they always do! The issue is how?

Questions to Answer Relative to an Employee's Retirement Plans

What are the employee's retirement intentions?

☐ Does the employee plan to leave the organization for another job or retirement? If so, when?

☐ Is the person unsure about his or her plans?

☐ Does the employee want to continue working with the organization?

If the person wants to stay on in the organization, what type of position does he or she desire?

☐ Full-time?

☐ Transition-to-retirement job (part-time, fewer hours)?

☐ Undecided?

Where in the organization would the individual like to work?

☐ Same job?

☐ Different job in the same unit?

☐ Different job in another part of the organization?

In organizations with conventional defined benefit plans, anticipating people's retirements is easier. A leader can calculate the date of an employee's retirement eligibility, and then very naturally ask what the person is planning to do once he or she becomes retirement eligible. In the conversation, the leader can bring up options of future part-time employment, if appropriate. Leaders working for organizations with defined contribution, amended defined benefit, or 401(k) plans face more of a challenge because their employees have more timing options; thus, leaders must ask those employees about their target dates and their plans.

When searching for answers, a leader should be clear that he or she is in no way encouraging the individual to retire. The leader should point out the need to know about the individual's retirement plans for his or her own planning purposes and also to offer assistance in implementing those plans. To assure employees that they aren't being pushed out the door, a leader should not link a retirement query in any way with a discussion of poor job performance or changes in job responsibility.

A best practice would be for the leader to start this conversation by stating that the organization's policy is to allow its people to retire at will. The leader might say something like this: "The organization encourages you to work as long as you can and want to, but we also encourage you to be thinking about your retirement and to be aware of all the options available to you. Have you thought about retirement at all?" If the answer is "no," then the leader might mention the increasing complications associated with retirement and the need to start planning as far in advance as possible. If the answer is "yes," then the leader might pursue the issue relative to the person's plans and timing. For example, an employee might mention that her son is an apprentice chef and that she plans to open a restaurant with him in about two years. Perhaps the organization can help prepare this individual for her change of career. For instance, if she is now an accountant, she might be assigned to audit the organization's food service operations to gain insight into the business.

Many leaders prefer to broach retirement plans in an informal setting, when they have some quality time with an individual (e.g., in a car or taxi ride, sitting at an airport, having coffee or a meal together). Often, a good time to discuss retirement is when someone else in the organization is retiring; then, the leader can refer to that and ask an older employee, "Have you thought about your own retirement?"

Can Organizations Legally Ask About Retirement Plans?

In two cases federal courts have ruled that asking about people's retirement plans is a legitimate inquiry for an organization. In a 1992 case, a federal appeals court ruled that a "company has a legitimate interest in learning its employees' plans for the future, and it would be absurd to deter such inquiries by treating them as evidence of unlawful conduct."[1] In a more recent case (2002), another appellate court said, "Certainly, company officials are permitted to gather information relevant to personnel planning without raising the specter of age discrimination."[2]

The date a person chooses for retirement will depend on many factors, including:

- The employee's own health.

- The health of the employee's relatives, because he or she might need to be a caregiver.

- The person's financial situation. Investment advisors routinely recommend that people should plan on living to be 100. This frightens many people who have a defined contribution retirement plan. After projecting their after-retirement income, many decide to work for a few more years to build up their nest egg.

- The lure of hobbies, such as golf, sailing, or antiquing.

- The success of friends who have tried retirement. Some friends might be thriving and loving retirement—"leading the good life," as it were. With the combination of Social Security and company benefits, these friends actually might have more disposable income than they did while working, and perhaps they're making good use of their money by traveling, playing sports, or pursuing education. On the other hand, other friends might seem to have physically and mentally deteriorated after leaving work, having lost their zest for life.

- Job opportunities outside the potential retiree's organization. If the person's friends have easily found interesting and remunerative jobs, if there's an opportunity to work with their children in a business, or if an opportunity surfaces to try an entirely new field (e.g., starting a franchise restaurant), then the temptation to leave the current job can be very strong.

- Faith that announcing a retirement date won't have negative repercussions. Some people are not forthcoming about retirement plans because they feel their boss will start giving them less-interesting assignments or freeze them out of development opportunities. Or, they might feel that if they make their retirement plans known, their peers or direct reports will treat them differently—possibly by not involving them in projects, not keeping them informed, or not respecting their judgments. In other words, they might be worried about becoming a "lame duck" on the job.

In general, people at lower organizational levels who have available retirement options tend to retire later than they had planned, likely because they become more realistic about their desires and financial situation.[3] On the other hand, senior managers and executives often surprise their organization by retiring earlier than expected.

Anticipating the Retirement of Senior Executives

Sometimes an organization has an upper limit on how long its executives can work, such as one imposed by a board of directors or an established precedent that says no one serves beyond a certain age. But often, exceptions are made.

However, most companies have no restrictions on how early an executive can retire, except where employment contracts are involved. Most executives can retire virtually any time they think they can afford to and feel like doing so, and many are taking an early retirement option, citing the stress of running large organizations in a very dynamic business world, the desire to be a big fish in a little pond by going to a smaller organization as CEO, or the yearning to use their leadership and management skills in a totally different environment, such as in education, health care, or a charity. Often, executives' retirement intentions are influenced more by when their stock options come due or when the organization's stock reaches a certain level, than by the company's retirement plan.

Trying to anticipate retirements at these senior levels can be difficult. Senior managers want to retire with dignity—and not appear to be pushed out the door. They want to choose their time to leave. Also, they don't like to telegraph their retirement intentions too far in advance for fear that their final months or years in the organization might be marginalized and that people will start planning around them rather than involving them. Time and again, I've heard stories from senior executives about how they plan to "surprise" their organization by retiring early and thus be able to do meaningful work up to their last day. This kind of surprise can be extremely costly to a company from a business operations standpoint. With an unexpected executive retirement, the organization might have to accelerate the development of a successor before that person is fully ready or make some other, less-than-optimum staffing move to fill the void.

I have found that a solution to this conundrum is for the CEO or COO to openly discuss the costs to the organization of being blindsided by a sudden senior management retirement. As smart as they are, many executives profess that they hadn't considered all the ramifications. The CEO or COO can then promise that he or she will personally make sure that managers who give adequate notice of their retirement will be fully utilized until their last day of employment.

As opportunities for transition-to-retirement positions become known, I believe individuals at all levels will have more incentive to share their retirement plans with their organization and actively seek input about their options from their leaders and the HR department.

The Effect of Peer Expectations on Retirement Date

Research has shown the importance of peer expectations on a person's retirement timing. If peers expect a colleague to retire at a certain age and assume that it is a foregone conclusion, then that retirement is very likely to happen.[4] Such peer expectations can be particularly strong in organizations that once had a conventional defined benefit plan.

A leader who would like some people to stay longer must counter others' expectations by ensuring people understand the options available to them in choosing their retirement time and by relating anecdotes about people who have stayed longer in the organization. After a few people in the organization resist their peer expectations and delay their retirement, the problem should resolve itself.

Determine Who Should Be Encouraged to Stay with the Organization (If They Want To)

Areas to consider in making retention decisions are covered in Chapter 11.

Find the Optimum Position for Each Individual

After understanding an individual's retirement intentions, a leader has to consider possible job opportunities for that person within the organization: In the same job? In a different job in the same unit? In a different job in another part of the organization?

Usually, a majority of potential retirees wish to stay in their current job (with many seeking changes in work hours, start times, etc.), which obviously makes it easier for the person's immediate leader. Even if a potential retiree requests a different job in that leader's unit, the leader's decision is relatively easy because he or she is intimately familiar with those jobs, knows if such openings are available, and is able to make a good judgment about whether the individual is qualified. However, as discussed in Chapter 11, I highly recommend that leaders check their thinking with their manager and HR.

The real challenge comes in looking at placement opportunities outside the unit. Here, of course, it's definitely appropriate for the leader to seek the advice of the HR department and higher management. If retaining the potential retiree is critical to the organization, his or her future position might well be decided by the organization's talent review committee; and in that sense, action is out of the immediate leader's hands. For the majority of potential retirees, the leader, the leader's manager, and HR representatives must review the options they can present to the person as well as to any other managers involved in the transfer.

Unfortunately, the potential retirees themselves often aren't sure what they want to do. Many have difficulty articulating their preferences and voice them only in vague generalities. It's not uncommon to hear something like this: "I'd love to stay with the organization, but I'm tired of doing what I'm doing. I want something different."

Of course, if an organization really wants to keep a potential retiree who is looking to do something different, it can always create a position. Jobs that are gaining popularity among organizations with an active retirement management strategy are coach and trainer. These roles often benefit everyone involved: They meet the individual's personal desire to leave a legacy, and they accommodate the company's need to preserve or disseminate technological and organizational knowledge to other employees who are not as experienced.

Why Older Workers Make Good Coaches and Trainers

Here are the most common observations by HR managers about why select older workers make good coaches and trainers:

1. **They want to leave a legacy.** As people mature, many are highly motivated to make a mark with their company. They not only want people to think well of them after they've gone, but they also want to look back with pride at the difference they've made. In general, as people age, they become more generous rather than more competitive.[5]

2. **They're "life smart."** They have the confidence that comes from accomplishment and pure survival. Older employees have handled good and bad times. They've had an abundance of experiences, which means they have meaningful and real stories to share.

3. **They're highly motivated to be a good coach or trainer and want to share newly learned skills and insights.** I know several older individuals who, after accepting an assignment as a trainer, have taken college classes, read books, and spent hundreds of hours on the Internet just to bolster their knowledge of what they are teaching. Although they were chosen for this position because of their

experience in a specific area, they became motivated to transform themselves into content experts.

4. **They're willing to give their time to overcome difficult "people" challenges.** Earlier in their careers, many people are too self-focused to give the extra time and effort it takes to really help someone else. In their later years they often have their jobs so under control that they feel comfortable taking the time to help others.

5. **They've learned the importance of sharing.** Older employees are more willing to open up and share their "life's adventures" (i.e., true stories of mistakes and misjudgments) because they know sharing is such an important communication device—and they know how much others will appreciate their openness. Sharing weaknesses or mistakes is not always politically prudent in an organization—people often think the information will be used against them. Older individuals, however, have more self-confidence and a more straightforward attitude. They often think, "What's the worst that can happen? Why shouldn't I tell it like it is?"

Note: Not all older workers are motivated to be trainers or coaches. Leaders need to carefully check people's degree of motivation before making such assignments (see Chapter 11).

Be Honest About Future Job Prospects for Marginal Performers

If an older employee's work seems to be on a downward path or performance appears to be sinking below par, then his or her leader needs to have an honest discussion with the person. This talk can help the individual realistically understand his or her ongoing job prospects—critical information for retirement planning.

This is an important issue because many age-related maladies come on slowly, and older people don't always realize they're not functioning as well as they once did or that their contributions are deteriorating. A good example is Myron Cope, a legendary sportscaster in Pittsburgh who for 35 years provided the radio color commentary for the Pittsburgh Steelers football games. At his retirement banquet, Myron cited his reason for finally calling it quits. He said he had made a deal with a friend in the Steelers organization that when his commentaries were not up to their usual quality, the friend would tell him so. Upon returning to the broadcast booth after experiencing a heart attack and other medical problems, Myron was taken aside one day by his friend, who told him that his work had slipped badly. Reflecting his high work standards, Myron immediately submitted his resignation. Subsequently, he's very happy about his decision and is enjoying his retirement.

Many people need such a reality check, and usually the information they need can come only from an immediate leader as part of a normal performance management discussion. In such a discussion, it's very appropriate for the leader to recognize all the person's past and present accomplishments, yet show that his or her performance or quality has declined. The leader should not mention retirement—just truthfully present observations and data showing a deterioration of performance.

In my experience, most people over 55 are not devastated when their declining performance is called to their attention (of course, this would depend upon their receptivity to feedback throughout their lives). In fact, people are usually very open to such feedback. They're very proud of what they've brought to the organization or to their job, and the last thing they want to do is ruin their reputation by staying on too long when they aren't pulling their weight.

Holding a performance discussion should be a naturally occurring process. After all, in performance management discussions, performance is what a leader talks about when reviewing job accomplishments against an individual's established goals. Nevertheless, such open and forthright talks often don't happen, especially with veteran employees. If there is a history of well-organized, candid performance management discussions, then bringing up more recent changes in behavior will be somewhat easier for a leader. If these meetings have not happened on at least a yearly basis, then such a discussion will be more difficult, but it is still needed.

Leaders can be encouraged to hold discussions about poor or deteriorating performance by:

- Providing them with appropriate training to build the skills and confidence they need to hold such talks.

- Coaching them to think through conversations beforehand and share their discussion plans with their manager or an HR representative before each meeting.

It's also wise to use a discussion planning form for these kinds of important interactions to be sure that the discussion is well thought out.

Together, the training, the planning form, and pre-meeting coaching give a leader the confidence needed to hold the discussion and make it a success.

How a leader handles an older employee's declining performance is nearly the same as the approach he or she should take with a younger employee in the same situation. The leader needs to make the individual responsible for addressing his or her own declining or unacceptable performance (e.g., quality, poor sales) or work habit (e.g., attendance, tardiness, lack of cooperation with others) that is affecting others and the organization.

Dealing with Poor or Deteriorating Performance

When conducting a coaching-for-improvement discussion:

1. Begin by stating the purpose of the discussion and identifying the positive impact—to the person, team, and organization—if the individual's performance improves.

2. Take a balanced approach of seeking and sharing information about the person's performance, the situation, or the task to clarify the details about the performance or work habit situation. Explore specific examples and maintain the employee's self-esteem by focusing on the facts. Discuss the natural consequences if the situation continues and explore the individual's specific concerns. Openly share your concerns.

3. Work together to develop ideas for improvement. Seek ideas and offer your own. Provide support in helping the person make the decision, but don't take over.

4. Decide on a specific course of action and a method for monitoring improvement. Consider how you as a leader will help the person obtain needed resources. Plan for contingencies if appropriate.

5. Finally, end the conversation by summarizing the important features of the improvement plan. End on a positive note by confirming your confidence in the person and your commitment to the plan. Establish a follow-up date.

If the discussion is handled correctly, by appropriately acknowledging the individual's past accomplishments and good reputation, then there is no way the leader can lose. Either the person starts to change his or her behavior to overcome the problem, or he or she starts to think about leaving the organization, feeling that it's not worth the effort to make the change.

The leaders I've interviewed said they found it particularly difficult to hold these discussions with older employees who really weren't poor performers; they just weren't performing as well as they could, and certainly not as well as their replacements probably would. It's very easy to let such performers ride out their time until retirement (often with their pay frozen), and sometimes that's the appropriate thing to do. However, as I have discussed, there's no assurance they will retire. The best thing for them and the organization would be for the leader to press for improved performance or perhaps find another job for them.

Another difficult situation for a leader occurs when an older employee drifts into poor performance not by traditional standards, but rather due to a rising performance standard driven by competitive pressure on the organization. For example, a salesperson who for years barely met the company's acceptable performance criterion of $1.5 million in annual sales suddenly becomes a substandard performer when the company must raise the bar for minimum acceptable sales performance to $2 million a year because it's beginning to offer larger, more complex, and more expensive products. Older workers might feel they've done just fine for many years and think the organization is unfair in pressing them to change. To address this, an effective leader would show that change has, in fact, been a constant throughout such an individual's career and that the person has adapted to it before and can do so again, particularly with the leader's support.

If an individual's performance fails to turn around despite several coaching-for-improvement discussions, then the leader must face the fact that terminating employment is a distinct possibility. The next chapter explores the issue of starting formal processes to end the employment of individuals—no matter what their age—who either are not contributing to the organization or are deterring the efforts of others.

Discussions regarding deteriorating or poor work habits or performance and discussions that could eventually lead to termination point to the absolute importance of having an effective performance management system. Such a system takes the surprises out of performance discussions and should be used with everyone in the organization, regardless of age. (Chapter 13 discusses what it takes for an organization to have an effective performance management system, pages 198–199.)

Encourage People to Plan for Retirement

As stated in Chapter 2, retirement planning is becoming more complicated because there are more variables to consider. People who have a defined contribution or 401(k) retirement plan must decide how best to invest the lump-sum payouts they receive upon retiring. For most people, paying for health care in their retirement will be an important decision, with many private and government-sponsored options to take into account. The pros and cons of moving to a location with lower taxes (e.g., Florida) raise other interesting and complicated issues. In addition to these and many other factors is a new variable for many people—decisions around when and how to retire (e.g., simply walking away or easing out over a number of years through a transition-to-retirement job).

Because of the growing complexities in this area, it's crucial that people get some kind of guidance. Leaders need to encourage attendance at internal and external programs that provide information to people within 10 years of normal retirement age on what to expect and the options available to them. Leaders often hate the thought of hassling their people to attend programs or get counseling, but on returning from such a session, most participants are glad they went. People commonly report that they didn't know all that they didn't know; that is, there were many variables they never considered. At the very least, a leader can make an effort to guide an older individual to the appropriate HR specialist within the organization for help.

Getting direct reports of all ages to start thinking about retirement is definitely a positive. Once they start to consider the important personal issues involved in planning, they might make lifestyle changes such as saving more money for retirement. Their attendance at retirement information meetings also is an advantage for the organization because once people start seriously thinking about their retirement, they can more accurately convey their plans to their leader.

I don't recommend that leaders do any serious retirement counseling themselves. Few have all the necessary information or the skills to do so. Also, the leader might not be a credible counselor regarding job-related decisions. There might be a bias toward keeping an individual or moving a person out of the organization. Leaders help most when they concentrate on guiding their people to the best resources. They should check with their HR department about what is available. (See Chapter 12 for more on retirement planning programs and the leader's role.)

Regularly Check in with Older Workers Regarding Job Performance, Job Satisfaction, and Changes in Retirement Intentions

I strongly recommend that, at all organizational levels, leaders of employees in their middle 50s and 60s hold a brief, informal, private meeting with them at least every four months to gauge how they're doing. The meeting can be in an office or a conference room, or a leader can just find time to have coffee with the person and have a friendly chat. After introductory remarks, perhaps about family or extracurricular activities, the meeting should focus on the person's job satisfaction—and job frustrations. The conversation might then go in a number of directions: job success, general happiness, motivation, career, learning progress, or retirement.

These quick "temperature checks" are particularly important when managing older workers because their situations often change rather rapidly. For instance, an older worker might be quite interested in keeping her job at one point in time, but that could change dramatically if her spouse becomes ill or some other family crisis arises. Life changes happen at all age levels, but occur more often as people get older.

Another possible reason for such quick-check conversations is the likelihood of a sudden deterioration in a person's skills and abilities due to health or other problems. Sometimes people can be reluctant to reveal they have a physical or mental problem and continue working beyond the time when they enjoy the work or can effectively do it. The stereotype of older people being proud and a little obstinate has some basis in reality. The motivations that make them work hard are not far from the motivations that keep them from admitting problems. The best way to deal with this is to give slightly more attention to older workers, particularly by routinely checking in to see how they're doing.

While I have no hard evidence of the effectiveness of so-called quick-check discussions in a retirement management context, such meetings have proven highly effective in cutting turnover in general populations. When leaders have been trained to conduct such discussions, turnover decreases because problems are identified and rectified before the damage is irreparable. The meetings are seen for what they truly are—opportunities for a leader to catch up with an employee and to see if there's anything he or she can do to make work life easier for the individual. In these situations the leader shouldn't be seen as rushing the employee's retirement; to the contrary, these discussions communicate that the leader and the organization value the individual and want him or her to be happy and satisfied on the job. If a person is struggling with work, then more frequent quick checks are appropriate.

It's important for a leader to follow up on information obtained in quick-check discussions. Because of the meeting's short duration, leaders rarely glean enough from them to take immediate, meaningful action beyond merely seeking more facts or having someone else (e.g., HR) take a deeper look into a situation. Usually, the next action for a leader is a more in-depth conversation with the person about the item that came up in the previous quick-check discussion.

Obviously, finding out about someone's retirement intentions is not the main purpose of quick-check discussions, but gaining advance information about the person's plans is definitely an extra benefit.

Outline of a Quick-Check Discussion Between a Leader and an Older Worker

When you are having a quick-check discussion and the person is satisfied with his or her job, you should follow these three steps:

> OPEN by stating that you want to talk about the person's job satisfaction (e.g., "How's your work going?").

> CLARIFY the situation and the person's needs. Don't take a quick "OK" for an answer. Ask about a specific aspect of his or her work (e.g., "How are you getting along with the IT department?").

> CLOSE by summarizing and confirming your commitment to the individual's success.

When an Issue Is Revealed

Complex Issue
When you uncover one or more issues that need to be addressed, AGREE on the next steps and responsibilities, which is usually a meeting on these issues.

Simple Issue
If you uncover an issue that can be resolved easily with the information at hand, you might take a few extra minutes to DEVELOP ideas and AGREE on next steps, responsibilities, and, if appropriate, a monitoring method.

Help People Implement Their Transition-to-Retirement Plans

Regarding older professionals and managers who have elected to work fewer days each week or fewer hours in a day, the biggest problem I've observed is keeping the number of hours they work under control. The fact that voice mail and e-mail improve people's connectivity to the office also presents a downside for some in transition-to-retirement jobs because it's easy for them to do company work at home on the two days they're not working at the office or another location. It's also sometimes difficult for people to adhere to a schedule of only three days at the office. What are they supposed to do when the team leader convenes an impromptu meeting or assigns them to a task force that will require them to work extra days? They likely will agree to do it because they are accustomed to being a team player and saying "Sure, I can do it," or they might want to say yes because they're interested in what's happening.

To really change their lifestyle, some people need a complete break from the office. One executive I know owns a cabin on a lake in Maine. He escapes there for many four-day weekends—more to psychologically and electronically disconnect from the office than to enjoy the beauty of the place, which, of course, he also does. He's told his organization that he doesn't even have a phone in his lakeside cabin—which is not true. Another executive told me that it was so hard to scale back his time that he finally just sent a memo explaining that on certain days he would be totally unavailable by any means of communication. Although it was difficult, he stuck with his decision, and much to his surprise, the company got along fine without him.

For the good of the organization and the individual, the actual hours worked by part-time employees must be closely monitored by the leader. For one thing, it's against the law to pay someone for part-time work and then have the person work full-time hours. But equally important, if restricted hours are not maintained, at some point a person in a transition-to-retirement job is highly likely to conclude that a gradual phaseout isn't working and then quit, thereby depriving the organization of the knowledge, experience, and contacts it had sought to maintain.

Challenges Facing Young Leaders Who Manage Older Workers

In 2005 there was a popular movie, *In Good Company,* starring Dennis Quaid as a 51-year-old advertising executive who suddenly found himself reporting to a manager who was half his age. In addition to being substantially younger, the new boss was significantly less experienced in advertising and leadership. How unique is this situation? And how extreme are the problems?

Ever since the modern organization structure was developed by Alfred Sloan, some leaders have found themselves in situations where they must supervise employees who are substantially older than themselves. It is inevitable. And the situation will become even more common in the next 20 years, fueled by the necessity to rapidly push high-potential younger managers up the organizational ladder to fill positions that are being vacated by baby boomers. Consequently, young, high-potential individuals will be managing groups of people in situations where they don't have extensive leadership experience or technical/professional knowledge. Here are some ideas about what these young leaders need to do to succeed:

Getting Started: Confront the Issue

While the new leader will probably want to have an individual meeting with each of his or her new direct reports, such meetings are particularly important with the older workers. In these individual meetings, a young, new leader should:

> Maintain the person's self-esteem by commenting on how much the person knows, has contributed in the past, and has the opportunity to contribute in the future.

> Empathize with the individual regarding how he or she might feel about reporting to a younger person.

> Draw the individual out to discuss his or her feelings about working for a younger boss.

> If appropriate, empathize with the individual regarding his or her frustration relative to not getting the leadership job.

> Find out what kind of leadership behavior has worked best with the person in the past. The leader can do this by asking questions about past leaders who were very successful in meeting the individual's needs and other leaders who weren't.

> Be sure that performance expectations and measurement methods are clear.

> Seek ideas relative to issues confronting the unit. Ask for the person's input and help in solving those issues.

> Listen for the older worker to mention special projects in which he or she could have an opportunity to shine and receive recognition.

It's important that the younger leader treats each older individual uniquely. Each older employee has different needs and expectations, and they all surely will compare notes after their meetings.

When making introductory remarks to the team, the leader should try to single out some older individuals for their contributions in getting the organization where it is, and make it clear that he or she will be looking for input from these individuals in the future.

Ongoing Management of Older Workers
After that start, an effective leader would use the six Leadership Constants to develop a solid working relationship with each direct report. (See Chapter 8.)

The new leader should conduct quick-check meetings frequently with the older individuals about how they are doing and feeling about their job. The leader must be careful not to appear to be checking the quality or quantity of work unless there's some particular reason to do so. These discussions should center more on each employee's feelings of accomplishment or how the leader can help solve his or her problems.

Sometimes it's possible for the new leader to use an older individual as an informal coach. Then, the leader can make comments like, "Well, I always check with Mary before I do anything in that area." This enhances Mary's self-esteem and probably helps the overall decision-making process. Several older coaches could be involved with the young leader relative to various parts of the leader's responsibility.

The leader shouldn't be afraid to ask for help from people of all ages. By asking for help from older workers, the leader will make it easier for them to return the favor when they need it.

Quality of leadership trumps age any time. There might be some initial resentment, fear, miscommunication, or misunderstanding due to generational differences, but these all can be resolved through good leadership—using the Leadership Constants and the leadership skills defined in this chapter.

Chapter 10

Taking a Stand with Poor Performers

An ongoing leadership challenge facing organizations in the early part of this millennium will be how to deal with older people who turn in marginal or poor performance, have failed to keep up to date on the technology or knowledge required for their job, or are physically unable to perform their work—even after job redesign to make it easier for them—yet want to continue working.

Extending the possibility for employees to work beyond the normal retirement age is a double-edged sword. On one side, it taps a previously unused labor source; but on the other side, it sparks leadership challenges that must be handled in a way that protects the interests of both the organization and its employees while also meeting government regulations.

In my interviews with more than 100 line and HR managers about the employment of older workers, almost all made a similar observation: "We would like some of our people to stay, but we're glad to see others go. We're afraid that if we make adjustments to keep the strong performers in critical jobs, we'll have to do the same for poor performers in the same jobs." Essentially, these leaders are saying they'd rather sacrifice the advantages from making better use of select older workers than to risk any legal problems that might ensue from confronting substandard older performers. This chapter tackles that issue, starting with a review of the legal situation in the United States.

U.S. Age Discrimination Legislation and Its Impact

In 1967 the United States Congress passed the Age Discrimination and Employment Act (ADEA), adding people over 40 to the list of groups protected from discrimination by the Equal Employment Opportunity Commission (EEOC). Since then, age discrimination has become a major source of complaints to the EEOC (see Figure 10.1).

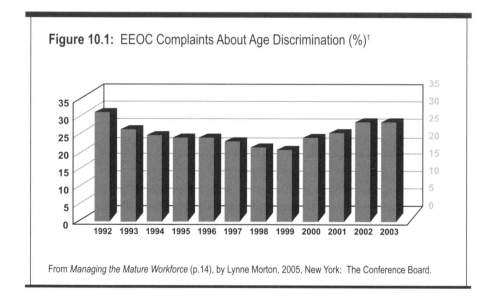

Figure 10.1: EEOC Complaints About Age Discrimination (%)[1]

From *Managing the Mature Workforce* (p.14), by Lynne Morton, 2005, New York: The Conference Board.

Basically, the law says that organizations can't make personnel decisions, such as hiring or firing, based on age. At the time of the ADEA's passage, attorneys expected that most complaints filed under it would focus on hiring issues, following the precedent set by complaints filed by gender- and race-protected classes, but that hasn't been the case. As reported by the EEOC's Office of General Counsel, most of the complaints recently filed with the organization have dealt with termination (44.1 percent in 2002, 62.9 percent in 2003, 46.6 percent in 2004, and 38.9 percent in 2005) as compared with hiring complaints (38.2 percent in 2002, 22.2 percent in 2003, 22.2 percent in 2004, and 19.4 percent in 2005).[2]

Summary of EEOC Laws

The Age Discrimination in Employment Act of 1967[3] applies to employers with 20 or more employees. The law protects job applicants and employees who are 40 or older from age-based discrimination by employers. These protections extend to all terms, conditions, and privileges of employment, including hiring, job advertisements, testing, recruiting, termination, promotions, layoffs, compensation, benefits, job assignments, transfers, use of employer facilities, and training. In addition, the ADEA prohibits retaliation against a protected individual for filing an age discrimination claim or participating, as a witness or otherwise, in such a claim or investigation.

Another law, the Older Workers Benefit Protection Act (OWBPA) of 1990, also outlaws age discrimination. The OWBPA amended the ADEA to specifically prohibit employers from denying benefits to older employees. What the law does permit, however, is an organization offering reduced benefits to older workers in some cases, so long as the cost of providing such reduced benefits to the company's older workers equals the cost of providing benefits to its younger workers.

I strongly suggest that you consult with experienced employment discrimination counsel before implementing any company policies in the protected areas of activity described above.

A survey of judicial decisions in non-jury, EEOC summary judgment cases dealing with age discrimination found that the great majority (73 percent) were won by the defendant organizations. The research found this outcome to be significantly related to such variables as the company having a formal performance appraisal system, a termination decision review process, and the presence of a concrete policy regarding layoffs.[4]

To the extent that these findings can be generalized, they reinforce the need for an organization to have an effective performance appraisal system, a formalized system dealing with employees' poor performance, and most of all, the involvement of its HR department to ensure that each step in its termination process is appropriately handled and documented.

Poor Performance Issues Often Are Avoided

In spite of the "profit-at-any-cost" mentality attributed to businesses by much of the media, the people I interviewed recounted many stories of their organization's allowing older, poor-performing employees to coast to their retirement even though they weren't meeting performance expectations. There are several primary reasons why companies essentially let retirement take care of their employees' performance or work habit problems:

- Respect for an employee's past loyalty and contributions.

- A reluctance to discuss poor performance because managers lack the confidence to handle such difficult situations well.

- Fear that actions such as radically changing people's jobs or terminating them will have a negative impact on the general morale of the unit (the leader seeming like a villain).

- Fear of the legal problems that can arise when people over 40, and especially those near retirement age, are fired.

Here is a common scenario that illustrates management's failure to take action with an older, poor performer: "Joe," a second-level leader in the claims processing department of a large insurance company, is one year from retirement. His unit usually ranks near the bottom in terms of quality and productivity. Employee turnover in Joe's unit is higher than in comparable units, and morale issues there show up more frequently in the organization's annual surveys. Recently, the organization sent a survey, called the $E3^{®}$, to all employees to measure their engagement (i.e., how involved they are in their jobs). The results, just released, show Joe's people to be third from the bottom of 35 comparable units. In spite of periodic discussions with his manager, Joe has made no changes in his managerial behavior. His manager has decided that taking action, such as threatening termination, is not worth the probable gains and is looking forward to the day when Joe retires.

One might wonder how Joe ever got to his current position. Even though he's shown a weakness in basic leadership skills for the past 20 years, he received little developmental feedback about his performance as long as his unit's output met the organization's minimal standards, which it did most of the time. Most annual performance appraisals rated him as "acceptable"; for a few review periods, his rating was actually "more than acceptable." Joe has never been warned, reprimanded, or put on probation about his performance. In times of a tight labor market, his unit's high personnel turnover was very costly to the organization; but, when many applicants were available to fill open positions, it caused no concern—at least not enough to warrant much management attention. Dr. Douglas W. Bray, who studied the progress of managers within the old AT&T structure, characterized Joe's situation as the "upward seep of mediocrity"—meaning that if you don't do something really bad and if you stay long enough, the bureaucracy of a large company will take care of you, and up the organizational ladder you'll go. You won't get to the top, but you'll make some significant progress upward.

The problem in Joe's case—and in many other situations like it—is that natural selection never happened. Time and again, when I asked managers how long an older leader's performance or work habits had been poor, the answer almost always was, "Oh, he (or she) has had that problem for years!"

Holding improvement discussions with older employees is difficult for leaders, the vast majority of whom have never had to face such interactions. So naturally, when they expect a subpar performer to retire relatively soon, most leaders try to postpone such conversations and instead deal only with those individuals whom they believe intend to continue working at the organization. A common rationale is "Why go looking for a problem that's going to resolve itself (i.e., with the person's retirement) in a short time anyway?" The catch here is that in the absence of an economic reason to retire (e.g., a conventional defined benefit plan), there is no assurance that poorly performing older workers will actually retire, no matter what they say in advance. As I have noted, it's quite common for people to change their minds as they approach their retirement date.

Such rationalizations for inaction with poor performers, multiplied many times throughout an organization, can be very costly in terms of productivity, quality, and morale, and can deny promotional opportunities for deserving others and even cause them to look for jobs elsewhere.

The High Cost of Avoidance

The costs to an organization of not facing up to performance or work habit problems can be high. For example, a poor-performing employee might be taking a salary that would be more wisely spent on a better researcher or engineer. Or, a leader's inaction might seem to be condoning poor performance, which could irritate or alienate other workers who see themselves as doing more than their fair share (see Chapter 8, pages 105–107). Just one employee's chronic performance or work habit problem can drag down the performance and morale of an entire work group. And dealing with this employee can dominate a leader's time, greatly increasing his or her frustration and stress.

Difficult Decisions Have to Be Made

As discussed in Chapter 1, retirement laws and regulations are changing. For many of the baby boomers reaching retirement age who still want to work, there now is no economic reason why they shouldn't continue their employment with their career organization rather than having to retire and then get a job with another company. After 2010 many more people whose defined benefit plans were frozen in 2005–2007 will have similar choices. The payout from their defined benefit retirement plans will not be enough to compensate for the money they could be making by staying with their current organization. Even more people will have the freedom to stay with their career company if it has amended its defined benefit plan to allow people to collect their pensions while still working. Thus, more people will stay with their career organization. Most will be good or great employees; some will be poor performers.

In organizations that allow their employees the option to continue working beyond retirement age, leaders must confront performance issues in older workers—as much as they would like to avoid it. The appropriate action for the leader will depend on the extent to which these performance issues have been discussed with the employee in the past.

The Retirement Management Era

Good performers:

> With qualified replacements, work as long as they want.

> Without qualified replacements, can work as long as they want and are offered special work arrangements (e.g., transition-to-retirement jobs) to entice them to stay longer.

Poor performers:

> Get an opportunity to improve—feedback.

> Are reassigned or released from employment.

For older employees who have a documented, long-standing history of unsatisfactory performance, there are two options, depending on the quality of the organization's performance management system and how well it's applied:

If past discussions of poor performance and lack of improvement are well documented:

- The leader should meet with the individual and express the organization's desire that he or she retire for reasons of performance, not age. Most people eligible for retirement benefits will accept the suggestion and resign. There's no humiliation, and the individual is probably uncomfortable knowing that his or her performance is not acceptable. In these situations, people will want to retire with the honor and the prestige they deserve. And if they really do want to work longer, for monetary or other reasons, there may be opportunities for them in other organizations.

- If the suggestion to retire is not accepted, despite the documentation, the leader should start the organization's multistep disciplinary process at the appropriate level.

If past discussions of poor performance and lack of improvement are *not* well documented:

- The leader should meet with the individual to discuss his or her current performance or work habit problems. The leader would explain the problem and help the person determine how to improve (such a discussion is described in Chapter 9). Past performance should not be broached if it either should have been dealt with when it happened or if it cannot be substantiated. In other words, this is the time to start the organization's disciplinary process at the first stage, giving the individual a full opportunity to improve.

- The leader should then conduct follow-up meetings until the problems are corrected or the disciplinary process reaches its conclusion with the employee's termination.

During these discussions it's very important for the leader to recognize the individual's long-time contributions to the organization.

A Structured Process for Discussing Poor Performance

When poor performance or work habits continue after one or more developmental discussions about the person's need for change, leaders must be able to manage a discussion about the ongoing problem. Such a discussion would flow like this:

1. The leader starts by stating the meeting's purpose, providing specific examples of the recurring problem, and describing the consequences (e.g., steps to termination). If appropriate, the leader should reference previous agreements regarding the performance or work habit problem. While it's important to be clear about why improvement must occur, the leader also must be careful to maintain the person's self-esteem. This means remaining focused on the facts and acknowledging the positives, when appropriate.

2. At this point, the employee might be feeling angry or disheartened, so the leader needs to empathize with these feelings without necessarily agreeing with them. If appropriate, the leader and employee should explore causes, rationale, or concerns around the performance or work habit problem.

3. If an improvement plan already exists, then both parties should develop ideas to adjust it. If not, the leader seeks and discusses new ideas for improvement, all the while thinking about how he or she can support the person's improvement efforts.

4. The leader and employee agree on a specific plan by a) identifying specific actions the person will take to improve, b) specifying the resources or support the leader will provide, c) agreeing how both parties will monitor progress, and d) agreeing on how the leader and employee will measure progress. The leader stresses accountability and shows support, yet does not remove responsibility for improvement from the employee.

5. Finally, the leader closes by asking the employee to summarize the agreements made. Again, the leader restates expectations regarding the employee's performance or work habits as well as the consequences of failing to improve. The conversation ends with the leader offering encouragement and confirming his or her confidence in and commitment to the employee

The key element of a termination process is having a number of documented discussions about the poor performance or work habit over a period of time that indicate the individual's opportunities and failure to improve.

No leader takes severing an employment relationship lightly. Leaders, no matter how experienced, need professional advice about this. Besides, it's good to have qualified people on your side if a legal problem arises in the future. Just as they should with people of any age, leaders need to consult with their manager and an HR representative when they implement a plan to deal with performance or work habit issues.

Chapter 13 further examines the need for a good performance management system that documents both good and poor performance and behavior.

A Function of Age or Good Performance Management?

Do people naturally perform better as they age? Or might older workers' higher performance ratings be a function of good performance management?

One interpretation of the positive work habit and customer relationship data presented in Figures 7.1, 7.3, and 11.2 is to assume that people actually improve their performance as they age. Because they are generally more serious about their jobs and life, they try harder to be good employees and team members, and they become more savvy through their accumulated wisdom.

Another view is that the figures represent the natural selection that occurs in an organization. People who had poor work habits and who didn't care about customers either were fired for their poor performance or left because they didn't like their jobs.

I don't know if either interpretation alone is correct; I suspect some combination of the two holds the answer. But the question underscores the importance of having an effective performance management system.

Expect Many More Lawsuits

Just responding to EEOC complaints can be costly to organizations—information must be collected, data compiled, and meetings held. Preparing cases that are headed for trial can incur incrementally larger costs and consume much valuable management time. Thus, most organizations want to avoid getting involved in litigation if possible—even if there's a very good chance they'll win. One way to do this is to simply do nothing special for older workers, in hopes that time will solve all problems. How far will this approach take organizations in the next 20 years?

With the removal of economic incentives to retire, more and more people will elect to stay with their organization, thus making companies more likely to encounter unintended age-related situations, such as an older worker being upset about being passed over for a promotion or feeling pressured to retire. Older workers are already suspicious of management. A 2002 AARP study found that two-thirds of workers over 45 believe that age discrimination exists in organizations, and they are concerned about it.[5] These suspicions along with some kind of negative personnel action, like a demotion, will lead some percentage of employees to take legal action.

Organizations that have an effective retirement management program will be in a better position to defend themselves against complaints, because they will have a documented policy and history of action demonstrating their fairness and concern for older workers. Also, they will have proactively dealt with performance issues at all organizational levels. Companies that don't try to manage retirements will find themselves blindsided by complaints. Their individual managers will make wrong decisions, be inconsistent, and won't have documentation when it's needed. These organizations will find themselves with no fewer legal problems than those practicing retirement management (some are inevitable), but they will have none of the advantages that will come as a result of tapping into the rich source of highly qualified older people they can retain for a few more years.

As stated previously, I'm not trying to give legal advice in this book; rather, I'm alerting organizations to some of the important laws with which they should become familiar. Therefore, organizations that seek to implement retirement management processes should first consult with their own legal counsel regarding age discrimination law.

Section IV

Getting Retirement Management Started

In this section I move to implementing a retirement management system: systematically determining who to try to retain, rehire, or hire from outside the organization; helping current employees prepare for retirement; and setting up a retirement management system.

- Chapter 11—Selecting the Best
- Chapter 12—Helping with Retirement Planning
- Chapter 13—How to Implement a Retirement Management System

Chapter 11

Selecting the Best

"Organizations turn into who they hire" is an old saying, but one I've found to be very true. To describe a company that practices effective retirement management, I would add to it: "Organizations turn into who they hire *and who they retain*." Decisions about whom to encourage to stay beyond normal retirement age and whether an older individual from outside should be hired to fill a position are important decisions that organizations and leaders practicing retirement management have to make. This chapter examines proven methods to help organizations make both decisions. The discussion is based on more than 35 years of DDI's research and experience in helping over 5,000 organizations (including 50 percent of the Fortune 500 companies) install selection and promotion systems.

Selecting People to Retain or Rehire

Chapter 13 describes how to do a retirement audit and match the results against your organization's knowledge and experience needs to identify candidates for retirement management. Sometimes, organizations find themselves with few retention choices; for example, Jane, whose current job performance is acceptable, is the only person with certain knowledge, experience, or contacts and thus needs to be retained in the job for a year or two, if possible. More often, organizations implementing a retirement management strategy are able to choose among several people who have unique knowledge, experience, or contacts, or whose skills will be difficult to replace. They don't need to keep *all* the people who are nearing retirement age—just a few. This coincides with what I've been careful to note throughout this book—that retirement management focuses on keeping *select* people.

Leaders considering a team member for retention and senior managers in a talent review meeting evaluating retention prospects will decide on one of three work situations for an employee:

- Make no changes in the person's job responsibility.

- Keep the person in virtually the same position but with a few new tasks, such as coaching younger people.

- Assign totally new responsibilities (e.g., becoming a trainer or taking on a public relations role).

Decisions pertaining to the first situation are relatively easy; usually, the individual wouldn't be considered for retention if his or her performance wasn't at least acceptable. The other two situations are much more difficult. Leaders often make selection mistakes by not considering unique job requirements of the new responsibilities (or roles) that are unrelated to people's current job performance.

All candidates for retention should be measured against a position's Success Profile. Even incumbents should be measured. Job requirements change; the factors that made a person successful for the last 20 years at an organization might be very different from the success factors he or she will need in the future.

Establishing a Success Profile

The first step in any selection decision is to define what you are looking for—the targets of the selection system. At DDI we call these targets the position's "Success Profile." A Success Profile has four components: the *competencies* (i.e., behavior required), *job challenges (experience)*, *knowledge*, and *personal attributes* (e.g., motivation) for a particular assignment. Figure 11.1 depicts the components of a Success Profile.

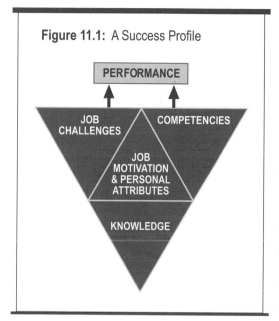

Figure 11.1: A Success Profile

PERFORMANCE

JOB CHALLENGES

COMPETENCIES

JOB MOTIVATION & PERSONAL ATTRIBUTES

KNOWLEDGE

A Success Profile defines what's required to succeed in a job in the future, not how people have succeeded in the position in the past. Thus, the best place to start in constructing a Success Profile is to consider how the organization's strategy intersects with the job's responsibilities.

Computerized programs are available to help organizations build Success Profiles. For more information on constructing a Success Profile, see my book, *Grow Your Own Leaders*.

Here are some of the considerations in evaluating an older individual against the position's Success Profile:

• **Job performance**—Has the person demonstrated a sustained, strong track record over a number of years and been successful in jobs similar to the one for which he or she is now being considered? Has the employee shown an ability to take on new responsibilities or deal with increasingly larger issues? Has the individual demonstrated the ability to get along with the kinds of people with whom he or she will interact in the job (e.g., people in their 20s)?

Performance trends are important. Has the individual's work taken a downswing, even though it is still acceptable? Or, has the person been a late bloomer, actually showing improved performance or output in recent years? The trend line is indicative of where people will be in five years. If it's heading downward, then the person's performance might, in the near term, sink below minimum standards; if the trend line is pushing upward, the individual's performance might be outstanding over the next few years.

Evaluating trends in job performance should be easy for leaders. Each year, effective leaders set measurable performance objectives for their direct reports and then measure their accomplishments against those objectives. Thus, leaders are in a good position to accurately observe employees' performance and interpret quantitative results.

- **Job challenges (work history)**—When thinking about an individual's future, it's important to look at his or her complete past, even though far greater weight should be placed on the most recent experiences and behavior. Too often, important features of a person's background are overlooked when he or she is under consideration for a new job assignment. For example, the organization might forget what an outstanding scientist an individual was before taking on a management job, or that a person came through the HR department rather than the usual route to a position in public relations.

At DDI, we like to think of the key areas of a person's background that are related to job success as "job challenges" that have been successfully handled or mishandled. Some examples might include negotiating agreements with clients, operating in a high-visibility situation, building and leading a team, or managing in an e-commerce environment. Targeting job challenges in an interview or in other parts of a selection system is much more precise then targeting job titles. People with the same job title perform a number of tasks, some of which might be related to success in the job for which they are being considered, while others might not be. Success against the job challenges must be carefully evaluated. Just because a person has had an opportunity to make a number of presentations about technical material doesn't mean that he or she was good at it.

- **Behavioral competencies (e.g., leadership, planning, decision making)**—Competencies most related to an individual's current performance can be observed by managers on the job. Competencies represent the "how" of performance because they are the means by which people meet their job's objectives. Many organizations evaluate these competencies as part of their performance management system.

It's more difficult for managers to evaluate competencies that are less important to a person's current job yet vital to the job for which he or she is being considered. For example, if someone is being considered for an assignment that includes public relations duties, then the person's influence and communication skills would be very important for the role and would need to be evaluated. But if these competencies aren't part of the person's current position, then they would be difficult for the immediate manager to observe and evaluate.

Trainability is almost always an important competency. Often, the transition-to-retirement job of an older worker will require learning new skills and abilities as well as relearning old ones. Almost all jobs in business are constantly changing, and the ability to adapt and thrive is a key one that can be effectively evaluated in a selection system. It's a lot better to identify resistance to training during selection than to identify and have to deal with it in the middle of a training program. Most organizations want people who are highly motivated to keep up to date—people who do not have to be motivated by their boss or others.

Table 11.1 provides examples of some of the competencies that might be important in evaluating a person taking on new sales responsibilities.

Table 11.1: Competency Examples for Sales Positions[1]

- **Active Learning**—Demonstrating zeal for new information, knowledge, and experiences; regularly seeking and capitalizing on learning opportunities; quickly assimilating and applying new information.

- **Compelling Communication**—Clearly and succinctly conveying information and ideas to individuals and groups in a variety of situations; communicating in a focused and compelling way that drives others' thoughts and actions.

- **Demonstrating Business Value**—Effectively influencing other people to accept a solution; clearly connecting solutions to business needs; expressing thoughts, feelings, and ideas in a convincing and engaging manner; demonstrating a professional demeanor that establishes credibility.

- **Devising Sales Approaches and Solutions**—Trying different and novel ways to deal with sales challenges and opportunities; taking courses of action or developing sales solutions that appropriately consider available facts, constraints, competitive circumstances, and probable consequences.

- **Exploring and Expanding Opportunities**—Engaging with customers to explore their situations and needs; probing underlying issues that suggest broader solutions; maximizing the productiveness of interactions by monitoring and building on customers' cues.

- **Seizing the Market**—Actively using one's understanding of key market drivers to create business and customer-focus opportunities and/or expand into new markets, products, or services.

- **Sustaining Customer Satisfaction**—Supporting customers during the implementation of sales contracts and throughout the relationship; seeking and taking appropriate actions on customer feedback; resolving difficult issues in a timely and professional manner; taking responsibility for customer satisfaction and loyalty.

As it is important to spot trends in the person's current job performance, it's also vital to look at trends in competencies to determine if the individual would be an appropriate fit for a position. Take the competency Coaching as an example. What kind of a formal or informal coach has the individual been? How's that changing? Do people seek help from this person? What positive impact from the coaching can be observed? Does the individual vary his or her coaching style according to the situation?

- **Job motivation**—Leaders must seek information to determine if a candidate has the required specific motivations to do the job. This is particularly important if the job for which the individual is being considered is very different from his or her current position. For example, after a person has been in a technical job all of his life, does he want to coach others or work as a liaison with government officials?

Simply asking something like, "Do you want to be a coach?" would not be the best way to obtain the most reliable and truthful data from a candidate. For many reasons, the person might give an untrue affirmative answer. Instead, the preferred method of assessing someone's motivation to coach others would be to ask questions about specific situations in which the person had the opportunity to help others through coaching. How did the candidate feel about the experience? What did the candidate like best? Least? Was the coaching session successful? How was success determined? It's also important to find out whether the individual acted out of self-interest and a personal, positive inclination toward coaching others, or if the coaching was merely an assignment the person had to take on.

Because many older employees who might be retained by organizations likely would be moving into some kind of coaching or consulting assignment, it's important to note that people who are good at a particular skill are not necessarily adept at coaching others in that skill. For instance, we all know of athletes who have made poor coaches as well as excellent coaches who were not very good players.

- **Personal attributes**—Beyond motivation to do a job, personal attributes include personality factors that either facilitate success (i.e., enablers) or impede effective performance (i.e., derailers). Some common personality factors are:
  - Teamwork orientation
  - Positive supervisory relationships

- Conscientiousness
- Extraversion
- Agreeableness
- Openness to experience
- Self-confidence
- Resilience

When selecting older people to retain or rehire, personality factors are particularly important to consider because personalities of people in their 50s and 60s tend to change. In a 2006 meta-analysis of 92 longitudinal studies of aging and personality, Roberts, Walton, and Viechtbauer found that "social vitality" (i.e., sociability, positive affect, gregariousness) and "openness to experience" both decline around age 55.[2] Also, a downward trend in personality test scores was observed in the classic management progress study conducted at AT&T.[3] For 38 years Drs. Douglas Bray and Ann Howard and their colleagues studied a group of college graduate managers and a group of non-college graduate managers as they rose through the management ranks at AT&T. Bray and Howard found that both groups of managers became less affiliative and more assertive, autonomous, argumentative, and willing to challenge authority as they grew older. Similar observations were reported in an AARP study in which HR executives described employees over 50 to be somewhat inflexible, adverse to change, and resistant to learning and understanding new technology.[4] DDI's cross-sectional (i.e., people in different age groups) surveys of 771–1,629 nonmanagement subjects in 31 organizations also found trends in the same direction.[5]

Using well-validated personality tests, DDI also has determined that the variability of some personality test scores markedly increases starting between ages 46 and 55; that is, there are bigger individual differences from the average in personality factors, both up and down.

All of this means that organizations will have to be more careful in establishing the personality and motivation job fit of older workers, whether they are using tests or interviews. As in evaluating employees' experience and competencies, leaders must consider apparent trends in personality: Some people in their 60s and 70s will become more difficult to manage—not necessarily poorer workers—while others will be easier to manage.

How Should Organizations Evaluate the Elements of the Success Profile?

The most common way for an organization to obtain information it needs about current employees relative to the elements of a Success Profile for a position is from manager observations, involving as many managers as possible. The accuracy of any decision depends on the breadth and depth of the information obtained about a person and, most of all, how the information is processed and how the retention decision is made. Generally, the more formal the discussion, the more accurate it is.

The entire talent review committee should be involved in making evaluation decisions about key employees being considered for retention or rehiring. The committee should hear the details about the individuals and match that information against the four Success Profile elements (i.e., competencies, job challenges [experience], knowledge, and personal attributes) for the particular job. The committee's collection of data and its presentation for discussion can be automated through a web-based inventory that summarizes managers' observations and provides expert guidance to the managers discussing an individual. If discussions are run efficiently and all the supporting material is available, retention decisions usually don't take a long time—20 to 30 minutes per person. The time devoted is a good investment for the organization. This process not only assures that the organization's resources are being allocated most effectively, but also captures the thinking of senior people on how best to use certain candidates and musters support for them from many parts of the organization, thus helping to position them for success.

While using a talent review committee to discuss the impending retirement of certain individuals might be a new idea, the methodology described so far in this chapter has been used effectively in hundreds of organizations for succession management purposes (see my book *Grow Your Own Leaders*).

The vast majority of retention and rehiring decisions are made by leaders one or two levels above the individual being considered. Like the talent review committee, their task is to match the individual against the Success Profile of the job for which he or she is being considered and to weigh the loss of the employee against the costs, such as managing someone who wants to take three months of vacation every year. The accuracy of retention decisions can be enhanced by adding appropriate people (e.g., another manager or a representative of the HR department) to bring an outsider's objectivity to the decision-making teams and by slightly formalizing the process.

The Importance of Systematic Data Integration and Decision Making

For both the talent review committee and individual leaders making retention and rehiring decisions, the key to accuracy is systematically reviewing data against the Success Profile and rating candidates against each Profile element (e.g., each of the competencies and background experiences defined as important to success) before a final decision is made. This formal, systematic discussion of information about an individual relative to the Success Profile is called *data integration*. Too often, managers are so enamored of a candidate's potential positive impact on the organization that they forget to consider facets of a position that might present problems for the person. The value of formal data integration before making a decision has been proven time and again in selection situations to be an investment with a significant payoff for the organization. The data integration discussion adds value because:

- Managers review information and observations about *all* elements of the Success Profile—the competencies, knowledge, job challenges (experience), and personal attributes important to success—before making a decision. Also, they discuss gaps in the data or possible problem areas.

- The judgments of several people about how an individual stacks up against a Success Profile are more accurate than those of just a manager acting alone.

- The decision-making process is slowed, thus keeping managers from jumping too quickly to decisions before all the data about a person are fully considered.

- Managers stick to real observations of behavior and tangible facts because they don't want to look bad to other managers by presenting their mere speculation as evidence.

- Race, gender, and age biases can be explored through the insistence that only hard evidence be presented. A person making a broad statement like, "Mary can't take that job because it would require her to learn a whole new technology" is asked to provide specific facts to support the generalization about Mary's learning ability: Has she ever been faced with learning a new technology before? If so, how did she respond? Asking for such details forces the person making the statement to consider the data on which the judgment was made and possibly exposes hidden biases.

Data integration sessions are time extremely well spent. Not only are the ensuing decisions more accurate,[6] but if the individual is placed in a job, potential problem areas are revealed so support mechanisms can be put into place to ensure the success of the individual selected.

Selecting Older Applicants from Outside the Organization

Except for the absolute need to have a well-thought-out Success Profile, hiring people from outside the organization is a completely different situation from deciding which employees to retain or rehire. To obtain information relative to the candidate, organizations must start from scratch. Because interviewing is the most common method of selecting older people, I'll focus on how an organization can improve its interviewing process. I'll also examine the use of tests and simulations.

First, though, a general comment: Organizations would be wise to use older employees to carry out parts of their recruiting, screening, and interviewing processes. They demonstrate the company's commitment to hiring people of all ages and represent living proof of the job opportunities open to senior hires. Their experience and knowledge of the company also can help candidates better understand the organization they hope to join.

Interviewing an Older Applicant

Job interviews can be quite stressful for older applicants because, often, they haven't had to go through an interview for quite a long time. Also, as noted earlier, many older candidates believe that organizations practice age discrimination, so they are very careful about what they say.[7] To alleviate this anxiety, the interview should be unhurried and the interviewer should do everything possible to put the candidate at ease. One way to do this is to recognize the achievements noted on the person's resume or application form.

For any given position, the job competencies, experience, knowledge, and personal attributes (i.e., the Success Profile) sought in the interview should be the same for all applicants, regardless of age. Interview questions and the interpretation of their answers should be totally related to the job requirements. Most organizations use some form of structured, behavior-based interviewing, such as DDI's Targeted Selection® program.

Targeted Selection interviewers cover all four elements of the Success Profile during their interviews, but they focus on the competencies and personal attributes that are related to job success. For each applicant, two or three interviewers seek examples of the person's past behavior relative to each assigned competency or attribute, and then follow up by asking more questions about each behavioral example proffered by the applicant until they understand each example completely. (Appendix 11A contains some examples of Targeted Selection behavioral questions.) Then, each interviewer uses the examples of past behavior to predict the candidate's future job behavior relative to each competency or attribute. After each interviewer has independently rated each assigned competency and attribute, all the interviewers convene in a data integration session to share their ratings as well as the behavioral data obtained to substantiate those ratings. Then they come to an agreement on each part of the Success Profile and, finally, make an overall decision about an individual. This data integration session is a very important feature of the Targeted Selection system. A computer-based system is available to accelerate data integration sessions.

Selling the Job and the Organization

When interviewing older workers, the interviewer also must sell the organization and the job. The organization is not just vying for talent against other employers; it's competing against nonpaying jobs where an individual might have more opportunity to make a socially important impact. And, it's competing against the enticements of full retirement. For many older job seekers, money is not the primary objective of working.[8]

Job candidates of all ages want to know about an organization's reputation and values, but older candidates seem to be particularly interested. Is the organization well managed? Do leaders "walk the talk"? According to a 2006 DDI survey, 65 percent of job seekers over 50 said they were very impressed by the quality of the leadership shown by prospective employers (20 percentage points more than younger workers).[9] Is the organization known for quality products? Is it responsive to its customers? Is it a technological leader in its industry? Does the organization participate in local charities? That same DDI survey of job seekers over 50 revealed that 81 percent were seeking an organization for which they would be proud to work. This was their most frequent expressed need and was significantly higher than the expressed interest of the younger workers surveyed.[10]

Third-party materials, such as article reprints from popular publications, help to convey and shape an organization's image. In addition, it's important to provide candidates with fact sheets that include:

- The organization's vision and values.

- A list of major products and services.

- Financial performance.

- Number of employees.

- Office locations.

- Major accomplishments.

- Cutting-edge technology or products the organization has developed.

- Market share of key products.

An effective interviewer also will carefully review areas of particular interest to most older workers, such as flexible hours, health benefits, growth opportunities, and a friendly atmosphere. For each area, the interviewer should be prepared to tell a brief story illustrating how these offerings have worked out for another older person in the same operation where the applicant would work. For example, rather than saying, "We give people a lot of training," an effective interviewer might tell the story of a woman, Ellen, who had been out of the workforce for 30 years and lacked job skills and confidence. But because of the extensive training she received along with the on-the-job coach every new person is assigned, Ellen was able to blossom and within a month was performing as well as any of her colleagues. But Ellen wasn't satisfied with that—she took more company courses and continued to learn. Within a year she had become a new-employee coach.

Testing Older Applicants

Along with interviewing, organizations use job-related testing to help select the best older candidates. Because of the large volume of positions to be filled and applicants to be processed (sometimes thousands per day), most large retail chains and national food service organizations use tests to qualify and screen entry-level applicants for both their first-level management and nonmanagement positions. Other heavy test users are call centers and new manufacturing plants.

The first rule of selection testing is that the test must be valid for its use; that is, it must reliably evaluate a relevant part of the position for which the individual is being considered.   There are several ways this can be established, depending on the test, the job in question, and the realistic threat of legal issues regarding selection fairness. I would strongly advise seeking professional help in establishing and documenting the validity of any tests used.

The age distributions on decision-making tests show why professionals are needed. As shown in Figure 7.3 (in Chapter 7), older applicants for supervisory jobs achieve the highest scores on the situational judgment test; conversely, they get the lowest scores on tests that focus on mathematical reasoning and interpreting charts and diagrams. Figure 11.2 shows similar results from when a customer service-related situational judgment test and a problem-solving test were administered to 3,346 candidates for customer service positions.

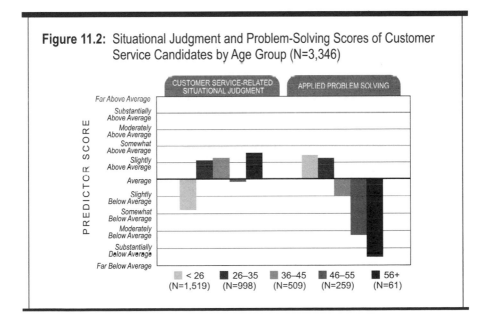

Figure 11.2: Situational Judgment and Problem-Solving Scores of Customer Service Candidates by Age Group (N=3,346)

Which test is better? Which is fairer? It depends on what spells the difference between a good performer and a poor one. If analytical reasoning is important, it is perfectly appropriate to use the applied problem-solving test, even while realizing that older workers' performance tends to be poorer. (Remember, this is not the case for all older workers. Many will be able to do better than the average younger worker, but an organization must work harder to find those individuals.) If customer service judgments are more important, then the customer service-related situational judgment test is more appropriate.

As you can see, it's very easy to choose the wrong test—one that systematically discriminates against older individuals for no job-related reason. That's why it's important to involve a highly skilled, experienced professional in test selection and in determining how the test scores are interpreted.

Tips for Adapting Selection Tests to Older Workers

1. Increase the font size of tests or any other instruments used in selection so that people with slight visual impairment are not unfairly disqualified.

2. Avoid tests requiring a quick recall of numerous facts unless that is an explicit job requirement. Instead, use text-based, situational judgment tests if they can produce the needed information.

3. If the test is administered by computer, offer the candidate time to practice using the technology.

4. Avoid using abstract reasoning tests in which people have to determine patterns in triangles and squares to make decisions. Older workers tend to perform disproportionately worse than younger people on these kinds of instruments. I've also observed that they particularly seem to dislike them—perhaps because they've never encountered such tests before and don't see the relevance.

Conducting Simulations

Many important elements of a Success Profile are difficult to evaluate through interviews or tests—particularly those that reflect aspects of a job that are new to the individual being evaluated. For example, because a person being considered for a training assignment might never have had any teaching or training responsibilities, seeking examples of past behavior in relevant competencies might be difficult. In this case, an organization could set up a situation in which the candidate could demonstrate training skills. For example, the person could be asked to train someone on some technology or procedure skills that he or she had developed in a current or previous job. Managers then could observe and evaluate the candidate's basic training skills in action. They also might make some suggestions for improvement and allow the candidate to repeat the training assignment, thus evaluating how well the person responds to feedback.

Simulations are particularly useful in evaluating older candidates who have been out of the job market for some time. These people might not sport an impressive resume, but in all likelihood they will have developed life skills to make them highly effective in many jobs. All they need is an opportunity to prove what they can do. Simulations provide that opportunity.

Many companies use phone-based simulations as part of their screening process. For example, a hiring organization might provide an applicant some basic information about a product and a potential client and ask the person to prepare for a brief sales phone call. Then, someone from the organization or a testing firm would act as the client in a role play over the phone and evaluate the applicant's sales ability during the call. DDI has observed thousands of people who have never had any formal sales experience or training do very well in these exercises, reflecting the skills they've developed over time in influencing others, selling ideas within a previous organization, or using innate interpersonal skills. Frequently, their performance in the simulation is enough to convince an organization that they have the potential to succeed—something the company wouldn't have accepted based solely on the individual's previous job experiences—and they get invited in for the next phase in the selection process.

Simulations also are used extensively at higher levels in an organization, with candidates going through an assessment center—a series of simulations mirroring the kinds of tasks and situations a person would typically encounter in a supervisory or management-level job. See *Grow Your Own Leaders* for a description of an Acceleration Center®—a special kind of "day-in-the-life" assessment center experience used to evaluate senior leaders and candidates with potential for senior leader positions.

On-Boarding

It's becoming increasingly more common that a selection system does *not* end with the acceptance of a job offer by a candidate. Rather, it goes beyond that, culminating in the transfer of information obtained from the person's screening, testing, and interviewing activities to his or her new supervisor, who uses the information to kick-start the new hire's development. In the best organizations, during the new hire's first week on the job, the leader and the new hire use the information from the selection system to provide insights into the individual's strengths and development areas. Together, they work out a plan to enhance the new hire's identified strengths and overcome or avoid the designated areas in need of development. This "fast start" development planning makes an excellent impression on new employees of all ages by demonstrating that the organization really wants them to be successful. It may be especially welcomed by older workers taking on new job activities in a new organization because it would help to alleviate their natural anxieties.

Appendix 11A

Examples of Targeted Selection®
Behavioral Interview and Motivation Questions

In the Targeted Selection system, an interviewer is given a number of questions to ask to prompt a candidate to provide specific behavioral examples. Not all the suggested questions for a competency need to be asked; instead, the interviewer moves on to the next competency when he or she has obtained enough behavioral data to evaluate the competency. Similarly, the interview ends when the interviewer has gleaned enough data from the applicant to evaluate all the target competencies.

Some of the most common competencies sought in interviewing older workers are Continuous Learning, Ability to Collaborate with People of Different Ages, and Motivational Fit. A few examples of Targeted Selection behavioral and motivational fit questions about these competencies follow, along with some general responses that both strong and weak candidates might likely have.

Continuous Learning

1. *What have you tried and failed at recently?*

   - Strong candidates make the attempt. It doesn't make any difference whether they were successful.

   - Weak candidates don't try.

2. *What have you learned lately? What new knowledge have you obtained?*

   - Strong candidates can cite specific examples of knowledge or skills they've obtained. The Targeted Selection interviewer looks for the more recent experiences (the more recent, the better) and checks to see if these examples occurred within the company or outside. The interviewer also checks to see if the individual has had an opportunity to learn and grow but didn't seize it. Strong candidates can produce a variety of examples throughout their lives and can particularly talk about their experiences in the last five years.

     Weak candidates can cite examples from earlier in their lives, but don't spontaneously recall relatively later examples. When probed, they might come up with one answer, but not much more.

Ability to Collaborate with People of Different Ages

1. *Tell me about your direct reports (work group).*

   - Strong candidates will describe younger people as well as older people. They will have stories to tell about individuals of all age groups and indicate a broad interest in people of all ages.

   - Weak candidates don't know much about their direct reports or colleagues. They concentrate their attention on people who are about the same age as they are.

2. *How long did it take you to get a significant leadership or technological (scientific) position? How long does it take current people? Do they miss anything by being developed much faster (or slower)? What were the advantages of the way you were developed?*

   - Strong candidates think that new, faster ways are better. They can see advantages and disadvantages.

   - Weak candidates look fondly on old ways.

3. *Who is the youngest individual you've worked with? What was the situation? What did you do to make your work relationship as positive as possible? How did it work out? Do you find it harder or easier to work with young people than it used to be? Why? What do you do differently?*

   - Strong candidates can name several young people they've worked with and can tell stories about their significant interactions. They like young people and enjoy working with them. They have adapted to younger colleagues' needs.

   - Weak candidates don't know many young people and have difficulty explaining how they are unique. Such candidates don't see the need to adapt to their younger counterparts.

4. *What does work-life balance mean? Where are most young people in terms of work-life balance?* If they see differences: *Provide an example of how you have taken the work-life needs of others into consideration.* (**Note:** Research says that work-life balance is more important to younger people—at least they bring it up more as something of great concern.)

   - Strong candidates recognize younger people's need for work-life balance and the additional pressures that younger workers might be under that they might not have experienced (e.g., husband and wife both work).

- Weak candidates haven't thought about the issue, nor do they have an opinion.

Motivational Fit

1. What are you looking forward to in the next few years? What are some examples?

- Strong candidates answer that they're looking forward to new learning, adventure, meeting and working with new people, etc.

- Weak candidates are less adventurous; they tend to give answers like "same old thing" or "doing less." They don't have a positive view of their life; they would be more likely to characterize themselves as "just living through it."

2. What part of your life gives you the most pride? Talk about specific situations.

- Strong candidates produce a broad range of answers, with work-related activities being part of them.

- Weak candidates don't take pride from their work. They might take pride in side benefits of work (e.g., prestige, travel), but not from the work itself. Also, they might take pride in accomplishments from earlier in their work career, but not recently.

3. What would you like to accomplish with the rest of your life? Where does work fit in?

- Strong candidates say they want to help others solve problems, develop people, or make a major scientific, technical, or business contribution. Often, they also relate that they want to be good grandparents and make a difference in their grandchildren's lives. They have goals on and off the job and can give examples of actions taken to achieve their goals.

- Weak candidates find this question difficult to answer. They see life as something to be endured. They can name very few goals.

4. How will you answer that question five years from now?

- Strong candidates assume they will still be active and working toward their goals. They can tell stories about putting their plans into action.

- Weak candidates are not as goal oriented or as planful.

Chapter 12

Helping with Retirement Planning (Next-Life-Phase Planning)

For baby boomers, retirement planning is far more complicated and presents infinitely more issues to consider than it did for their parents. As they reached retirement age, more than 80 percent of the previous generation was covered by some kind of defined benefit retirement plan, which provided a guaranteed income for life.[1] All they had to do was stop working and then cash the monthly checks. Any savings they had would have expanded their retirement opportunities, but most people felt they could live a fairly comfortable life with modest savings.

Retirement planning for that generation meant calculating the type of lifestyle they could afford with the combination of their employer pension, Social Security, personal savings, and any other pensions, such as those resulting from time served in the U.S. Armed Forces. People didn't show a great deal of interest in company-sponsored retirement planning programs until their retirement was in sight. They had no doubt that the government and their employer would take care of them. Much of the time spent in company-sponsored retirement planning programs dealt with how people could enjoy their retirement (e.g., taking up hobbies, doing community service work, etc.).

Unfortunately, life will not be so sweet for many of the younger baby boomers. Over the next 30 years, the number of private sector retirees who leave their jobs for a comfortable retirement from a defined benefit pension will dramatically shrink, placing a premium on the potential retirees' ability to prepare for the days when they no longer will be working. They will be personally responsible for decisions that will affect their financial future through decisions about how much they contribute to their retirement and where the money is invested. They also will have to decide when to start taking money out of their retirement plans and how long they will work full-time and part-time in order to comfortably live out their 60s and 70s. In Chapter 2 I called this time the period of "high anxiety" because very few things will be certain, particularly people's retirement income from investments and the amount of money they will need to finance their future medical expenses. A 2006 McKinsey study documented this rise in anxiety, finding that in the two years prior to the study's publication, concern about whether people will have enough income for retirement had doubled and concern about the viability of Social Security had tripled.[2] This heightened anxiety should spur people to start their retirement planning much earlier and do a better job of sticking to their plans.

When Should Retirement Planning Start?

Of course, the answer is "as early as possible" so people can determine how much they must save to enable them to have the lifestyle they want when they retire; then, they need to start saving the money. In a survey conducted by McKinsey, about half of the respondents under the age of 45 reported they had started to formally plan for retirement. However, the survey also found that their plans were often based on some serious miscalculations about the amount of money they will need and their chances of earning it before age 65.[3] Higher-income people (over $100,000 per year) are more likely to engage in both formal and informal retirement planning than people with lower incomes, and men are more likely to plan for their future than women.[4]

When People Plan to Retire[5]

A 2005 *New York Times* poll of 1,000 people came up with this distribution of people's retirement age goals:

> Before 60 years: 20%

> Between 60–64 years: 20%

> 65–69 years: 30%

> 70 or older: 12%

> Never: 11%

> Have not given retirement much thought: 7%

A 2006 AARP poll came up with exactly the same percentage of people planning to retire at age 65 or later—42 percent. The AARP research also found that age has a lot to do with retirement targets, with younger workers thinking they will retire earlier and older workers later.[6] The difference between the younger and older groups is probably a function of older workers' more realistic estimates of the cost of retirement and the money they will have available.

As people get serious about planning their retirement, they will have a lot to think about. Here are some questions they'll need to ask themselves:

- How long will I live? Obviously, this is difficult to predict. But people can estimate by looking at statistical information and their family history. Life expectancy tables that predict a life span of 20 years after age 65 give *mean* data; by definition, then, there is a 50 percent chance that a person will live longer than that. Some financial planners tell people to add two years to their parents' life span as a good guess of how long they will live, assuming their parents had a natural death. Other planners tell people to plan to live to be 100. How much risk should a person take? There's no agreement among experts.[7]

- What monthly income can I expect after retiring?

- What other financial resources are available (e.g., first or second home, inheritance)?

- How will I pay my health care costs? What might these costs realistically be? What about the possibility of a long-term illness?

- What work opportunities past age 65 are available within my career organization?

  - Full-time work?

  - Transition-to-retirement jobs (full- or part-time), including the possibility of going through periods of working and not working before I finally reach full retirement?

- What work opportunities exist outside my career organization?

  - Types of paid full- and part-time jobs that seem interesting (e.g., possibly serving on a board of directors or doing part-time retail work with lots of people contact)?

  - Ability to predict the job market when I decide to seek reemployment?

  - Opportunities for self-employment?

- What about the psychological factors associated with my missing various aspects of work (e.g., loss of camaraderie, sense of achievement, personal identification)?

- What opportunities exist for unpaid work at nonprofit, cultural, or other organizations (e.g., Executive Service Corps, community food bank, etc.)?

- What are my non-work alternatives?

  - Relaxation, travel, hobbies, visiting grandchildren, etc.?

  - Help family members who are ill or who have small children?

All these issues must be factored into the individual's personal situation (personal health, family, dependents, choice of place to live, etc.) before appropriate decisions can be made. In fact, for baby boomers the term *retirement planning* really isn't a very good descriptor of what needs to be considered; rather, *next-life-phase planning* more accurately depicts the kinds of decisions to be made.

A 2005 Fidelity Investments poll of retirees revealed that 57 percent wish they had done more to prepare themselves for retirement, and 17 percent said they wished they had retired later.[8]

Retirement Planning Must Be Ongoing

An important insight for people considering retirement is that retirement planning is not a one-time event; the world moves too quickly for that. For instance, U.S. government rules and programs change, and companies continually offer new and "improved" retirement packages. Think about people who have recently found themselves with "frozen" retirement benefits—whose retirement plans are being shifted to 401(k) plans—and now need to totally revamp their plans. Also, people's personal situations and the general economic climate often change, causing them to rethink their plans.

Should Organizations Provide Retirement Planning and Counseling?

Currently, I don't believe organizations are in a very good position to directly provide retirement planning services to their own employees, because company-sponsored programs might be seen as biased relative to the employment opportunities they discuss. They may push too hard for people to leave or stay. Rather, I see the most appropriate role for an organization is to provide help in finding appropriate counselors or classes for potential retirees. Of course, there will be many exceptions, particularly companies that have a long history of offering retirement planning programs and that have adapted them to fit the new realities of retirement facing baby boomers.

Certainly, an organization can help finance the cost of retirement planning if it wants to make that a benefit of employment. It's not unusual for senior managers to have their company assume the costs of their retirement planning efforts, mainly focusing on financial planning.

Organizations will find that they benefit from having older employees who have thoughtfully considered their retirement options and directions. With this aspect of their lives under control, these people will be able to focus on their work rather than being increasingly more anxious about their future. And, they'll be more accurate about their retirement plans, thereby enabling their company to then do a better job of retirement forecasting and management. Retirement planning certainly will benefit the individuals themselves and thus will be seen as a meaningful employee benefit. Organizations that don't promote retirement planning very likely will find themselves with some very unhappy employees in a few years when they near retirement.

How to Get People to Plan for Retirement

How can an organization help its employees think about retirement? One major way would be to provide assistance by making a qualified expert available to talk to potential retirees about the need to plan their retirement and to inform them about the help that is available through the company or outside groups.

The policy in some organizations is to have a trained HR representative interview employees about their retirement plans when they reach a certain age and then again every year afterward. Generally, the first interview is scheduled 5 to 10 years from the age that most people in the organization retire (which is too late for many people). In the subsequent annual interviews, employees are offered help in executing their retirement plans. The interviewers also can serve as a sounding board for employees' concerns or anxieties about retirement.

By setting a fixed time for this discussion and then holding it at relatively the same time for everyone, the organization avoids legal problems inherent in discussing retirement. The interviewer should clearly state the organization's policy of having no fixed retirement date for its employees and emphasize that because almost everyone has to retire at some point, the company wants to help people get ready for an enjoyable life when they finally do retire. There should be no organizational agenda in these talks, and if people don't want to discuss retirement planning, they shouldn't be forced to. The interviewer should be absolutely neutral about the age at which people would retire. However, there's no reason an organization can't use the information gleaned in these interviews to plan for backups and other contingencies.

There are numerous other actions organizations can take to prepare their employees for retirement. They can:

- Print frequent articles in the company newsletter or magazine about the need for employees to consider retirement planning, particularly by contributing to a 401(k) program in which a portion of their savings is matched by the organization.

- Use a variety of communication vehicles to feature people who have chosen to stay with or return to the organization. Their stories might be included in company magazines, at company events, or just through managers who can refer to them when talking with people who are considering retirement options. It can be very helpful for potential retirees to talk with people who've decided to work past retirement age so they can hear both the pros and cons of what these people have experienced. Communication about retirement models can be the start of a "virtuous cycle." That is, the more people know about the opportunities to be flexible regarding retirement, the more they'll want to avail themselves of those opportunities; they, in turn, will become models for others approaching retirement.

- Stock how-to books and articles about retirement in the company library or make them available through some other means.

- Offer a list of reputable retirement counselors and programs in areas where the organization has a large population. Choosing the right counselor can be difficult for people. The HR department should be able to provide guidance about which counselors or programs would be best for a particular individual.

- Allow outside organizations that offer retirement guidance the opportunity to make presentations to people after hours and then promote employee attendance at those meetings. The host company should be clear that it is not endorsing the outside organization or services; rather, it is merely giving the firm a chance to talk about what it can do relative to guiding people's retirement.

- Train leaders to encourage their direct reports to thoughtfully consider available retirement options. This does not mean offering specific retirement advice. Leaders should limit their help to getting their people to think about retirement and assisting them on where they can get good advice.

- Offer clear, understandable financial information so people can accurately calculate the income they can expect from the company, Social Security, or any other sources. The information people need to plan for retirement goes beyond the basic information they receive possibly once or twice a year in a benefits statement.

- Provide access to computer programs that can help people project their financial needs and resources. Understanding retirement benefits can be quite complicated, thanks in great part to how the government has set up a number of its programs. For example, the more income individuals over 65 earn, the less they will receive in Social Security payments because Social Security becomes taxable beyond a certain earning level.

There are many computer programs that can help people project their likely future situation. It's relatively simple for a human resource department to acquire such a program and to help people use it.

- Use yearly (or more frequent) defined contribution and 401(k) statements that show the progress of employees' investments to remind employees of the longer-range financial counseling that is available.

Starting a Business

My interviews of professional and managerial retirees found many of them are starting their own business rather than returning to their career organization or going to work for another company. I don't know how much of a choice they had in this decision, but those who have chosen to start their own business, often with a family member, profess to be very happy. Many say they're working harder than they ever did in their previous job, but they love being their own boss and seeing the direct results of their efforts.

Retail is often the business of choice (e.g., opening an ice cream store, a battery store, or a restaurant). Others have launched themselves on a much grander scale by buying a ski resort, purchasing a fleet of houseboats for rental, or conducting tours of Antarctica.

These individuals, all of whom retired with fairly good assured incomes, say that they didn't make the decision to go into their own business to make money; instead, they just wanted to keep busy and do something different or to help a relative get a start in business.

It's probably a good thing they didn't have high expectations about making money, because most of the people I talked with have realized only meager earnings. They are working for a lot less than they had earned during their earlier career.

Why People Don't Plan for Retirement

I've heard some very interesting rationale for people's failure to plan for their senior years:

- Being in denial (e.g., "Retirement is for old people!").

- Failing to see the need. They experience some general anxiety about retirement, but it's not focused enough to get them to plan.

- Being too busy in their current job; thus, thinking about retirement is not a high priority.

- Feeling afraid of what they will have to do if they figure out they're lacking in what they need for retirement. It's like being afraid to go to the doctor to get a medical test result: They don't want to hear bad news.

- Believing there's nothing they can do about their future retirement situation; they're already working as hard as they can.

- Thinking they aren't ready for the tough decisions that must be made. At this stage in their life, it's too late to make easy decisions.

- Underestimating their chances of living a long life after retirement. According to *New York Times* columnist David Leonhardt, people in their early 70s and younger consistently underestimate their chances of living to 85.[9]

- Thinking they have a plan when they really don't.

- Assuming their spouse has everything worked out for their retirement years.

Counseling for One or Both?

Retirement is not an individual affair. It involves the person who is leaving the organization as well as his or her dependents, particularly a spouse or significant other. Of course, situations differ, but in general many experts have found that a couple being involved together in retirement counseling will help the two people come to better decisions about their future direction. It also can be a trigger for them to have more meaningful conversations about their future.[10]

Should Job Search and Interview Training Be a Pre-Retirement Service?

Many baby boomers who take advantage of pre-retirement counseling will find that to meet their projected lifestyle needs, they must get a transition-to-retirement job in or outside their current organization. As is typical for this generation, they probably have changed jobs several times in their career. Few have followed their parents' hierarchical (i.e., one career) trajectory. Thus, because of their experience, they should have considerable ability to seek new opportunities and responsibilities within or outside their current organization. Yet, if they are like the recent retirees I've talked with, the thought of being interviewed for a new position will be frightening for many of them.

Many organizations that have reduced their workforce have offered terminated employees training on how to find another job as well as on how to make a good impression and sell themselves in future job interviews. But I know of only two organizations that offer similar benefits to their potential retirees. Such training could be particularly meaningful to people who plan to seek a transition-to-retirement position in another part of their organization. One very large U.S. company has found that training potential retirees on preparing a resume and making an impression during an interview has paid off for both the company and its older employees. Those who complete the training are much more confident when they seek job openings in other parts of the company, and they fare better in their interviews.

I've written a book, *Landing the Job You Want*,[11] that describes how people can prepare for job interviews. Older workers who want to do their best in upcoming interviews for inside or external positions will find it quite useful.

Making Retirement Plans Happen

Many people in their 70s and 80s can tell sad stories about failed retirement plans—how in retirement they found themselves in situations very different from what they had hoped: having a lower standard of living, depending on others, and living in a state of constant anxiety. Many didn't plan very well (i.e., they failed to consider all the variables), and most didn't follow through on their plans (e.g., to develop new skills for a post-retirement job or to save more money).

I believe that one of the snags for people in following through on their retirement plans is the time frame of their implementation strategy. Generally, retirement planning encompasses long-range issues: how long people will live, how much money it will take to provide for their desired lifestyle, etc. That long-term horizon usually leads to long-range goal setting, which is not very motivating for many people. An alternative might be helpful. Perhaps people should plan sequential and overlapping three- to five-year strategies. Such goals are much more actionable, measurable, and motivating. They might include getting a real estate license so that upon retirement a person can become a realtor, returning to school in hopes of eventually becoming a college professor, taking on more overtime assignments to increase yearly retirement savings by 25 percent, or writing a short story as preparation for working on a novel that's been percolating for years. Other goals might include sampling some new job areas within the organization, such as assuming more writing assignments if a person is considering a transition to marketing, or trying out the role of a project coordinator if that is an area of possible interest.

In a 2003 research study, retirement planning programs that emphasize explicit and realistic goal setting were found to lead to more meaningful actions on the part of potential retirees than programs that only provided useful information. Programs that push individuals into goal setting are probably particularly important for people whose day-to-day positions don't require much planning.[12]

Many People Fail to Take Advantage of Their Organization's Retirement Planning Assistance

Financially oriented retirement planning classes supported by organizations with defined benefit plans are not nearly as popular as one might think. Most companies report that less than 50 percent of their retiring people actually take advantage of such classes. The number of people who partake of individual counseling supported by their organization is somewhat higher, but far from 100 percent. This may be due in part to the lack of effective communication about the availability of these services.

I believe this situation will change because:

- The baby boomer generation is, in general, much more demanding of services and has higher expectations of their "rights" than their parents' generation ("veterans"), which was more prone to just take what they were given.

- There are now many more options open to people, thus requiring more information to be provided.

- Government programs are extremely complicated, and often qualified people are needed to figure them out.

- Individuals with defined contribution or 401(k) plans often leave their organization with a large lump sum of money (for some, it's $1 million or more). The decisions they make in investing this money are crucial.

- Baby boomers have had more experience with career counseling than their predecessors, and they might be more open to seeking outside advice.

Group meetings about financial and life planning likely will soon be retired themselves and replaced by individual counseling. Financial and life planning is so complicated, with so many variables to consider, that an individual approach is virtually a must. Many people might find that a combination of personalized guidance provided by a trained, experienced counselor plus insights gained from a computer-based program is the best answer to meet their needs.

The Pension Protection Act of 2006 allows a plan administrator to make professional investment advice available to defined contribution plan participants and be protected from liability for breaching fiduciary duty.[13] There are many unscrupulous people offering retirement planning advice, and it can be difficult for people to weed them out from advisors who will work in the employees' best interests. It seems like the least an organization should do is to lead its employees to reputable firms that can provide the guidance they need and to suggest questions they should ask of advisors to check for a good fit of skills, knowledge, and experience.

The AARP web site (www.aarp.org) is a good source of retirement information. Another source is the SHRM pre-retirement planning tool kit (http://www.shrm.org/hrtools/Toolkits_published/CMS_014954.asp).

Any retirement help would be better than the situation currently facing many American workers. In a 2005 poll conducted by Fidelity Investments, 77 percent of the retirees polled reported they didn't seek help from their employers in planning their retirement; however, of those that did, 92 percent reported that the guidance they got was valuable.[14]

Chapter 13

How to Implement a Retirement Management System

If what you've read to this point has convinced you to be proactive about confronting the expected labor shortage brought about by looming baby boomer retirements, then it's time to consider implementing a retirement management system in your organization.

There are three primary and several secondary steps involved in getting a retirement management system up and running:

1. Develop a plan and obtain top management's commitment.

    a. Conduct an audit to estimate how many people the organization stands to lose to retirement over the next 2–10 years.

    b. Make an economic case for retaining or rehiring select older employees for specific jobs.

    c. Make an economic case for hiring select older candidates from outside the organization for specific jobs.

    d. Write a plan, have it reviewed and approved by experienced legal counsel, and present it to top management.

2. Set up the required infrastructure, provide training, and ensure management support.

    a. Clarify responsibilities, align systems, and set goals.

    b. Expand the responsibilities of the talent review committee to include retirement management decisions.

    c. Ensure that the right people, below the talent review committee, are involved in retirement management decisions.

    d. Train leaders throughout the organization in their responsibilities and help them develop the retirement management skills they need.

    e. Develop leaders' competency and confidence to take action with poor performers.

    f. Encourage retirement management applications through ongoing measurement and communication of successes. Produce an annual report on the progress and status of the retirement management system.

3. Ensure that annual performance reviews happen and result in action.

Following is an in-depth description of each of these steps and a discussion of important implementation issues. Later in this chapter, I describe the roles of the HR department in retirement management.

1. Develop a plan and obtain top management's commitment.

    a. Conduct an audit to estimate how many people the organization stands to lose to retirement over the next 2–10 years.

        Organizations need to know how many people will retire and when as well as how these anticipated retirements will be distributed across units and job specialties. This knowledge will allow them to anticipate problems and take prompt actions to address them, such as implementing a retirement management or succession management program. Organizations also need data to gain their top management's commitment to the actions required to manage retirements— particularly, establishing or expanding talent review meetings to deal with retirement issues and training leaders to effectively handle the challenges they will face with an aging workforce. The content of a retirement audit as well as how to conduct it differs across companies. First, I describe how to mine existing organizational data for an estimate of an organization's situation, and then I explain how to conduct a more formal retirement audit.

For organizations with a conventional defined benefit retirement plan, conducting an audit of the current situation can be relatively simple. The HR department should be able to assemble information on individuals who are 2, 5, and 10 years away from being eligible for retirement. A graphic output of what such data might look like is shown in Figure 13.1.

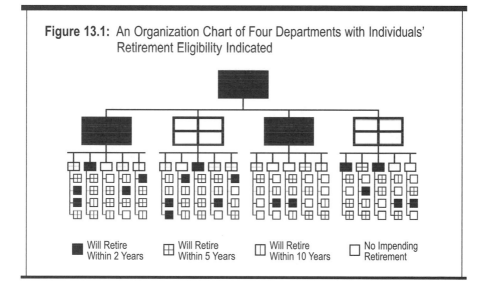

Figure 13.1: An Organization Chart of Four Departments with Individuals' Retirement Eligibility Indicated

■ Will Retire Within 2 Years   ⊞ Will Retire Within 5 Years   ⊡ Will Retire Within 10 Years   ☐ No Impending Retirement

Figure 13.2 shows individuals in the same departments and designates those with new plant start-up experience and with experience operating in Asia, particularly China.

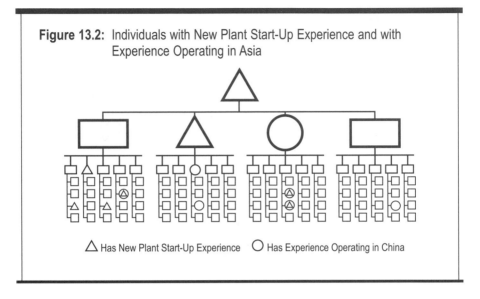

Figure 13.2: Individuals with New Plant Start-Up Experience and with Experience Operating in Asia

△ Has New Plant Start-Up Experience   ○ Has Experience Operating in China

Figure 13.3 shows a combination of Figures 13.1 and 13.2.

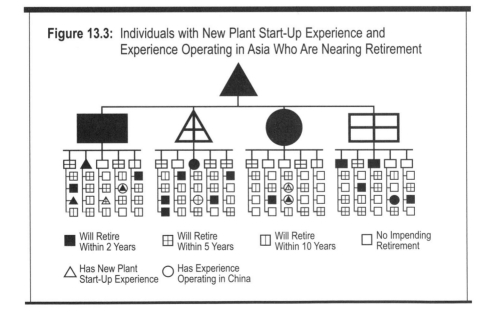

Figure 13.3: Individuals with New Plant Start-Up Experience and Experience Operating in Asia Who Are Nearing Retirement

■ Will Retire Within 2 Years   ⊞ Will Retire Within 5 Years   ⊟ Will Retire Within 10 Years   ☐ No Impending Retirement

△ Has New Plant Start-Up Experience   ○ Has Experience Operating in China

The organization shown in this example is planning to open five plants in China over the next 10 years. It hasn't opened a new plant anywhere in the world in the last 15 years, and considerable new-plant expertise has already left the company, mainly in the form of retirements. The remaining expertise is not widely distributed, and the people who have it are nearing retirement age. As a matter of fact, most of them are within two years of retirement, and only one of the people with plant start-up experience who will remain for about 10 years has experience working in China. It's through analysis like this that organizations can make meaningful decisions about how to handle the outflow of older talent.

Predicting when people will retire from companies that provide no economic incentive to retire can be more difficult. An organization facing such a situation can make a somewhat educated guess from looking at its overall age distribution. How many people are over 55, 60, 65, or 70? Where are they located, and what are they doing? This information gives an organization a rough idea of what it's facing relative to impending employee retirements. Such information can be quite frightening when age data are superimposed over key positions in the organization as shown in Figure 13.4. Note in this example how everyone in the department on the extreme left is about the same age. What knowledge will be lost when they retire? Who will be the backup for the senior manager, who is already over 65?

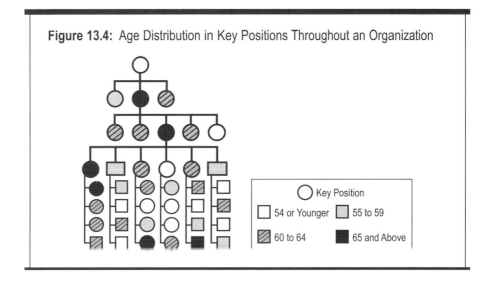

Figure 13.4: Age Distribution in Key Positions Throughout an Organization

Key Position

54 or Younger   55 to 59

60 to 64   65 and Above

The problem with relying on age data and even retirement eligibility data is that baby boomers, as I have noted, often will leave organizations earlier or stay longer than did people their age in previous generations. Increasingly, age will become a less accurate predictor of retirement; thus, many organizations will find that "noninvasive" data mining cannot produce the information they need relative to their employees' potential retirement dates. Instead, they'll need to find other ways to get information about their employees' retirement plans.

A few organizations survey their employees to collect information about their retirement plans. For example, the management of TVA realized that 40 percent of its workforce could be eligible for retirement by 2008 and felt compelled to find a way to keep vital technical knowledge from leaving the company. "TVA needs to retain critical technical knowledge to make sure the power supply is reliable and plentiful," stated TVA Media Consultant Gil Francis. Starting in 2003, TVA began to survey its employees annually regarding their retirement plans. Of the employees who returned the survey, 80 percent provided a nonbinding planned retirement date. TVA then was able to match the expected retirements against a "position-risk factor," which was based on the need to retain technical knowledge for operating its plants, and to determine the necessity for action. It's important to note that TVA's practice is to survey all its employees.[1]

Other companies I've looked at are more subtle (and much less accurate) about employees' retirement plans. They conduct internal surveys in which each level of management is required to estimate the retirement dates of their direct reports over age 50. Managers are told to rely only on their knowledge of people's current plans and *not* to interview them about their retirement plans. Both the reliability and validity of these estimates are highly suspect.

I believe the best survey is one that collects data from managers at every level who have been encouraged to discuss retirement plans with their people as appropriate. Chapter 9 cites court decisions that have upheld the right of management to collect data regarding their employees' retirement intentions.

Directly asking people about their retirement plans has several advantages. It:

- Reaps more accurate information.

- Forces leaders to start thinking about retirements in their units.

- Compels leaders to have meaningful, future-oriented meetings with potential retirees—an activity I believe is very important.

- Boosts leaders' confidence in talking about retirement plans with their employees so they will continue holding such discussions on a regular basis and get more in-depth information about their reports' preferred job options and timing.

For the initial audit, a manager might be asked to provide answers to questions, like the following, relative to each of his or her direct reports:

- Plans to retire:

  - In less than 2 years?

  - In 2 to 5 years?

  - In 5 to 10 years?

  - Hasn't thought about it./Has no plans to retire.

- Importance of keeping the individual past planned retirement:

  - Highly important?

  - Somewhat important?

  - Not important?

Once all the surveys are in, it's a good idea to look at the expected retirement numbers by different job categories and units. Often, there is considerable variance (see Figure 13.4). Some parts of the organization are pockets of younger people, while others are populated with a large number of more seasoned employees.

Faulty Assumptions

What false assumptions keep organizations from working harder to retain their older employees? Here are a few that I've heard:

> We believe there won't be a labor shortage because:

  ► Boomers won't retire; they'll need the money.

  ► New labor-saving technology will eliminate enough jobs.

  ► Increased productivity of the remaining workers will make up the shortfall.

> We believe the labor shortage will be resolved by:

  ► Hiring from outside—there won't be a shortage of applicants with the needed skills.

  ► Outsourcing.

  ► Hiring immigrants.

  ► Hiring replacements who are currently in the pipeline.

> We're afraid we might violate federal law if we take action to keep select older individuals.

---

b. **Make an economic case for retaining or rehiring select older employees for specific jobs.**

Table 13.1 summarizes the arguments, pro and con, of retaining or rehiring older workers versus replacing them from outside the organization. As noted in Chapter 5, research by Towers Perrin has found that, in general, the weight of the argument is on the side of retaining or rehiring older workers.[2] But, of course, that does not hold true in all cases, and top management will quite correctly require company-specific information on each of the cost factors (if they can be obtained or even estimated) before they will be totally convinced.

Table 13.1: Relative Cost Factors Associated with Retaining or Rehiring Nonexempt Older Employees Versus Hiring Replacements from Outside the Organization	
Let People Leave *Replace from Outside*	**Manage Retirements** *Retain or Rehire Select Older People*
• New nonmanagement hires are usually paid less than experienced people.	• No productivity is lost while positions are open.
• New nonmanagement hires are eligible for less vacation.	• No recruitment/training costs associated with hiring replacements.
• No need to create part-time, transition-to-retirement jobs.	• No productivity is lost while new employees get up to speed.
• New hires might have skills or experience that older individuals lack.	• No loss of knowledge, experience, or contacts.
• Younger workers carry lower health care costs.	• Lower turnover and absenteeism costs associated with older workers.
	• Older workers typically have better work habits than younger workers.
	• Retaining or rehiring older workers will have a positive effect on team morale.

Similar comparisons can be made relative to the retention or rehiring of managers, executives, and professionals. For these key people, the arguments for retention management are much stronger because of the higher cost of recruitment, on-boarding, etc., and the high compensation rates of hard-to-find replacements. As with consideration of retaining or rehiring nonmanagement individuals, organizations would be well-advised to weigh the arguments relative to exempt-level individuals based on their own data.

The economic case is much different if people retiring are replaced by qualified people from within. Then, most of the advantages of retaining or rehiring disappear. Only the potential loss of knowledge, experience, and key contacts remains as a major factor.

c. **Make an economic case for hiring select older candidates from outside the organization for specific jobs.**

Table 13.2 summarizes the arguments, pro and con, of increasing the age diversity of new hires from outside the organization, in particular by hiring more younger (under 26) and older (over 56) workers. As discussed in Chapter 7, Towers Perrin, in looking at the general tradeoff between hiring older versus younger workers, found that the increased health care costs of workers over 50 is about 1 percent of their compensation. This cost, Towers Perrin believes, is outweighed by older workers' performance factors.[3]

Table 13.2: Relative Cost Factors Associated with Recruiting and Hiring a Broad Range of Age Groups into Nonmanagement Positions[4]	
Hire People of All Ages, with More Emphasis on Those Under 26	**Hire People of All Ages, with Less Emphasis on Those Under 26 and More Emphasis on Those Over 56**
• Lower health care costs. • Better applied problem-solving skills. • More rapid assimilation and application of new job-related knowledge.	• More reliable (e.g., follow through on commitments). • Better attendance. • Better punctuality. • Fewer disciplinary actions. • Better safety awareness. • Better customer focus. • Better customer service-related situational judgment. • Better planning and organizing. • Better teamwork/collaboration. • Better retention. • A positive effect on team morale.

Organizations should assemble their own company-specific data on health care expenditures by age group and come to their own conclusions. Also, they should consider only the factors in Table 13.2 that are important to job performance in the specific job or job category for which an individual is being considered for employment.

For example, planning and organizing and teamwork/collaboration might not be important to a specific position.

An important issue in determining the value of hiring more older workers is the population against which the older workers are being compared. Obviously, if the alternative is to hire workers under 26, then the argument for hiring more people over 56 would be much stronger than if the alternative is to hire people between 26 and 56.

At this point, management ought to be able to make a thoughtful, data-based decision about retirement management. I believe the correct decision would be to implement retirement management for select positions. For many jobs or individuals, the reasons for making a concerted effort to retain, rehire, or hire from the outside are simply too strong. Management also should have enough information to develop a well-conceived implementation plan, which should drive its next steps.

d. **Write a plan, have it reviewed and approved by experienced legal counsel, and present it to top management.**

The last actions in Step 1 are relatively easy: Pull together the arguments for retirement management (made in points "a," "b," and "c" above) and develop an implementation plan. Such a plan would address the following questions:

- Would the retirement management program focus on retention, rehiring, hiring from outside the organization, or a combination?

- Would the program be implemented globally or strictly in the U.S.?

- What organizational levels would be targeted?

- How would the talent review committee be oriented to its new responsibilities?

- How will leaders at all levels be oriented/trained in their new responsibilities?

- What kind of general communication (if any) would have to be made about the plan?

- How quickly would the program have to be up and running?

Management will expect examples of and information on the costs and benefits of various scenarios (e.g., the costs involved with putting 10 people in part-time, transition-to-retirement jobs), the financial risks associated with providing health care coverage to older people, how much more two part-time people cost than one full-time employee, etc.

A best practice at this point is to ask a consultant or some other experienced person to review the plan to be sure nothing has been overlooked. Then, as a final step before presenting the idea to top management, I would recommend that the plan be reviewed and approved by a legal advisor who is familiar with pensions, benefits, and EEOC law. It is a virtual certainty that members of top management will have questions about the legality of the effort.

2. **Set up the required infrastructure, provide training, and ensure management support.**

   a. **Clarify responsibilities, align systems, and set goals.**

   Like all management initiatives, the accountability for a viable retirement management system must be established by senior management, with goals set, actions planned, and methods for measuring progress approved. Usually, the implementation responsibilities fall to the human resource department, while senior management stays involved by participating on the talent review committee, reviewing reports provided by HR, and following up to ensure the retirement management system is operating appropriately.

   Because retirement management is a fairly new concept, many organizations find that their compensation, vacation, training, and other HR systems are either not aligned with it or, in some cases, actually act to thwart its efforts. For example, an organization might find that its lack of medical coverage for part-time workers is a problem in recruiting or rehiring older employees; the company might respond by establishing a special "bridge" benefit that will cover employees only until they reach 65 and are eligible for

Medicare. Alignment and improvement of various systems to make an organization attractive to older workers is clearly an HR responsibility and an opportunity for some organizational creativity.

b. Expand the responsibilities of the talent review committee to include retirement management decisions.

Attendees at talent review meetings usually include the CEO or the COO, and managers directly below them. Large organizations can have several talent review committees, organized by divisions or geography.

The most common purpose for talent review meetings is succession management—to identify people to populate the organization's Acceleration Pool® and to periodically review their development. (For a description of how talent review meetings operate to facilitate succession management, see Chapter 15 in *Grow Your Own Leaders*.)

The second most common responsibility of a talent review committee is retention. The executives develop a "watch list" of individuals who are high retention risks and take appropriate action—in the form of increased compensation, recognition, new assignments, or relocation to try to keep them.

When the issue of retirement comes up in talent review meetings focused on succession or retention, it's usually in the context of the organization being able to use the soon-to-be-vacated jobs as development opportunities for Acceleration Pool members or individuals who are at a high risk of leaving. Typically, there is little or no discussion about persuading people not to retire.

However, once top executives understand the problems they face relative to potential baby boomer retirements and realize that these retirements can, indeed, be managed, they will agree to add time on their committee agendas to discuss actions that can and should be taken relative to retaining certain individuals.

Figure 13.5 shows how the talent review meeting relates to all components of an organization's talent management systems.

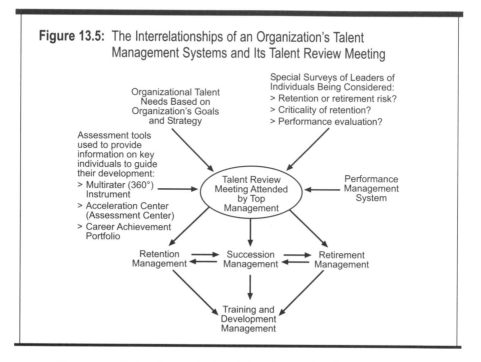

Figure 13.5: The Interrelationships of an Organization's Talent Management Systems and Its Talent Review Meeting

Organizational Talent Needs Based on Organization's Goals and Strategy

Special Surveys of Leaders of Individuals Being Considered:
> Retention or retirement risk?
> Criticality of retention?
> Performance evaluation?

Assessment tools used to provide information on key individuals to guide their development:
> Multirater (360°) Instrument
> Acceleration Center (Assessment Center)
> Career Achievement Portfolio

Talent Review Meeting Attended by Top Management

Performance Management System

Retention Management

Succession Management

Retirement Management

Training and Development Management

Because of the interrelationships shown in Figure 13.5, I believe that retention, succession, and retirement should be considered in each talent review meeting, even though at any given time there might be a focus on one over the others.

Managers tend to enjoy participating in talent review meetings even though the meetings take them away from their other duties. Managers realize that they are accomplishing important work for the company while getting new insights into the people to whom they are entrusting the organization's future success.

Obviously, in large organizations top management cannot be concerned with each and every retirement. The talent review committee must focus on the impact of key retirements as defined by their management level, unique knowledge, and if they are in difficult-to-fill positions. Other retirement issues must be delegated downward just as retention responsibility is. (Chapters 8 and 9 discuss the retirement management responsibilities of individual leaders.)

For a description of how talent review committee meetings can facilitate retirement, succession, and retention management, see Appendix 13A. For more information about the sources of information used in talent review committee meetings, see Appendix 13B.

c. **Ensure that the right people, below the talent review committee, are involved in retirement management decisions.**

Chapter 11 examines the advantages of involving several people in key retirement management decisions, such as which older employees to retain and what job alternatives to discuss with each potential retiree. More accurate decisions result from involving several people who can share and discuss data about a particular person before reaching a decision. The potential retiree's immediate manager and his or her second-level manager are obvious choices to be involved. The higher-level manager is apt to be more familiar with the organization's strategy and direction and, therefore, will have a better understanding of the knowledge, experience, skills, and contacts that will be needed in both the short and long term—and, thus, recognize the importance of keeping certain people.

The immediate leader of a person under consideration almost always is a key person in the discussion, but might not be the best person to talk with the employee about his or her particular retirement plans. In such situations this responsibility should revert to the manager at the next higher level. Here are some examples of situations in which higher-level involvement might be appropriate:

- If the higher manager has a long and close relationship with the potential retiree.

- When the immediate leader is new and, thus, unfamiliar with organizational policies and practices.

- If there have been personality or performance problems that have caused difficulties between an immediate leader and the individual that might prevent the potential retiree from being candid with him or her.

- When the organization wants to indicate its special interest in the person. One way to do this is by having higher management involved in discussions about retirement.

d. Train leaders throughout the organization in their responsibilities and help them develop the retirement management skills they need.

Training leaders in the skills required to effectively lead and meet the special needs of older workers is a major HR responsibility. Some of the areas that need to be covered include:

- Being sensitive to the unique needs of older workers, effectively displaying the leadership behaviors they desire.

- Determining employees' retirement intentions and what options they are considering.

- Guiding older workers to appropriate retirement planning help.

- Encouraging select older people to stay with the organization by discovering the incentives that will meet their unique needs and, if appropriate, providing them.

- Taking action with individuals who want to stay beyond retirement age but whose performance (or the availability of jobs within the organization) does not warrant that possibility.

In particular need of leadership training in this area are new leaders who are substantially younger than many of the people they will supervise (i.e., an intergenerational workforce). They face a potentially difficult situation with their older workers and will need all the coaching and training they can get (see Chapter 9).

All the leadership skills pertaining to retirement management are trainable. If a program is going to be successful, then training must be combined with management reinforcement and coaching—actions that should be encouraged by the HR department. Higher management and HR can support the leaders' training by:

- Making sure all leaders understand the organization's commitment to utilizing older workers where appropriate.

- Being proactive in dealing with the needs of older workers.

- Modeling the Leadership Constants (presented in Chapter 8) in their interactions with lower-level leaders.

- Providing leadership training that builds skills and confidence.

Diversity Training for Leaders

Many organizations periodically offer their leaders training on the importance of valuing diversity—particularly regarding gender and race—and their role in achieving it. It also would be appropriate to offer comparable training regarding various age-related issues and to identify the barriers to the success of older workers so they can be minimized. This training should not only focus on what cannot be said to older workers (e.g., making age-related jokes), but also address what can be done to make each older employee's career as satisfying as possible.

Organizations essentially have three options relative to building awareness of diversity issues associated with an aging workforce:

- Make available a discrete training course that deals specifically with the issue of aging, its opportunities, and potential problems.

- Include aging along with gender and race in a valuing diversity program.

- Discuss issues relative to managing older workers at the same time that leaders are developing skills to handle common leadership issues. For example, age issues can be discussed as part of a training program in the Leadership Constants so participants can see how each Constant uniquely applies to older workers and can practice the needed behavioral skills in situations where older individuals are involved. The unique legal issues regarding dealing with older workers that are covered in traditional diversity programs often can be added to a course on performance management or selection.

I strongly believe the third alternative for building awareness is the best single option because it builds the skills and confidence leaders need to take action. It also emphasizes that the fundamentals of leadership are the same for everyone, with only minor nuances separating age groups; one doesn't have to learn a whole new set of skills. The second and third alternatives represent the best combination of options.

A key aspect of almost all programs dealing with aging is the issue of stereotypes. There is no question that a major obstacle for organizations trying to use more older workers is overcoming lingering stereotypes about people who are older than 40, older than 50, older than 60, and older than 70. A variety of creative methods can be used to expose these stereotypes and correct them. Even something as simple as having participants list well-known people over 70 who are still fully functional in business, government, and the arts is a start.

e. **Develop leaders' competency and confidence to take action with poor performers.**

The big challenge for higher-level managers is how to get the leaders below them to confront poor performance, no matter what an individual's age. Many leaders put off holding such discussions, hoping that some miracle will occur and the employee's performance will turn around. The manager of the leader who needs to hold a difficult discussion about performance or other matters should work with the leader to plan it. I recommend they use a discussion planning form that will enable them to think through all aspects of the discussion beforehand, including possible next steps. Then, the manager should role-play the interaction with the leader and discuss the underperforming employee's probable reactions and how best to handle them. Following repeat (or serious first-time) discussions regarding poor performance or work habits, the manager should insist that the leader writes a follow-up letter describing agreements and the next steps. The leader should give the letter to the individual and also put a copy in the person's file.

f. **Encourage retirement management applications through ongoing measurement and communication of successes. Produce an annual report on the progress and status of the retirement management system.**

Retirement management won't happen unless top management sees it as a priority. To communicate its importance, senior leaders must at least annually review:

- The organization's overall situation relative to retirements (e.g., if certain departments will be particularly affected).

- The performance of managers or units relative to managing retirements, and then recognize those who are doing an especially good job.

- The ongoing fairness of processes and procedures relative to older workers.

- Retirement planning and referral services being offered to people approaching retirement age.

- The alignment of various HR systems (e.g., selection and benefits) with retirement management efforts.

I highly recommend that the human resource department be asked to produce an annual report showing retirement management's progress in the organization against measurable and meaningful goals. For example, top management should insist that training success in building leaders' retirement management skills be measured on outcomes—not simply on the number of people who attend classes.

3. **Ensure that annual performance reviews happen and result in action.**

Performance management is a key step in helping all employees feel empowered and that they are growing professionally and contributing to the organization's success. It involves setting and reviewing meaningful, measurable performance and behavioral goals, with appropriate follow-up actions if they are not achieved. If an organization has an effective performance management system, then everyone's work will be aligned with its strategy, vision, and values. People will feel they're making meaningful contributions to help the company succeed.

If a company has had an effective performance management system in place over the years, there should be few performance problems as employees grow older. When their job duties change to require different skills and knowledge, they'll set new goals and expectations with their leaders to accommodate their new responsibilities. Over the years poor performance or work habits would have been corrected, and consistently underperforming employees would have been either moved to less-demanding jobs or terminated.

An effective performance management system provides a documented history that can be used to establish the rationale for allowing a person to stay with or leave an organization. If the documentation is solid, then there's no problem. It's perfectly legal to encourage a good employee to stay or to terminate an individual who is underperforming.

Alas, well-implemented performance management systems are not universal. According to a DDI survey, nearly 25 percent of respondents rated their organization's performance appraisal system as ineffective.[5]

Thus, for many organizations a major roadblock in the realization of a retirement management system is the need to improve their performance management system. How else can they decide who to encourage to stay or leave? Performance management is clearly the responsibility of every employee and manager, but a lot of help is also needed from the HR department and top management.

Higher management and HR can support the implementation of a performance management system simply by modeling it—that is, by using the same interaction skills and wording of performance goals with their direct reports as those leaders should use with their own reports. Top management and HR also must provide support systems and coaching around how to deal with especially difficult employee situations.

What It Takes to Have a Successful Performance Management Program

DDI has consulted with hundreds of organizations, including some of the world's largest companies, on realizing their goals for their performance management system—that is, making the system produce the desired results. Here's what DDI has found to be necessary for success:

> Communicate the importance of both goal setting and reviewing people's progress toward achieving those goals as well as the expectation that goals will be set once a year and reviewed at least twice a year. Make a case for the benefit of having all employees' efforts aligned with the organization's strategy and values.

> Include three components in performance management plans: specific, strategy-related outcomes to work toward; behavioral expectations to achieve the desired outcomes, which align with the organization's values; and each employee having a development plan.

> Train everyone at all levels in the skills they need to effectively set their own goals and behavioral expectations and evaluate their results. Also, train managers in the coaching skills they will need to guide their direct reports to set goals and to review their progress toward accomplishing them. The performance plan should be "owned" by the individual, not the leader; the leader's role is to coach and help the person to achieve the goals set forth in the performance plan. A combination of classroom and e-learning can be used to provide the training.

> As much as possible, automate the performance management system. Electronic programs are available to walk individuals through the preparation of goals (quantitative, qualitative, and behavioral), their midyear reviews, and their final evaluation of goals. Such programs make the performance management process easier for both the individual and the leader and facilitate communication through the elimination of paper. One key advantage of automation is that business goals throughout the organization are clearly and visibly aligned. Automation also allows HR and senior management to know who has followed through on their performance management commitments and who hasn't.

> Audit the quality of at least 10 percent of the completed performance management documentation (i.e., plans, reviews) each year. The best performance management systems have such a quality audit built in. Following an annual performance cycle, a skilled auditor reviews randomly selected performance documentation to see if the goals are clear, measurable, and realistic and if the actions taken by the employee to achieve those goals were appropriate. The auditor then meets (face-to-face or over the phone) with the employees whose plans were audited and the managers who approved the forms and provides them with feedback. Once a year the auditor also makes an overall report to higher management about the general quality of the overall performance management system and any organizational problem areas. Management has a great deal riding on having a successful performance management system. It needs to know what percentage of people are completing the plans and with what quality as well as where any noncompliance is located. Often, management finds pockets within the organization where people are not following through on their performance management obligations.

While these steps might seem a bit heavy on management scrutiny and control, anything less would invite a breakdown in the system. Even if everyone believes that performance management helps individuals focus their work on what's really important and gives them a sense of achievement through realistic goal setting and reviews, the fact remains that, unless encouraged by higher management, people still put off scheduling their performance review discussions. Often, they come up with imaginative rationalizations about why goal setting is not needed or not implemented. It takes a clear, top-level commitment and the modeling of effective performance management practices by upper management to realize the intended goals of the system.

For more information about what it takes to achieve the full benefits of a performance management system, I highly recommend the book, *Realizing the Promise of Performance Management* by Robert W. Rogers.[6]

Role of the Human Resource Department

HR's support is critical to any retirement management initiative. The rest of this chapter focuses on some key activities for which a human resource department is responsible.

Provide Information for Talent Review Meetings

HR plays a staff role in talent review meetings by preparing information on each employee who will be discussed and progress reports on people whom the committee has put into transition-to-retirement jobs. Also, HR is responsible for analyzing data obtained through the talent management system relative to broader considerations of retirements in the organization. For example, if a number of people in a unit are eligible to retire but it looks like there's a good chance that most of them will continue in their jobs, there's less pressure to rapidly accelerate the development of replacements to fill those jobs. People still should be groomed, but at a pace that emphasizes quality over speed (i.e., the organization doesn't try to rush people to be ready in one year when three years is really needed to impart the necessary skills and experience). It's also HR's job to measure the success of retirement management interventions and report progress to senior management.

Identify Whom to Keep and Whom to Let Go

Part of HR's responsibility is to help line organizations make decisions about which potential retirees they should try to retain, which they should make no effort to keep, and which they should encourage to leave (see Chapters 9 and 10). For this responsibility, HR needs to take a strategic view. For instance, if an organization's strategy is to return its focus to a product area that has been deemphasized for 20 years, it's likely that there are very few employees left who remember the old product or have experience with it. For this strategy to succeed, it might be very important for the organization to retain some people with that specific product knowledge, at least long enough for them to pass on what they know. A line organization unaffected by such a shift in product focus could easily miss this consideration.

Support Leaders in Their Retirement Management Responsibilities

It is incumbent upon HR to be available to consult with leaders throughout the company relative to each of the special challenges described in Chapter 9. HR personnel need to be involved because they understand the organization's retirement practices as well as the degree of job flexibility that can be offered to potential retirees. They also have expertise in avoiding the two legal pitfalls leaders face in holding retirement discussions: the appearance that they are forcing people to retire (a form of age discrimination) and the issues around offering special work arrangements to some individuals and not to everyone (see Chapter 5). At the very least, leaders should consult with HR representatives before making any transition-to-retirement offers to potential retirees.

Sometimes, leaders need to either invite an HR representative to attend a discussion they are planning with a potential retiree or ask a human resource associate to hold certain talks without the leader being present (e.g., a discussion about positions available outside the leader's responsibility). The degree of HR's direct involvement varies depending on the older person's position in the organization.

Shell Oil: An Example of Retirement Management[7]

Shell Oil has created the position of Global Skill Pool Manager and given the people in that role the responsibility of ensuring the viability of six skill pools in the exploration and production areas of the company: five technical skill pools (such as petroleum engineering, production engineering, and field engineering) and one commercial skill pool. On a worldwide basis, the Global Skill Pool Managers identify critical jobs in their assigned skill area and make sure there are backups ready to step in when needed. While the Global Skill Pool Manager has a multinational responsibility, Shell also has Regional Skill Pool Managers.

While Global Skill Pool Managers concentrate on the senior-level employees, Regional Skill Pool Managers meet regularly with each assigned technical employee at their sites to assess the individual's current and future career interests. In addition to thinking of retirements, Regional Skill Pool Managers act as coaches regarding skill development and job opportunities.

Help Individualize Work-Retirement Options

As I've noted, there's no one-size-fits-all solution to retirement management. Transition-to-retirement packages often must be crafted to a particular individual's needs. HR must have people who can stimulate leaders' thinking about options they can offer. Creativity is needed, but not so much as to set expensive precedents for the organization.

While providing incentives to keep people in their present jobs is often quite easy, moving people into transition-to-retirement jobs in different units can be a particularly troublesome situation in some companies. For many organizations it represents a big leap to start an older worker in a new job in which he or she is untested. A lack of faith in the ability of older individuals to make such a transition is probably a factor in keeping some people out of many job opportunities. HR often has to do some real selling to move the individual (e.g., describing scenarios in other parts of the organization where such a move has worked, sharing the evidence used to make the retention decision).

Ensure the Implementation of Planned Personnel Actions

A large part of HR's responsibility in retirement management is following up with line managers on their commitments to take action relative to older employees. As more and more people decide not to retire at 60 or 65 and work an additional 5 or 10 years, organizations inevitably will have a few individuals whose poor performance must be addressed (see Chapters 9 and 10). HR will have to take major responsibility in ensuring that decisions made about confronting a poor performance or work habit situation are implemented in a timely, prudent manner. There's usually no problem with getting managers to implement a positive retirement management decision in which individuals are encouraged to stay longer and are given incentives to do so. It's the negative side of the picture—managers dealing with poor performance—that HR must make sure takes place. Also, HR must make certain that leaders have the skills and confidence to effectively handle these interactions. This usually involves coaching before a leader's meetings with the individual.

Support the Organization's Responsibilities to Provide Help in Retirement Planning

If an organization has retirement-planning classes, offers retirement consulting to people, or just provides suggestions to retirees on where they can get help, the HR department should coordinate the activity.

As the baby boomers approach retirement in greater numbers, there will be considerably more interest in retirement and an acute need for accurate information on what people can expect and what options are open to them—all areas of HR expertise. People who are approaching retirement eligibility need to receive all possible assistance to make the right decision relative to retirement and life.

Be Watchful for Age-Related Biases

Inadvertent age bias can be revealed by looking at data readily available to human resource departments—for instance, data on participation in company-sponsored training and development activities. As noted in Chapter 8, training is very important to older workers. It's HR's responsibility to be sure they aren't being systemically excluded from appropriate training programs delivered within and outside the organization. Several academic studies and data from the Bureau of Labor Statistics seem to indicate that older workers sometimes get less training than their younger compatriots.[8]

Also, HR groups need to start collecting more age data in their surveys. For example, an organization that collected the ages of people responding to a 360° instrument (when there were enough people participating in all age groups to maintain anonymity) found this to be a useful way of identifying supervisors with an apparent bias against older workers. A similar finding was obtained when a certain organization started to collect age data in engagement surveys and saw that some departments had their older workers more consistently engaged than other departments.

Provide a Benefits Package Appropriate for the Organization

Benefits are always trade-offs—costs versus the actual perceived impact on employees. All an organization's benefits should be reviewed relative to retirement management's objectives and costs. There are many possibilities that hold special appeal to an older working population, such as elder-care for aging parents, "bridge" health coverage, and financial/retirement/life planning. HR's responsibility is to consider these options, model all costs, and estimate tangible and intangible benefits (based on solid research data).

Provide Training and Development Programs That Keep All Workers Up to Date

As I discuss in Chapter 8, older workers want meaningful, practical training. Generally, they don't want or need special training programs just because they're older. To illustrate this, CVS, the large drugstore chain, tried new-employee training programs tailored for its older recruits, but then eventually reverted to programs that include all age groups. Providing training that covers all age groups enables all new employees, older and younger, to learn from one another.[9]

Best Practices in Training Older Workers

DDI associates train hundreds of thousands of supervisors and managers each year in leadership skills. It's not uncommon to find individuals in the classroom who are over 60 and occasionally over 70. We surveyed 42 DDI trainers about special techniques that seemed to be required or that work well with older workers. The overwhelming response was that there are no major differences. A skilled instructor always responds to the particular needs and situations of his or her trainees. Some older learners lack confidence, but so do many very young workers. Some older workers haven't been in the classroom for a long time and fear the consequences, but so do many middle-aged workers. And, just like many other learners, some older workers aren't very good at separating the wheat from the chaff in terms of pinpointing the training's key learning points.

Several points emerged time and again in discussions with the DDI trainers:

> It's important to show the importance and application of the material being presented to all individuals *and* to the organization. DDI's trainers suggest starting programs with a discussion of how the material can be applied. If possible, they have each learner write a description of a particular situation to which he or she would apply the skills that the class is about to learn. Older workers seem to have less patience for theoretical material because they often can't see an immediate use for it.

> Some older individuals who have been away from training for some time won't jump into group discussions and management games as quickly as people who are more recently out of school. However, while the older individuals might start slowly, they soon gain confidence and are fully participating by the second or third learning session.

> There are no differences in how older workers respond to simulations and management games, role-playing opportunities, and other kinds of activities.

> As a training device, behavior modeling is equally effective at all age levels. Of course, it's helpful if some of the models reflect the age of the older learners.

We specifically asked about physical changes that need to be attended to, such as larger print in overhead slides, better lighting, etc. Most trainers said that they routinely check on these things throughout the first session of the training, and that they could not recall any major problems.

Speed of learning is often discussed as an issue relative to technical training. Considerable research shows that older workers learn more slowly, but others have found that if the overall time it takes to reach a skill criterion is measured, an older worker's performance is no worse than that of other learners. Because most older workers have a higher skill base to begin with, they often have less to learn; therefore, they can spend more time on the skills that they don't know.

For examples of how training can overcome or avoid issues relative to older learners, go online to http://www.ddiworld.com/70thenew50/trainingolderworkers.asp

Publicize the Organization's Position Regarding the Employment and Treatment of Older Workers

HR should use a variety of media to communicate the organization's values and policies relative to its employment, reemployment, and hiring of older workers. An excellent approach is to publish stories about older individuals in the company who are models of successful continued employment. Also, HR should use its company newsletters and other communication vehicles to publicize the availability of retirement counseling and guidance resources for employees. Such communication makes it easier for leaders to bring up the issue in casual conversations.

Open Lines of Communication About Retirement and Its Options

I believe the best way to foster more open communication about the subject of retirement is for HR to encourage the quick-check discussions described in Chapter 9. If an individual and his or her leader get accustomed to talking about retirement in an informal way, it becomes much easier to hold a more formal discussion when either side finds it necessary.

Be the Retirement Management Champion

Because retirement management is a new strategy for most organizations, it needs a strong, persuasive champion; HR is the logical choice to fulfill that role. But it won't be easy—management at all levels will have to be convinced of both the need for retirement management and the viability of HR's recommendations. I have written this book to help with this process.

Appendix 13A

How Talent Review Meetings Facilitate Retirement, Succession, and Retention Management

The members of the talent review committee (i.e., the CEO and/or COO and their direct reports):

1. Consider organizational strategies (e.g., growth plans or new technologies), and then identify people who are key to implementing them. These individuals might be at many different organizational levels; more often, they are in positions where they perform a key communication, coordination, or knowledge function.

2. Make tentative determinations about key people, labeling individuals as follows:

    a. Candidate for accelerated development (i.e., provide bench strength).

    b. Retention risk (i.e., the organization wants to keep this person who, for one reason or another, is at risk of leaving).

    c. Retirement risk (i.e., the person is nearing retirement age, and the organization wants to retain him or her for at least a few years).

    d. Not a problem, either because the person is expected to stay in the job or there are qualified backups in place.

3. Review the following information about individuals in groups "a," "b," and "c" above:

    • Job assignments in current organization and past organizations, if relevant.

    • Performance and potential ratings from their leaders and confirmed by higher management. Often they use a special computerized rating system, such as the Leadership Potential Inventory from DDI.

    • Assessment data from an Acceleration Center® (assessment center) or multirater (e.g., 360°) instruments. (This is particularly important for Acceleration Pool® candidates.)

- Self-reports of skills (e.g., language skills) and experience (e.g., time spent in a foreign country). The Career Achievement Portfolio (CAP) might be used to systematically capture data if people know they are being reviewed.

- Expressed desire for advancement or movement within the organization.

- Personal priorities.

4. Make one of the following final determinations for each person being considered:

   a. Accelerate development.

   b. Make a special effort to retain.

   c. Try to delay retirement.

   d. Take no action.

5. Plan actions (e.g., increased compensation, new assignment, transition-to-retirement opportunities, new boss or location, special recognition, placement in an Acceleration Pool® to speed the development of high potentials, assignment of an executive coach).

6. Define how success will be measured for each individual and clarify responsibilities.

Most organizations need to consider employees at all organization levels, but it's best to start at the top so the talent review committee will know how many spots it must fill.

SECTION V

WHAT THE GOVERNMENT AND ORGANIZATIONS NEED TO DO

I conclude by speculating on the impact of retirement management on the U.S. gross domestic product (GDP) and on the viability of the U.S. Social Security and Medicare programs. I also discuss how U.S. government laws and regulations need to be changed to allow all organizations to fully implement retirement management.

- Chapter 14—Retirement Management and the U.S. Government
- Chapter 15—Final Thoughts

Chapter 14

Retirement Management and the U.S. Government

So far, this book has emphasized the value of a well-conceived retirement management strategy not only for potential retirees, but also for their organization. To briefly recap, an effective retirement management strategy allows *individuals* to:

- Make their own decisions about the timing of their retirement.

- Ease into retirement through transition-to-retirement jobs, which can be tailored to their needs (e.g., cycling between periods of work and retirement).

- Stay in their current job or try out a new job in their present organization.

- Build a bigger nest egg to finance later retirement options by working longer and collecting pension benefits while still working.

A solid retirement management initiative allows *organizations* to:

- Employ the skilled people they need to move ahead, even when faced with a worldwide skills shortage.

- Retain knowledgeable, motivated talent.

- Delay recruiting and selection costs associated with replacing their retiring baby boomers.

- Delay training costs related to on-boarding new people and bringing them up to speed.

- Spend more time preparing backups to fill key positions that will open up because of retirements.

- Hire people of all ages for key open positions.

- Take more time to collect knowledge and information about key contacts that will be lost when baby boomers retire.

In this chapter I first discuss the impact of retirement management on the the nation's economy and government programs. Then, I examine how government regulations and laws will need to be changed to open the door for more organizations to implement retirement management.

The U.S. government stands to reap two significant benefits from the broad practice of retirement management:

1. Projected labor shortages from retirements would be mitigated by the longer participation of baby boomers in the workforce.

2. Projected deficits in Social Security and Medicare funding would be delayed or eliminated.

Each of these benefits is explained further on the next few pages.

1. **Projected labor shortages from retirements would be mitigated by the longer participation of baby boomers in the workforce.**

    If the demographers are correct, the growth rate of the U.S. workforce is declining and will continue to drop until 2025.[1] See Figure 14.1.

Figure 14.1: Ongoing Decline in the U.S. Workforce Growth Rate Through 2025

Growth Rate Percent (5-year moving average)

From GAO analysis of data from the Office of the Chief Actuary, Social Security Administration, 2005.
Note: Percentage change is calculated as a centered five-year moving average of projections based on the intermediate assumptions of the 2004 Trustees' Reports.

If the labor force growth continues to decline as projected, relatively fewer workers will be available to produce goods and services in the future.

According to the U.S. General Accounting Office, without a major increase in worker productivity and/or higher-than-projected immigration, the decline in the U.S. labor force growth will lead to slower growth in both the economy and federal revenues. This, in turn, will accelerate the overall pressure on the federal budget.[2]

An alternative, of course, would be for people to work longer. It's estimated that if 25 percent more people over 55 would continue on in the labor force for five years, a constant ratio of employees to the U.S. population would be maintained.[3] Participation of older workers in the workforce is already on the rise. After steadily declining for more than 50 years, in 1994 the percentage of men over 65 in the workforce reached 16.9.[4] Since then it has increased to 19 percent, and the Bureau of Labor Statistics predicts it will rise to nearly 25 percent in 2014. Similar, but smaller, increases are projected for older women.

BusinessWeek has estimated that the increased productivity of older Americans and their heightened participation in the workforce could boost the nation's gross domestic product by an additional 9 percent by 2045.[5] This would add more than $3 trillion a year in today's dollars to the country's economic output.

There are two ways to bring about increased participation of older workers in the workforce:

The Push Method

The U.S. government could increase the eligibility age for receiving full Social Security benefits while maintaining viable options for people who need to retire early (e.g., if their jobs require considerable physical exertion or they have health problems).

Under current law, the retirement age of eligibility for full Social Security benefits rose to 67 in 2007. Some people feel that this target age is not high enough—that the age for full retirement payout should be pegged at 70 and that the rate of increase to that target should be dramatically accelerated. It's also been suggested that further increases beyond 70 would be pegged to longevity. According to this logic, as average life span lengthens, the Social Security target age would rise proportionately.

However, changes in the retirement age are highly unpopular. According to a *New York Times*/CBS News poll in 2005, nearly 8 of 10 respondents said they would oppose raising the age of eligibility for Social Security benefits.[6]

The Pull Method

Organizations could make continued employment so attractive to older workers that the participation of 65- to 75-year-olds in the workforce would dramatically—and voluntarily—increase. Not everyone would continue working, but many would work for an additional 5 or 10 years, which would increase older workers' participation to 25 percent or more. The adoption of retirement management programs would be a key factor in such an effort.

The War for Talent: Global Implications

The impending labor shortage carries serious implications for the worldwide trade deficit and general U.S. competitiveness in the global market. If the United States, Europe, and Japan simultaneously experience a major war for talent, as each year fewer highly educated, motivated individuals come into their workforces, there will be an inevitable increase in worldwide wages as countries compete for talent. This will be particularly true at top management levels, as executives who can lead global organizations will be highly coveted. In such a scenario U.S. companies would have great difficulty finding or affording top-flight managers to import.

Even more important will be the impact on the trade deficit caused by the retirement of baby boomers. High labor costs caused by a skilled labor shortage will propel the outsourcing of manufacturing, technical, communications, and other services out of the United States, exacerbating the already large trade deficits with China and India.

2. Projected deficiencies in Social Security and Medicare funding would be delayed or eliminated.

As baby boomers retire, the number of people paying into the Social Security and Medicare programs will decline and, as shown in Figure 1.2 (in Chapter 1), the number of benefit recipients will increase, eventually leading to higher payments by employers and employees and to higher general taxes to support the payout to program recipients. Figure 14.2 projects when the Medicare and Social Security programs will eventually become insolvent if the government does nothing to fix them.

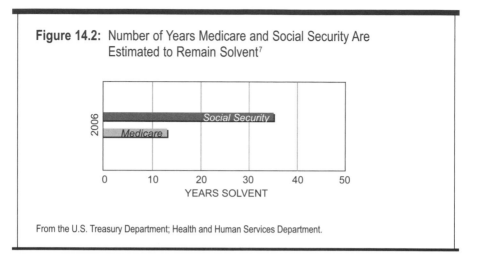

Figure 14.2: Number of Years Medicare and Social Security Are Estimated to Remain Solvent[7]

From the U.S. Treasury Department; Health and Human Services Department.

An increase in the workforce participation of individuals in their 60s and early 70s would boost government income and help alleviate the drain on these programs. Here's how:

- Workers over 65 who remain on the job would continue to pay into Social Security, even as they are collecting retirement funds from it.

- People who continue to work would have more income from their employer to be taxed, and their income from Social Security, if they are receiving it, also would be taxed.

- Many employed workers over 65 would be covered by their employer's health coverage, thus saving Medicare expenditures.

According to MIT economist Jonathan Gruber, who was quoted in *The New York Times,* encouraging people to work until they are 70 would produce an annual gain for the Social Security system of about 30 percent of the program's total cost. This increase would come from reduced benefit costs and more taxes paid by workers who are still on the job.[8]

While there is some debate about the absolute impact, there's no question that offering interesting, challenging, and rewarding opportunities to older people who want to remain with their career companies would be a big step toward improving the solvency of Social Security and would help to alleviate the growing challenge of funding Medicare.

The U.S. Government Can Promote Retirement Management

There are several things the U.S. government can do to encourage retirement management:

- Finalize the currently proposed IRS phased retirement rules, which allow individuals who reach a certain age to begin collecting their company's defined benefit pensions while continuing to work there. These rules would complement the provisions of the Pension Protection Act of 2006 (PPA), which permits in-service distributions from amended defined benefit plans to participants who have reached age 62.

  These proposed rules and the provisions of the PPA give recognition to the sweeping changes facing the U.S. in the near future. The old rules concerning pensions were devised in times when many people were looking for work. The provisions met a national need to encourage older workers to leave their employment, thus opening jobs for younger workers. Today, the U.S. is facing the opposite situation.

  The United States is not the first country to encourage people to work longer. Chile revamped its retirement regulations to allow employees to collect their retirement funds and continue working. The Chilean government has reported a 20 percent increase in labor force participation by workers 55 to 65.[9]

- Make it clear that companies can convert conventional defined benefit plans to cash balance plans, which have no built-in incentive to retire. There have been conflicting court rulings in this area that inhibit companies' actions.

- Allow individuals to keep their money in tax-favored plans longer without mandatory withdrawals. Currently, working people must begin to cash in their 401(k) plans when they reach 70½ and pay taxes on the money. The rule is unfair to the increasing number of people in their 70s and 80s who choose to continue working. A better solution would be to allow these older workers to delay recovery of their money until they are retired and in a lower tax bracket.

- Change laws and regulations to clarify the legality of transition-to-retirement jobs involving fewer work hours, more vacations, or other variations. As I've explained in earlier chapters, many older people want different vacation schedules, flexible hours, the ability to work from home, or permission to take unpaid leave, depending on their situation. Organizations must be sure they can offer these opportunities without violating the Age Discrimination in Employment Act (ADEA) or the Equal Employment Opportunity Commission (EEOC) rules.

And If No One Does Anything Differently . . .

By 2030, the projected cost of Social Security and Medicare could easily consume—via high taxes—one-third of workers' future earnings and salary increases, reports noted economist Robert Samuelson, as quoted in *The Washington Post*. According to Samuelson, "Baby boomers' children and grandchildren face massive tax increases. Social Security and Medicare spending now equals 14 percent of [an individual's] wage and salary income.... By 2030, using the trustees' various projections, that jumps to 26 percent." He compared the future situation to people feeling like they are on a treadmill: They won't be gaining anything from working harder, and they'll complain about this to their government.[10]

Will Washington Take Action?

A key driver of the need for reform legislation is the inequity created by the direction that retirements are taking in America. While many recent retirees and older baby boomers will spend the rest of their lives reveling in the relative luxury of defined benefit plans, most younger baby boomers and the generations that follow them won't have the benefit of these plans and, worse, will be footing the bill for increasingly higher Social Security and Medicare costs to fund the boomers' retirements. At the same time, they will be shouldering the responsibility of funding and managing their own 401(k) accounts and individual savings plans so that someday they too can enjoy their retirement. The younger generations will look on the older generation very wistfully and, at some point, might even turn on them, saying, "Enough is enough. It's not fair!" I can understand this point of view—both sides should be sharing the burden of our financially strapped Social Security and Medicare systems instead of the younger generation having to assume most of it.

Will Congress have the fortitude to take on the Social Security monster and attempt to fix Social Security and Medicare? I doubt it. The over-50 voting block, led by the AARP, is large—and they vote. In 2000, 72.2 percent of U.S. citizens age 65–74 voted; in contrast, only 36.1 percent of citizens age 18–24 cast ballots.[11] I believe an easier solution for Congress and the Executive Branch would be to make the relatively minor adjustments I've proposed to encourage retirement management. I don't think it's important for government to pass laws to encourage retirement management; it just needs to adjust and clarify existing laws so the perceived current legal risks are eliminated.

Chapter 15

Final Thoughts

What's Preventing Organizations from Implementing Retirement Management?

Let's look at some common assumptions about what might be inhibiting organizations from implementing retirement management practices.

- **Concerns about violating government discrimination and fairness laws and regulations.** These concerns are largely unwarranted. Certainly, government processes could be streamlined and rules clarified, but with a little boldness and planning by organizations, government regulations are not a major impediment to the implementation of retirement management. Many organizations throughout the United States are proving this every day.

- **Risk of deteriorating efficiency, quality, and innovation from large numbers of older workers who stay in their jobs past their prime.** As economic reasons for retirement are removed and increasingly more people realize they are psychologically or financially unprepared for retirement, the number of older people continuing to work is going to increase, no matter what organizations do. A well-functioning retirement management program, however, will cultivate a source of people who will represent a major, quantifiable benefit. Retirement management will not materially increase the number of poorly performing older workers. In fact, it will encourage leaders to face up to employees' performance or work habit problems early enough that they can be corrected or dealt with in a fair and equitable way. Companies that fail to strategically manage retirements will both increase their problems from marginal older employees and lose the advantages of retaining older workers who still have much to contribute.

In all scenarios, management will have to markedly improve its performance management systems for workers at all organizational levels. Leaders must ensure that people understand their job responsibilities and contributions to the organization, are placed in the appropriate jobs, receive the feedback and training necessary to continue to learn and grow, are able to evaluate their success, and are appropriately recognized for it.

- **Fear of making tough people decisions.** Retirement management means that some employees will be asked to stay with the organization longer while others will not. Inevitably, some feelings will be hurt. Some people will be forced into retirement. Many senior managers don't want to face up to the tough decisions involved.

  Special arrangements with older employees are being made every day, and often they're not very strategic, particularly with regard to the consequences that will be felt if older workers with important knowledge and key information or contacts are allowed to leave the organization. These decisions are neither centralized nor guided by senior managers. In many organizations, marginal performers are being retained simply because they took the initiative to ask for special consideration, while invaluable people are being allowed to leave.

  Retirement management would ensure that decisions being made every day about people are more explicit, just as a succession management program makes decisions more explicit and more aligned with the organization's strategy. An effectively functioning retirement management system provides the knowledge and structure a company needs to guide the selection of people and decisions about special incentives for key individuals.

While retirement management might occasionally bring about legal claims from marginal performers who weren't retained, an organization's careful application of the system also can provide solid, documented defenses against those claims.

- **Fear that health care costs will increase.** Older workers do incur higher health care costs, but they are not significantly more until they reach 75 or 80. As I've discussed, it's a risk-reward trade-off. Organizations must weigh the additional health care costs against the cost savings of not having to recruit, select, and train new people in a tight labor market. When replacements for retirees are drawn from a pool of young workers (under 26), the difference in performance and work habits between them and the older workers can be quite significant. Older workers have a clear advantage, even considering their increased health care costs.

  Less easy to quantify, but perhaps even more important, is the trade-off for middle and senior managers and professionals; because of their accumulated knowledge, experience, and industry contacts, these individuals are much more difficult and expensive to replace, particularly in a tight labor market. Also, health care costs of older executives and professionals are the same or less than those of individuals at lower organizational levels (generally, because they tend to take better care of themselves and are in positions that are less physically demanding). Again, it seems reasonable that an investment in retaining *select* older managers and professionals is a good one.

- **Concerns that maintaining a large number of older workers in part-time jobs will lead to increased wage and benefit costs.** Often, having two part-time older employees will cost an organization more than one full-time younger employee because they've benefited from salary increases over the years. Also, their health care costs might be two or three times what the company pays for the younger employee, but not necessarily (see Chapter 7).

  Relative to people, however, calculating cost versus value to the organization is not as cut and dried as, say, comparing widgets, where both the costs and the value of two half-widgets is the same as one widget. The comparative value of two older people working half-time can be much higher. Because older people often bring unique skills and knowledge to their part-time assignments, two of them might be more expensive than a single worker doing the same job; yet, they also might be more productive.

- **An expectation that people will become less engaged with their work when they're in part-time, transition-to-retirement jobs.** Will previously excellent employees lose focus and zeal if they convert to part-time employment? Will they start to retire while still on the job? Although not statistically significant, DDI's research on engagement levels of managers and professionals shows a slight downward trend as people age. I think that one's engagement in work does decrease over time, particularly when people accept part-time employment. But DDI's data indicate that the average engagement level of older workers remains relatively high and totally adequate for organizations. For most older workers, engagement seems to dip from very high levels to more moderate levels, but not down to low levels. An organization can stave off low engagement by providing challenging, empowered jobs and with an effective selection system in which people's propensity to be engaged in a job is evaluated along with other factors. This is why I've emphasized looking at motivation and other personal attributes in considering potential candidates for transition-to-retirement positions.

The Final Case for Retirement Management

I see retirement management as a win-win-win situation: a win for older workers who don't want to quit their career company or who want to return to work with it; a win for organizations because they'll be better able to survive an anticipated tight labor market and curb their losses of key knowledge and contacts; and a win for the United States government, as increased participation in the U.S. workforce would propel the economy upward and generate needed tax revenue to support Social Security, Medicare, and other struggling federal programs that are important to retiring baby boomers and future generations.

Retirement management is not a strategy guaranteed to have a positive impact on *all* working people above the age of 60. Rather, just like succession management and retention management, it's a strategy geared toward select members of a target group: in this case, motivated older people—solid performers who can continue to add value to their organization. Companies practicing retirement management should not necessarily measure success by the *volume* of older workers they retain, but rather by the *quality* of such workers.

End Notes

Introduction

1. From "98—Expectation of Life and Expected Deaths by Race, Sex, and Age: 2002," presented on *The 2006 Statistical Abstract (The National Data Book)* web site by the U.S. Census Bureau. According to this table of data from 2002, a 60-year-old is expected to live 22 more years; a 65-year-old, 18.2 more years to reach 83. This table, Table 98, is included in an archived edition of the 2006 report, available online at: http://www.census.gov/prod/2005pubs/06statab/vitstat.pdf

2. From *Cracking the Consumer Retirement Code* (p. 8), by McKinsey & Company, 2006, New York: Author. This report is available online at: http://www.mckinsey.com/clientservice/bankingsecurities/latestthinking/retirement.asp

3. From "Old. Smart. Productive." by Peter Coy, 2005, *BusinessWeek*, (3939), pp. 78–86.

4. From "Britons Are Living Longer, but They Face an Unhealthy Old Age," by Nicola Smith, 2006, *The Sunday Times*, p. News 5.

5. From *Retirements at Risk: A New National Retirement Risk Index* (p. 11), by the Center for Retirement Research at Boston College, 2006, Boston: Author. This statistic also was highlighted in a CNN online feature, available at: http://money.cnn.com/2006/06/06/retirement/risk_index/

6. From *The 2006 Merrill Lynch New Retirement Study: A Perspective from Individuals and Employers* (p. 5), by Merrill Lynch, 2006, New York: Author. This report is available online at: http://www.ml.com/media/66482.pdf

7. From *Baby Boomers Envision Retirement II: Survey of Baby Boomers' Expectations for Retirement* (p. 24), by the AARP (as prepared by Roper ASW), 2004, Washington, DC: AARP. This research is available online at: http://www.aarp.org/research/work/retirement/aresearch-import-865.html

   See also *Staying Ahead of the Curve: The AARP Working in Retirement Study* (p. 15), by S. Kathi Brown, 2003, Washington, DC: AARP. This study is available online at: http://www.aarp.org/research/reference/publicopinions/

8. From *A Micro-Level Analysis of Recent Increases in Labor Force Participation Among Older Men* (p. 33), by Kevin E. Cahill, Michael D. Giandrea, and Joseph F. Quinn, 2006, Washington, DC: U.S. Bureau of Labor Statistics. This report is available online at: http://www.bls.gov/ore/abstract/ec/ec060120.htm

9. From *Voices of Experience: Mature Workers in the Future Workforce* (p. 22), a research report by Deborah Parkinson, 2002, New York: The Conference Board.

   Also see "Phased Retirement: A Retention Strategy Whose Time Has Come," a 2004 article featured in the Watson Wyatt journal *Insider, 14,* p. 6. Available online at: http://www.watsonwyatt.com/us/pubs/insider/pdfs/2004_04.pdf

10. This research is included in a soon-to-be published manuscript, *Age Effects on Competency-Based Job Performance,* by Evan F. Sinar and William C. Byham of Development Dimensions International.

11. From *Managing the Mature Workforce: Implications and Best Practices* (p. 7), by Lynne Morton with Lorrie Foster and Jeri Sedlar, 2005, New York: The Conference Board. While many corporations agreed to speak to The Conference Board on the record for this study, the majority requested anonymity. Many issues preclude corporations from having open dialog with their employees about their retirement or future plans, including benefits, the Age Discrimination in Employment Act (ADEA), and the Employee Retirement Income Security Act (ERISA). Both corporations and employees expressed a desire to have effective, legal ways to openly discuss future plans and work options, particularly when an employee's decision would affect organizational plans.

Chapter 1

1. From *Retirement: Reasons, Processes, and Results* (p. 8), edited by Gary A. Adams and Terry A. Beehr, 2003, New York: Springer Publishing. The information was taken from the chapter "Contexts and Pathways: Retirement as Institution, Process, and Experience," written by Maximiliane E. Szinovacz.

2. From "Evolution of Employer-Provided Defined Benefit Pensions," by Patrick W. Seburn, 1991, *Monthly Labor Review, 114,* pp. 16–23 (also available online at: http://www.bls.gov/opub/mlr/1991/12/art3exc.htm). Selected quotations:

   - *"In 1930, some 2.7 million active workers, or about one-tenth of the workforce, were covered by private pension plans."* (p. 19)

   - *"In 1940, more than 4 million people, or about one-seventh of the active workforce, were covered by private pensions. . . ."* (p. 19)

   - *"By the end of 1950, private pensions covered 10.3 million persons, more than one-fourth of all persons employed in commerce and industry in the United States."* (p. 20)

   As cited in the article, all these figures are from *1987 Pension Facts* by the American Council of Life Insurance in Washington, DC.

3. From "Changing Retirement Age: Ups and Downs," by William J. Wiatrowski, 2001, *Monthly Labor Review, 124,* p. 4. This article is also available online at: http://www.bls.gov/opub/mlr/2001/04/art1full.pdf

Also, 2006 research has reported the same figures (*Cracking the Consumer Retirement Code* [p. 8], McKinsey & Company, 2006, New York). This report is available online at: http://www.mckinsey.com/clientservice/bankingsecurities/latestthinking/retirement.asp

4. From *The Coming Generational Storm: What You Need to Know About America's Economic Future* (p. 111), by Laurence J. Kotlikoff and Scott Burns, 2005, Cambridge, MA: The MIT Press.

5. From "The Broken Promise," by Donald L. Barlett and James B. Steele, 2005, *Time, 166,* pp. 32–47. In the article Barlett and Steele quote a study produced in December 2004 by The Henry J. Kaiser Family Foundation and Hewitt Associates called *Current Trends and Future Outlook for Retiree Health Benefits: Findings from the Kaiser/Hewitt 2004 Survey on Retiree Health Benefits.*

6. From an online abstract of an issue brief called *The Impact of the Erosion of Retiree Health Benefits on Workers and Retirees,* by Paul Fronstin, 2005, Washington, DC: Employee Benefit Research Institute. Available at: http://www.ebri.org/publications/ib/index.cfm?fa=ibDisp&content_id=3497 (The issue also is available online at: http://www.ebri.org/pdf/briefspdf/0305ib.pdf)

7. From "The Broken Promise," Barlett & Steele, p. 47.

8. From "Verizon to Halt Pension Outlay for Managers," by Ken Belson and Matt Richtel, 2005, *The New York Times,* pp. A1, C5.

9. From "The End of a Dream," by Geoffrey Colvin, 2006, *Fortune, 153,* pp. 90, 92.

The Watson Wyatt *Retirement Attitude Survey* was completed by roughly 8,000 employees from a national panel in the summer of 2003. Findings from the survey, including the data from this citation, can be found in an article called "How Do Retirement Plans Affect Employee Behavior?" (pp. 14–23) in a Watson Wyatt publication called *Insider: Trends in Pensions 2005* [Special Edition]. This report is available online at: http://www.watsonwyatt.com/us/pubs/insider/pdfs/pensionsSE.pdf

10. From "Workers Acknowledge Move to Defined Contribution," by David Shadovitz, 2006, *Human Resource Executive, 20,* p. 63.

11. From both "Bill Would Boost 401(k) Plans," by William Neikirk, *Chicago Tribune,* August 17, 2006, p. 4, and "Pension Protection Act of 2006: Long-Term Implications for the PBGC," by Jonathan Rose and Ryan Liebl, 2006, *Employee Benefit Plan Review, 61,* p. 9.

12. From "Ailing GM Looks to Scale Back Generous Health Benefits," by Julie Appleby and Sharon Silke Carty, 2005, *USA Today,* p. 1B.

13. From "A New Twist on Retiree Health Care," by Howard Gleckman, 2006, *BusinessWeek,* (3995), p. 68. The 2005 Mercer survey, *2005 U.S. National Employer-Sponsored Health Plans Survey,* is available for purchase online at: http://www.mercerhr.com/summary.jhtml?idContent= 1051300#highlights

For information regarding the U.S. health benefit costs rising 7.5 percent in 2004, which was the lowest increase in five years, see the following Mercer press release from November 18, 2004: http://www.mercerhr.com/pressrelease/details.jhtml?idContent=1162 645

14. From "New Twist," Gleckman, p. 68.

15. From *Redefining Retirement: Options for Older Americans* (p. 9), by the United States Government Accountability Office, 2005, Washington, DC: GAO. This is the testimony of Barbara D. Bovbjerg, Director of Education, Workforce, and Income Security, as she went before the Special Committee on Aging in the U.S. Senate on April 27, 2005.

Chapter 2

1. From *The Business Case for Workers Age 50+: Planning for Tomorrow's Talent Needs in Today's Competitive Environment: A Report for AARP* (p. 8), by Roselyn Feinsod, Tom Davenport, Rich Arthurs, Towers Perrin, and the AARP, 2005, Washington, DC: AARP.

   Also see "Predictors of Planned Retirement Age: An Application of Beehr's Model," by Mary Anne Taylor and Lynn M. Shore, 1995, *Psychology and Aging, 10,* p. 81.

2. From *Grow Your Own Leaders: How to Identify, Develop, and Retain Leadership Talent* (pp. 3–4), by William C. Byham, Audrey B. Smith, and Matthew J. Paese, 2002, Upper Saddle River, NJ: Prentice-Hall. This book is available through DDI's Client Service group by calling 1-800-944-7782.

3. From *Valuing Experience: How to Motivate and Retain Mature Workers* (p. 11), by Howard Muson, 2003, New York: The Conference Board.

4. From two AARP reports, specifically *Staying Ahead of the Curve: The AARP Work and Career Study* (p. 8), prepared by Roper ASW, 2002, and *Staying Ahead of the Curve: The AARP Working in Retirement Study* (pp. 6–7, 23), by S. Kathi Brown, 2003. Both were published in Washington, DC, by the AARP and are available online at: http://www.aarp.org/research/reference/publicopinions/

5. From "*The New Retirement Survey* from Merrill Lynch Reveals How Baby Boomers Will Transform Retirement," a press release promoting a 2005 survey released by Merrill Lynch, conducted by Harris Interactive. It is available online at: http://www.ml.com/?id=7695_7696_8149_46028_46503_46635

6. From *Voices of Experience: Mature Workers in the Future Workforce* (pp. 30–31), a research report by Deborah Parkinson, 2002, New York: The Conference Board.

7. From the report *Staying Ahead of the Curve: The AARP Work and Career Study,* prepared by Roper ASW, 2002, Washington, DC: AARP.

8. An unpublished DDI retirement practices study, conducted in 2007, of 600 workers between 50 and 65 found that almost 50 percent would prefer part-time work to just leaving the workforce altogether.

9. From interviews conducted by DDI during the research for this book.

10. From a presentation "The Quad Deficits: Why They Matter and What to Do About Them," by Pete Peterson, given during the *Business and Finance: America and the Fiscal Future* lecture theme week at Chautauqua Institution, Chautauqua, NY, in August 2006.

11. From "Is the American Dream Still Possible?" by David Wallechinsky, 2006, *PARADE,* April 23, p. 5. PARADE commissioned Mark Clements Research Inc. to administer the "Middle Class Study" in October 2005. It was conducted among a national online panel. The results are based on a sample of 2,203 adults, age 18 and over. Results are accurate to within +/− 2 percent at the 95 percent level of confidence. This article is available online at: http://www.parade.com/articles/editions/2006/edition_04-23-2006/Middle_Class_feature

12. The ABC News/*USA Today* poll of 1,000 adults was conducted October 12–16, 2005. The results are mentioned in "To Retire Well, Start Saving Yesterday," by John Waggoner, 2005, *USA Today,* October 26, pp. 1B–2B.

13. From *Encouraging Workers to Save: The 2005 Retirement Confidence Survey* (p. 5), by Ruth Helman, Dallas Salisbury, Variny Paladino, and Craig Copeland, 2005, Washington, DC: Employee Benefit Research Institute.

14. From a special section about retirement called "Want to Retire Early and Hang a Shingle? It'll Cost You," by John O'Neil, 2006, *The New York Times, 155,* p. E4.

15. From "Will Health Care Costs Erode Retirement Security?" (p. 2), by Richard W. Johnson and Rudolph G. Penner, 2004, *Issue in Brief, 23,* Chestnut Hill, MA: Trustees of Boston College, Center for Retirement Research. The document is available online at: http://www.urban.org/url.cfm?ID=1000699

16. From "Retire in Style? Maybe Not Quite So Soon," by Hubert B. Herring, 2005, *The New York Times, 154* (Special Section 2), p. 2.

17. From "Public Pension Plans Face Billions in Shortages," by Mary Williams Walsh, 2006, *The New York Times, 155,* pp. A1, C10.

Chapter 3

1. From the *SHRM/NOWCC/CED Older Workers Survey* (p. 12), by Jessica Collison, 2003, Alexandria, VA: Society for Human Resource Management (SHRM).

2. From *EEOC Issues Fiscal Year 2003 Enforcement Data,* by the Equal Employment Opportunity Commission, March 8, 2004 (as cited in *The Aging Workforce,* p. 37, by Jerry W. Hedge, Walter C. Borman, and Steven E. Lammlein, 2006).

3. From "EEOC Approves Targeting of Older Workers for Recruitment," by Alan Smith, 2006, HR *Magazine, 51,* pp. 29, 36.

Chapter 4

1. From *Phased Retirement: Aligning Employer Programs with Worker Preferences* (p. 1), by Watson Wyatt Worldwide, 2004, Washington, DC: Author.

2. From the study *Living Longer, Working Longer: The Changing Landscape of the Aging Workforce* (pp. 6–7), by David DeLong & Associates and Zogby International, 2006, Westport, CT: MetLife Mature Market Institute. This MetLife study finds that retirement is more a "state" than a "date," as stated in an April 3, 2006, MetLife press release, which is available online at: http://www.metlife.com/Applications/Corporate/WPS/CDA/PageGenerator/0,,P250~S813~AP,00.html

3. From *Legal and Institutional Impediments to Partial Retirement and Part-Time Work by Older Workers* (p. 17), by Rudolph G. Penner, Pamela Perun, and C. Eugene Steuerle, 2002, Washington, DC: Urban Institute. The report is available online at http://www.urban.org/publications/410587.html

4. From "Get a Life!" by Jody and Matt Miller, 2005, *Fortune, 152,* p. 112.

5. From "Employers Respond to Caregivers' Complex Needs," an article that appeared in a 2005 issue, entitled "A Profile of Caregiving in America," of *The Pfizer Journal, 9,* p. 23. The issue was edited by Salvatore J. Giorgianni. The article is available online at: http://www.thepfizerjournal.com/default.asp?a=article&j=tpj43&t=Employers%20Respond%20to%20Caregivers%u2019%20Complex%20Needs

6. From "They'll Just Keep Going, and Going, and Going . . .," by Ed Frauenheim, 2006, *Workforce Management, 85,* p. 26. (This article is also available online at: http://www.workforceonline.com/section/09/feature/24/55/67/245573.html)

   Frauenheim's article is based on findings from a survey that was conducted by Princeton Survey Research Associates International from March to April 2005, involving 1,000 people ages 50 to 70. The results were published as the *New Face of Work Survey* by MetLife Foundation/Civic Ventures in 2005 (available online at: http://www.civicventures.org/publications/surveys/new-face-of-work.cfm).

7. From *Attitudes of Individuals 50 and Older Toward Phased Retirement* (p. 3), by S. Kathi Brown, 2005, Washington, DC: AARP. Available online at: http://www.aarp.org/research/work/retirement/attitudes_of_individuals_50 and_older_toward_phase.html

8. From *Living Longer, Working Longer,* MetLife, p. 15.

9. From *Making Flexibility Work: What Managers Have Learned About Implementing Reduced-Load Work* (pp. 12–13), by Ellen Ernst Kossek and Mary Dean Lee, 2005, East Lansing, MI: Michigan State University and McGill University. Summary of findings from Phase II of Alfred P. Sloan Grant #2002-6-11.

10. From a personal conversation with John Deere's Rick McAnally, director of human resources, and Mary Leonard, manager of news services, on July 13, 2006.

11. From *Staying Ahead of the Curve 2003: The AARP Working in Retirement Study* [Executive Summary] (p. 7), by S. Kathi Brown, 2003, Washington, DC: AARP.

12. From *Organizational Structure of the Workplace and the Older Worker*, by James L. Farr, Paul E. Tesluk, and Stephanie R. Klein, 1998 (as cited in *The Aging Workforce*, p. 105, by Jerry W. Hedge, Walter C. Borman, and Steven E. Lammlein, 2006).

13. From an e-mail communication on June 19, 2006, with Sonja Sorrel, who worked in the Investor Relations area at Principal Financial Group.

14. From the "Women and Work" issue by Jennifer Schramm, 2006, of SHRM's *Workplace Visions, 3*, p. 7. Schramm includes a table displaying family-friendly benefits that organizations have offered from Shawn Fegley's *2006 SHRM Benefits Survey Report.*

Chapter 5

1. From *The Business Case for Workers Age 50+: Planning for Tomorrow's Talent Needs in Today's Competitive Environment: A Report for AARP* (pp. 18–19), by Roselyn Feinsod, Tom Davenport, Rich Arthurs, Towers Perrin, and the AARP, 2005, Washington, DC: AARP. This report is available online at: http://www.aarp.org/research/work/employment/workers_fifty_plus.html

2. From a personal conversation with Judy Gonser, benefits coordinator for Aerospace Corporation, on April 5, 2006.

3. From an e-mail correspondence with Daniel Mucisko, senior manager of national public relations for Deloitte Services, on April 17, 2006.

4. From *Retirement: Reasons, Processes, and Results* (p. 8), edited by Gary A. Adams and Terry A. Beehr, 2003, New York: Springer Publishing. The information was taken from the chapter "Contexts and Pathways: Retirement as Institution, Process, and Experience" (pp. 26–29), written by Maximiliane E. Szinovacz.

Szinovacz reviewed the current research on retirement decision processes. He looked at how the institutionalization of retirement as well as labor markets, work history, and marital/family characteristics influence individuals' retirement decisions and pathways.

5. From *Attitudes of Individuals 50 and Older Toward Phased Retirement* (p. 3), by S. Kathi Brown, 2005, Washington, DC: AARP.

This information also was covered in the testimony of Laurie Barr, SPHR, before The Special Committee on Aging, United States Senate, April 27, 2005. This is available online as *Best Practices in Retention of Older Workers* at: http://aging.senate.gov/public/_files/hr140lb.pdf

6. From "Phased Retirement: Leaving the Labor Force," by David Rajnes, 2001, *EBRI Notes, 22,* p. 4. This newsletter by the Employee Benefit Research Institute is available online at: http://www.ebri.org/pdf/notespdf/0901notes.pdf

The Mercer study cited is *Capitalizing on an Aging Workforce: Phased Retirement & Other Options* (2000).

7. From *The Aging Workforce* (p. 154), by Jerry W. Hedge, Walter C. Borman, and Steven E. Lammlein, 2006, Washington, DC: American Psychological Association.

Studies cited include "The Course of Adult Intellectual Development," by K. Warner Schaie, 1994, *American Psychologist, 49,* pp. 304–313; "Aging and Work: An Overview," by Carmi Schooler, Leslie J. Caplan, and Gary Oates, in *Impact of Work on Older Adults* (pp. 1–19), K.W. Schaie and C. Schooler (Eds.), 1997, New York: Springer Publishing; "Age, Work, and Mental Health," by Peter Bryan Warr, in Schaie and Schooler's *Impact of Work on Older Adults* (pp. 252–296); Warr's "Age and Work Behaviour: Physical Attributes, Cognitive Abilities, Knowledge, Personality Traits and Motives" in *International Review of Industrial and Organizational Psychology* (pp. 1–36), Cary L. Cooper and Ivan T. Robertson (Eds.), 2001, London: Wiley; and "Commentary: Age, Work, and Well-Being: Toward a Broader View," by James S. House, in Schaie and Schooler's *Impact of Work on Older Adults* (pp. 297–303).

8. From *My Time: Making the Most of the Rest of Your Life,* by Abigail Trafford, 2003, Cambridge, MA: Basic Books.

9. From a 2007 DDI retirement practices study.

Chapter 6

1. From *Cracking the Consumer Retirement Code* (p. 10), by McKinsey & Company, 2006, New York: Author. This report is available online at: http://www.mckinsey.com/clientservice/bankingsecurities/latestthinking/retirement.asp

2. From an e-mail correspondence between Gary J. Gunnett, Esq, of the Houston Harbaugh law firm in Pittsburgh, PA, to David Thomas, manager of benefits at Development Dimensions International, Pittsburgh, PA, on April 9, 2006.

3. The wording of this text has been approved by Brad Lawson, president and CEO of YourEncore™.

4. From a personal conversation with Deb Lebryk, head of Monsanto's Retiree Resource Corps, on May 12, 2006.

5. From a personal conversation with Judy Gonser, Benefits, Aerospace Corporation, on April 6, 2006.

6. From *The New Retirement Mindscape*^{SM} (pp. 1–6), by Ameriprise Financial in conjunction with Age Wave and Ken Dychtwald, Ph.D., and Harris Interactive, Inc., 2006, Minneapolis, MN: Ameriprise Financial.

   This groundbreaking study found that retirement is characterized by five distinct stages: Imagination, Anticipation, Liberation, Reorientation, and Reconciliation. The report is available online by visiting http://www.ameriprise.com/amp/global/sitelets/dreambook/study.asp

7. From *Retirement: Reasons, Processes, and Results,* edited by Gary A. Adams and Terry A. Beehr, 2003, New York: Springer Publishing. The information was taken from the chapter "Contexts and Pathways: Retirement as Institution, Process, and Experience" (pp. 26–29), written by Maximiliane E. Szinovacz, which cites Robert C. Atchley's *The Sociology of Retirement* (1976); David J. Ekerdt, Raymond Bossé, and Sue Levkoff's "An Empirical Test of Phases of Retirement: Findings from the Normative Aging Study" from *Journal of Gerontology* (1985); and Virginia E. Richardson and Keith M. Kilty's "Gender Differences in Mental Health Before and After Retirement: A Longitudinal Analysis" from *Journal of Women and Aging* (1995).

Chapter 7

1. This research is included in a soon-to-be published manuscript, *Age Effects on Competency-Based Job Performance,* by Evan F. Sinar and William C. Byham of Development Dimensions International.

2. See "Age Discrimination in the Workplace" (pp. 203–225), by Lynn M. Shore and Caren B. Goldberg, 2004, which is featured in Robert L. Dipboye and Adrienne Colella's *Discrimination at Work: The Psychological and Organizational Bases,* 2005, Mahwah, NJ: Lawrence Erlbaum Associates.

   For more information, see "They Don't Retire Them, They Hire Them," by Joe Mullich, 2003, *Workforce Management, 82,* pp. 49–54.

3. From *Age Effects on Competency-Based Job Performance,* Sinar & Byham.

4. Ibid.

5. From "Career Issues Facing Older Workers," by Terry A. Beehr and Nathan A. Bowling, 2002 (as cited in *The Aging Workforce,* p. 65, by Jerry W. Hedge, Walter C. Borman, and Steven E. Lammlein, 2006).

6. From "Establishing the Positive Contributory Value of Older Workers: A Positive Psychology Perspective," by Suzanne J. Peterson and Barry K. Spiker, 2005, *Organizational Dynamics, 34,* p. 154. This shows the results of a nationwide survey of 774 human resource directors that Harris Interactive conducted in 1999.

7. From *Age Effects on Competency-Based Job Performance,* Sinar & Byham.

8. See *The Business Case for Workers Age 50+: Planning for Tomorrow's Talent Needs in Today's Competitive Environment: A Report for AARP,* by Roselyn Feinsod, Tom Davenport, Rich Arthurs, Towers Perrin, and the AARP, 2005, Washington, DC: AARP. See also the MacArthur Foundation Study on Aging as reported in "Establishing the Positive Contributory Value of Older Workers," by Peterson and Spiker, p. 158.

9. From the *SHRM/AARP Older Workers Survey,* 1998, Alexandria, VA: Society for Human Resource Management.

10. From *Age Effects on Competency-Based Job Performance,* Sinar & Byham.

11. See Jack Botwinick and K. Warner Schaie's research referenced in Shore & Goldberg's "Age Discrimination in the Workplace," which is in Dipboye & Colella's *Discrimination at Work*, p. 214.

12. From "Practical Intelligence at Work: Relationship Between Aging and Cognitive Efficiency Among Managers in a Bank Environment," by Regina Colonia-Willner, 1998, *Psychology and Aging, 13,* pp. 45–57. See also "Old. Smart. Productive." by Peter Coy, 2005, *BusinessWeek,* (3939), pp. 78–86.

13. From "Turning Boomers into Boomerangs," 2006, *The Economist, 378,* p. 66. This article is available online at: http://www.economist.com/business/displaystory.cfm?story_id=5519033

14. From *Business Case for Workers Age 50+,* Feinsod et al, p. 50.

15. Ibid., p. 49.

16. From "Establishing the Positive Contributory Value of Older Workers," by Peterson & Spiker, p. 154.

In a personal communication on November 22, 2006, Dan Smith, the Senior Vice President of Human Resources for the Borders Group, said, "In the long-term, we found that, overall, the cost of health care for older workers is outweighed by the higher retention rate. There is much lower turnover of older workers than younger workers; therefore, the associated costs of turnover are less for older workers. We have found that those workers over 50 have a turnover rate of six times less than those under 30."

17. See "Equal Employment Opportunity Commission (29 CFR Part 1625, RIN 3046-AA78)—Coverage Under the Age Discrimination in Employment Act" (Federal Register, Vol 71, No. 155, Friday, August 11, 2006, Proposed Rules). The amendment is available online at: http://edocket.access.gpo.gov/2006/pdf/E6-13138.pdf

18. From *The Aging Workforce,* Hedge, Borman, & Lammlein.

19. From *SHRM/NOWCC/CED Older Workers Survey* (p. 5), by Jessica Collison, 2003, Alexandria, VA: Society for Human Resource Management (SHRM).

Chapter 8

1. In addition to thousands of job analyses, client interviews, and organizational surveys, DDI has administered more than 30 large-scale, cross-organizational studies of workplace performance issues and has published the results. DDI study titles include *Selection Forecast, Retaining Talent, A Survey of Trust in the Workplace, Managing Performance: Building Accountability for Organizational Success, Workforce Development Practices, Job/Role Competency Practices,* and various editions of *Leadership Forecast.* A listing of executive summaries for these studies can be found on DDI's web site at: http://www.ddiworld.com/thoughtleadership/hrtrendresearch.asp. Complete reports are available by calling 1-800-944-7782.

2. See *Empowered Teams: Creating Self-Directed Work Groups That Improve Quality, Productivity, and Participation* (pp. 13–15, 32), by Richard S. Wellins, William C. Byham, and Jeanne M. Wilson, 1991, San Francisco: Jossey-Bass. This book is available through DDI's Client Service group by calling 1-800-944-7782.

3. From *Voices of Experience: Mature Workers in the Future Workforce* (p. 32), by Deborah Parkinson, 2002, New York: The Conference Board.

4. See "Relationship Between All-Cause Mortality and Cumulative Working Life Course Psychosocial and Physical Exposures in the United States Labor Market from 1968 to 1992," by Benjamin C. Amick, III, Peggy McDonough, Hong Chang, William H. Rogers, Carl F. Pieper, and Greg Duncan, 2002, *Psychosomatic Medicine, 64,* pp. 370–381. Available online at: http://www.psychosomaticmedicine.org/cgi/content/abstract/64/3/370?ijkey=90b64eb9c23905ab9595584a131a50144a9e4d57&keytype2=tf_ipsecsha

5. From *Selection Forecast 2006–2007,* by Scott Erker, Ann Howard, and Neil Bruce, 2007, Pittsburgh, PA: Development Dimensions International.

6. From *Voices of Experience,* Parkinson, pp. 4, 15.

7. These data are presented in DDI's *Selection Forecast 2006–2007,* by Erker, Howard, & Bruce.

8. These data will be presented in the report *Age Effects on Competency-Based Job Performance,* by Evan F. Sinar and William C. Byham, which is being prepared at Development Dimensions International.

9. DDI's research in *Age Effects on Competency-Based Job Performance* (Sinar & Byham) indicates that people over 56 score lower on the personality factor, adaptability, which includes questions dealing with openness to abstract, rather than concrete, information.

10. See "An Examination of the Role of Age in Mentoring Relationships," by Lisa M. Finkelstein, Tammy D. Allen, and Laura A. Rhoton, 2003, *Group and Organization Management, 28,* p. 249.

11. These conclusions are based on both DDI's research and experience in implementing performance management in many organizations and a performance management study by the Corporate Leadership Council. See *Managing Performance: Building Accountability for Organizational Success,* by Paul R. Bernthal, Robert W. Rogers, and Audrey B. Smith, 2003, Pittsburgh, PA: Development Dimensions International, and *Closing the Performance Gap: Driving Results Through Performance Management* (p. 44), by the Corporate Leadership Council, 2002, Washington, DC: Author.

12. From *Age Effects on Competency-Based Job Performance,* Sinar & Byham.

13. These are some of the concepts explored in *Empowered Teams* (1991) by Wellins, Byham, & Wilson.

14. From *Empowered Teams,* Wellins, Byham, & Wilson, pp. 13–15.

15. From "They'll Just Keep Going, and Going, and Going . . .," by Ed Frauenheim, 2006, *Workforce Management, 85,* p. 26. (This article is also available online at: http://www.workforceonline.com/section/09/feature/24/55/67/245573.html.) Frauenheim's article is based on findings from a survey that was conducted by Princeton Survey Research Associates International from March to April 2005, involving 1,000 people ages 50 to 70. The results were published as the *New Face of Work Survey* by MetLife Foundation/Civic Ventures in 2005 (available online at: http://www.civicventures.org/publications/surveys/new-face-of-work.cfm).

Chapter 9

1. From Colosi v. Electri-Flex Company, 965F.2d500, 502 (7th Cir. 1992). The ruling is available online at: http://www.projectposner.org/case/1992/965F2d500/

2. From Wallace v. O.C. Tanner Recognition Company, et al, 299F.3d96, 100 (1st Cir. 2002). The ruling is available online at: http://www.ca1.uscourts.gov/cgi-bin/getopn.pl?OPINION=01-2624.01A

3. From *Cracking the Consumer Retirement Code* (p. 10), by McKinsey & Company, 2006, New York: Author. This report is available online at: http://www.mckinsey.com/clientservice/bankingsecurities/latestthinking/retirement.asp

4. From "Influences on the Bridge Employment Decision Among Older USA Workers," by Joelle R. Weckerle and Kenneth S. Shultz, 1999, *Journal of Occupational and Organizational Psychology, 72,* pp. 317–329.

5. From *My Time: Making the Most of the Bonus Decades After 50* (p. 26), by Abigail Trafford, 2004, New York: Basic Books.

Chapter 10

1. From *Managing the Mature Workforce* (p. 14), by Lynne Morton with Lorrie Foster and Jeri Sedlar, 2005, New York: The Conference Board. The chart originates from the Office of Research, Information, and Planning from the EEOC's Charge Data System's quarterly reconciled Data Summary Reports. **Note:** The age discrimination complaints include all charges filed under the ADEA as well as those filed concurrently under the Title VII, ASA, and/or EPA. Therefore, the sum of complaints for all statutes will exceed the total charges received.

2. Data compiled from the *Office of General Counsel Annual Reports* for fiscal years 2002, 2003, 2004, and 2005, by the Equal Employment Opportunity Commission, Washington, DC: Author. These reports are available online at: http://www.eeoc.gov/litigation/reports.html

3. The EEOC has made the *Age Discrimination in Employment Act of 1967* available online at: http://www.eeoc.gov/policy/adea.html

4. From "Organizational Downsizing and Age Discrimination Litigation: The Influence of Personnel Policies and Statistical Evidence on the Litigation Outcomes," by Peter H. Wingate, George C. Thornton, III, Kelly S. McIntyre, and Jennifer H. Flame, 2003, *Law and Human Behavior, 27,* pp. 87–108. The cases did not include jury trial or adverse impact law cases, ADA cases after 1998, or state age law cases. The study dealt only with cases in which defendants were seeking a summary judgment, and then only with organizations that were undergoing reductions in their workforce.

5. From an Executive Summary of *Staying Ahead of the Curve: The AARP Work and Career Study* (p. 2), by Xenia Montenegro, Linda Fisher, and Shereen Remez, 2002, Washington, DC: AARP. The whole study is a national survey conducted for AARP by RoperASW.

Chapter 11

1. These typical competencies (dimensions) for a sales position are from Development Dimensions International's *Sales Dimension Library,* 2006.

2. From "Patterns of Mean-Level Change in Personality Traits Across the Life Course: A Meta-Analysis of Longitudinal Studies," by Brent W. Roberts, Kate E. Walton, and Wolfgang Viechtbauer, 2006, *Psychological Bulletin, 132,* pp. 1–25.

   Sometimes after age 55, the variability of scores on many personality factors goes up markedly, particularly for conscientiousness, extraversion, and openness to experience. The only exception is self-confidence, which shows a decrease in variability.

3. From *Managerial Lives in Transition: Advancing Age and Changing Times* (p. 162), by Ann Howard and Douglas W. Bray, 1988, New York: Guilford Press.

4. See the *American Business and Older Employees Survey* (p. 4), by the AARP, 2000, Washington, DC: Author.

5. This research is included in a soon-to-be published manuscript, *Age Effects on Competency-Based Job Performance,* by Evan F. Sinar and William C. Byham of Development Dimensions International.

6. The importance of systematic data integration before making selection, retention, and rehiring decisions is illustrated by considerable research into the effectiveness of DDI's Targeted Selection® (TS) interviewing system. Data integration is a key component in TS. Some of this research is presented in the following DDI material: a monograph entitled *Targeted Selection: A Behavioral Approach to Improved Hiring Decisions (Basic Concepts and Methodology)* [Revised edition] by William C. Byham (2004), and a white paper titled "Selection: The Validity of Behaviorally Based Interviews" by DDI's Center for Applied Behavioral Research (CABER) (1998), which is a bibliography of research articles.

7. From *Staying Ahead of the Curve: The AARP Work and Career Study* (p. 6), prepared by Roper ASW, 2002, Washington, DC: AARP. The report is available online at: http://www.aarp.org/research/reference/publicopinions/aresearch-import-416.html

8. See "Butting Heads Over Retirement Plans," by Jacqueline Durett, 2006, *Training, 43,* p. 8. This article mentions the following study regarding why older people want to continue working: *The 2006 Merrill Lynch New Retirement Study* (available online at: http://askmerrill.ml.com/ask_merrill_2006/5_total_merrill/retirement_illustrator/retirement_main.asp?cpao=RETPR).

9. From *Selection Forecast 2006–2007,* by Scott Erker, Ann Howard, and Neil Bruce, 2007, Pittsburgh, PA: Development Dimensions International.

10. Ibid.

Chapter 12

1. From "The End of a Dream," by Geoffrey Colvin, 2006, *Fortune, 153,* p. 86. This article is available online at: http://money.cnn.com/2006/06/12/magazines/fortune/pension_retirementguide_fortune/index.htm

2. From *Cracking the Consumer Retirement Code* (p. 6), by McKinsey & Company, 2006, New York: Author. This report is available online at: http://www.mckinsey.com/clientservice/bankingsecurities/latestthinking/retirement.asp

3. Ibid., p. 7.

4. See the following: *Baby Boomers Envision Retirement II: Survey of Baby Boomers' Expectations for Retirement* (p. 80), prepared by Roper ASW, 2004, Washington, DC: AARP; "Gender Differences in Factors That Influence Time Spent Planning for Retirement," by Joy M. Jacobs-Lawson, Douglas A. Hershey, and Kirstan A. Neukam, 2004, *Journal of Women and Aging, 16,* pp. 55–69; and *The Cornell Retirement and Well-Being Study: Final Report 2000,* by Phyllis Moen with William A. Erickson, Madhurima Agarwal, Vivian Fields, and Laurie Todd, 2000, Ithaca, NY: Brofenbrenner Life Course Center, Cornell University (available online at: http://www.human.cornell.edu/che/BLCC/Research/Publications/upload/crwbreport.pdf).

5. From "Retire in Style? Maybe Not Quite So Soon," by Hubert B. Herring, 2005, *The New York Times, 154* (Special Section 2), p. 2. The retirement age expectations were based on a survey of 1,000 randomly selected adults from June 13–19, 2005. This article is also available online at: http://www.globalaging.org/pension/us/private/2005/style.htm

6. From "When You'll Retire—A Guessing Game," by Carole Fleck, 2006, *AARP Bulletin, 47,* p. 6.

7. From "A Surprising Secret to a Long Life: Stay in School," by Gina Kolata, 2007, *The New York Times, 156,* pp. A1, A16.

8. From *Retirement Readiness: Fidelity Survey Provides Real-Time Look at the Retirement Readiness of Today's Recent Retirees,* by Fidelity Investments, 2005, Boston: Author. A summary of the study is available online at: http://www.fidelity.com/workplace/drillDown.html?http://www.fidelity.com/workplace/PublicSites/MainWrapper/0,,CSN2646_PSN2638_SSN2639_PID20371,00.html

   The study was conducted for Fidelity Investments by Richard Day Research, Inc., in November and December of 2004. The organization surveyed 749 pre-retirees within one year of retiring and 755 retirees within three years of having retired. These people either worked for or have retired from an employer that had more than 5,000 employees, and they had a defined contribution or defined benefit plan from their employer.

   The Retirement Transition Study was cited in "Recent Retirees Wish They'd Been Better Advised by Employers" on the SHRM Compensation & Benefits Forum (March 2005).

9. From "Acting Like There's No Tomorrow When There May Be Many Tomorrows Left," by David Leonhardt, 2005, *The New York Times,* p. C5. This article is available online at: http://www.globalaging.org/pension/us/private/2005/acting.htm

10. See the following:

   "Setting Goals Together," by Nicole Lewis, 2006, *Black Enterprise, 36,* pp. 79–80. (This article is available online at: http://www.blackenterprise.com/ArchiveOpen.asp?Source=ArchiveTab/2006/02/0206-38.htm)

   "Split Decision: He Quits, She Keeps Working," by Joan Caplin, 2005, *Money, 34,* pp. 41–45. (This article is available online at: http://money.cnn.com/magazines/moneymag/moneymag_archive/2005/02/01/8231623/)

"EVOKE™: A Life Planning Methodology for the Coming Revolution in Client Relationships," by George Kinder and Susan Galvan, 2005, *FPA Journal of Financial Planning, 18,* pp. 46–55. (This article is available online at: http://www.lifewealthcommunity.com/mc/page.do?sitePageId=29892)

11. *Landing the Job You Want* (1997), by William C. Byham with Debra Pickett, is available through DDI's Client Service group by calling 1-800-944-7782.

12. From "An Experimental Comparison of Retirement Planning Intervention Seminars," by Douglas A. Hershey, John C. Mowen, and Joy M. Jacobs-Lawson, 2003, *Educational Gerontology, 29,* pp. 339–359.

    See also "Adaptation to Retirement: Role Changes and Psychological Resources," by Mary Anne Taylor-Carter and Kelli A. Cook, 1995, *Career Development Quarterly, 44,* pp. 67–82.

13. From "Pension Protection Act of 2006: Mandates and Options for Retirement Plans" by Antoinette M. Pilzner, 2006, October/November, *Legal Report,* p. 3.

14. From *Retirement Readiness,* Fidelity Investments.

Chapter 13

1. From a personal conversation with Gil Francis, TVA media consultant, on May 4, 2006.

2. From *The Business Case for Workers Age 50+: Planning for Tomorrow's Talent Needs in Today's Competitive Environment: A Report for AARP* (p. 19), by Roselyn Feinsod, Tom Davenport, Rich Arthurs, Towers Perrin, and the AARP, 2005, Washington, DC: AARP.

3. Ibid.

4. The data for Table 13.2 came from DDI samples ranging between 1,218 and 3,346 people and described in the research notes in this book (pp. 261–266). The lower health care costs come from Figure 7.4 (p. 88), garnered from data found in *The Business Case for Workers Age 50+,* by Feinsod et al, 2005.

5. See *Managing Performance: Building Accountability for Organizational Success* (p. 23), by Paul R. Bernthal, Robert W. Rogers, and Audrey B. Smith, 2003, Pittsburgh, PA: Development Dimensions International. An executive summary for this study can be found on DDI's web site at: http://www.ddiworld.com/thoughtleadership/hrtrendresearch.asp. A complete report is available by calling 1-800-944-7782.

6. *Realizing the Promise of Performance Management* (2005), by Robert W. Rogers, is available through DDI's Client Service group by calling 1-800-944-7782.

7. From a personal conversation with Chris Clark, manager for talent resourcing and learning for Shell EP Americas, on May 5, 2006.

8. See "Learning, Not Litigating: Managing Employee Development and Avoiding Claims of Age Discrimination," by Todd J. Maurer and Nancy E. Rafuse, 2001, *Academy of Management Executive, 15,* pp. 110–121.

9. From "They Don't Retire Them, They Hire Them," by Joe Mullich, 2003, *Workforce Management, 82,* p. 50.

Chapter 14

1. From *Redefining Retirement: Options for Older Americans* (pp. 5–6), by the United States Government Accountability Office, 2005, Washington, DC: GAO. This report is available online at: http://www.gao.gov/new.items/d05620t.pdf

2. From *Redefining Retirement,* the GAO, p. 7.

3. From a chapter called "Recruiting and Retaining Older Workers" (p. 43), by Mary Ann Taylor, Kenneth S. Schultz, and Dennis Doverspike, in Paulette T. Beatty & Roemmer M.S. Visser's (Eds.) book *Thriving on an Aging Workforce: Strategies for Organizational and Systemic Change,* 2005, Melbourne, FL: Krieger Publishing.

Also see *The Economic Impact of Trends in Retirement and Expected Life,* Rudolph G. Penner's testimony before the Senate Finance Committee on June 18, 1988 (available online at: http://www.urban.org/url.cfm?ID=900273), and "Tapping a Silver Mine: Older Workers Represent a Wealth of Talent—but May Require Increased Flexibility from HR," by Alison Stein Wellner, 2002, *HR Magazine, 47,* pp. 26–32.

4. From the *Civilian Labor Force Participation Rates by Sex, Age, Race, and Hispanic Origin* by the U.S. Department of Labor, Bureau of Labor Statistics, 2005. This table displays U.S. labor force rates from 1984, 1994, and 2004, and projects the data for 2014. Available online at: http://www.bls.gov/emp/emplab05.htm

5. From "Old. Smart. Productive." by Peter Coy, 2005, *BusinessWeek,* (3939), p. 81. This article is also available online at: http://www.businessweek.com/magazine/content/05_26/ b3939001_mz001.htm

6. From "In Overhaul of Social Security, Age Is the Elephant in the Room," by Robin Toner and David E. Rosenbaum, 2005, *The New York Times, 154,* p. 1.

7. From data included on *Status of the Social Security and Medicare Programs: A Summary of the 2006 Annual Reports,* by the Social Security and Medicare Boards of Trustees, 2006, Baltimore, MD: Social Security Administration. Available online at: http://www.ssa.gov/OACT/ TRSUM/trsummary.html

8. From "The Late, Great 'Golden Years,'" by Steve Lohr, 2005, *The New York Times, 154,* p. 6.

9. From "The Old and the Rested," by John Tierney, 2005, *The New York Times, 154,* p. A23.

10. From "Economic Death Spiral," by Robert Samuelson, *The Washington Post,* April 6, 2005, p. A19.

11. From *Voting and Registration in the Election of November 2000* (p. 6), by Amie Jamieson, Hyon B. Shin, and Jennifer Day, 2002, Washington, DC: U.S. Census Bureau. This report is available online at: http://www.census.gov/prod/2002pubs/p20-542.pdf

Bibliography

AARP. (2000). *American business and older employees survey.* Washington, DC: Author.

AARP (as prepared by Roper ASW). (2004, May). *Baby boomers envision retirement II: Survey of baby boomers' expectations for retirement.* Washington, DC: AARP.

Adams, G.A., & Beehr, T.A. (Eds.). (2003). *Retirement: Reasons, processes, and results.* New York: Springer.

Ameriprise Financial (with Age Wave, Dychtwald, K., & Harris Interactive). (2005). *The new retirement mindscape*^{SM}. Minneapolis, MN: Author.

Amick, B.C., III, McDonough, P., Chang, H., Rogers, W.H., Pieper, C.F., & Duncan, G. (2002). Relationship between all-cause mortality and cumulative working life course psychosocial and physical exposures in the United States labor market from 1968 to 1992. *Psychosomatic Medicine, 64*(3), 370–381. Available at: http://www.psychosomaticmedicine.org/cgi/content/abstract/64/3/370?ijkey=90b64eb9c23905ab9595584a131a50144a9e4d57&keytype2=tf_ipsecsha

Appleby, J., & Carty, S.S. (2005, June 23). Ailing GM looks to scale back generous health benefits. *USA Today,* p. 1B.

Barlett, D.L., & Steele, J.B. (2005, October 31). The broken promise. *Time, 166*(18), 32–47.

Belson, K., & Richtel, M. (2005, December 6). Verizon to halt pension outlay for managers. *The New York Times* [late edition—final], pp. A1, C5.

Bernthal, P.R., Rogers, R.W., & Smith, A.B. (2003). *Managing performance: Building accountability for organizational success.* Pittsburgh, PA: Development Dimensions International.

Brown, S.K. (2003). *Staying ahead of the curve 2003: The AARP working in retirement study* [Executive summary]. Washington, DC: AARP.

Brown, S.K. (2003). *Staying ahead of the curve: The AARP working in retirement study.* Washington, DC: AARP.

Brown, S.K. (2005). *Attitudes of individuals 50 and older toward phased retirement.* Washington, DC: AARP.

Burke, M.E. (2005). *SHRM 2005 benefits survey report.* Alexandria, VA: Society for Human Resource Management.

Byham, W.C., Smith, A.B., & Paese, M.J. (2000). *Grow your own leaders.* Pittsburgh, PA: DDI Press.

Cahill, K.E., Giandrea, M.D., & Quinn, J.F. (2006, October). *A micro-level analysis of recent increases in labor force participation among older men.* Washington, DC: U.S. Bureau of Labor Statistics. Available at: http://www.bls.gov/ore/abstract/ec/ec060120.htm

Caplin, J. (2005, February). Split decision: He quits, she keeps working. *Money, 34*(2), 41–45.

Center for Retirement Research at Boston College. (2006, June). *Retirements at risk: A new national retirement risk index.* Boston: Author.

Collison, J. (2003). *SHRM/NOWCC/CED older workers survey.* Alexandria, VA: Society for Human Resource Management.

Colonia-Willner, R. (1998). Practical intelligence at work: Relationship between aging and cognitive efficiency among managers in a bank environment. *Psychology and Aging, 13*(1), 45–57.

Colosi v. Electri-Flex Company, 965F.2d500, 502 (7th Cir. 1992).

Colvin, G. (2006, June 26). Ready or not, here it comes! [2006 retirement guide]. *Fortune, 153*(12), 29–30.

Colvin, G. (2006, June 26). The end of a dream. *Fortune, 153*(12), 85–92.

Cornell Law School's Legal Information Institute. (n.d.). Smith v. City of Jackson (03-1160) 544 U.S. 228 (2005) 351 F.3d 183, affirmed. Available at: http://www.law.cornell.edu/supct/html/03 1160.ZS.html

Corporate Leadership Council. (2002). *Closing the performance gap: Driving results through performance management.* Washington, DC: Author.

Coy, P. (2005, June 27). Old. Smart. Productive. *BusinessWeek,* (3939), 78–86.

David DeLong & Associates, & Zogby International. (2006). *Living longer, working longer: The changing landscape of the aging workforce.* Westport, CT: MetLife Mature Market Institute.

Development Dimensions International. (2005). *Leadership research summary.* Pittsburgh, PA: Author. Available at: http://www.ddiworld.com/pdf/ddi_leadershipresearchsummary rr.pdf

Doering, P.B. (1990). *Bridges to retirement: Older workers in a changing labor market.* Ithaca, NY: Cornell University, ILR Press.

Durett, J. (2006, July). Butting heads over retirement plans. *Training, 43*(7), 8.

Dychtwald, K., & Kadlec, D.J. (2005). *The power years: A user's guide to the rest of your life.* Hoboken, NJ: John Wiley & Sons.

Equal Employment Opportunity Commission. (1967). *Age Discrimination in Employment Act (ADEA) of 1967.* Washington, DC: Author. Available at: http://www.eeoc.gov/policy/adea.html

Equal Employment Opportunity Commission. (2002, 2003, 2004, & 2005). *Office of general counsel annual reports.* Washington, DC: Author. Reports available at: http://www.eeoc.gov/litigation/reports.html

Erker, S., Howard, A., & Bruce, N. (2007). *Selection forecast 2006–2007.* Pittsburgh, PA: Development Dimensions International.

Feinsod, R., Davenport, T., Arthurs, R., Towers Perrin, & AARP. (2005, December). *The business case for workers age 50+: Planning for tomorrow's talent needs in today's competitive environment: A report for AARP.* Washington, DC: AARP.

Fidelity Investments. (2005, March 8). *Retirement readiness: Fidelity survey provides real-time look at the retirement readiness of today's recent retirees.* Available at: http://www.fidelity.com/workplace/drillDown.html? http://www.fidelity.com/workplace/PublicSites/MainWrapper/ 0,,CSN2646_PSN2638_SSN2639_PID20371,00.html

Finkelstein, L.M., Allen, T., & Rhoton, L.A. (2003). An examination of the role of age in mentoring relationships. *Group and Organization Management, 28*(2), 249–281.

Fleck, C. (2006, September). When you'll retire—a guessing game. *AARP Bulletin, 47*(8), 6.

Frauenheim, E. (2006, October 9). They'll just keep going, and going, and going . . . *Workforce Management, 85*(19), 26.

Fronstin, P. (2005, March). *The impact of the erosion of retiree health benefits on workers and retirees* [EBRI Issue Brief No. 279]. Washington, DC: Employee Benefit Research Institute.

Giorgianni, S.J. (Ed.). (2005). Employers respond to caregivers' complex needs. In an issue entitled A Profile of Caregiving in America. *The Pfizer Journal, 9*(4), 23. Available at: http://www.thepfizerjournal.com/ default.asp?a=article&j=tpj43&t=Employers%20Respond%20to% 20Caregivers%u2019%20Complex%20Needs&l=en

Gleckman, H. (2006, July 31). A new twist on retiree health care. *BusinessWeek,* (3995), 68.

Hedge, J.W., Borman, W.C., & Lammlein, S.E. (2006). *The aging workforce: Realities, myths, and implications for organizations.* Washington, DC: American Psychological Association.

Helman, R., Salisbury, D., Paladino, V., & Copeland, C. (2005, April). *Encouraging workers to save: The 2005 retirement confidence survey* [EBRI Issue Brief No. 280]. Washington, DC: Employee Benefit Research Institute.

Helyar, J. (2005, May 16). 50 and fired. *Fortune, 151*(10), 78–90.

Herring, H.B. (2005, July 17). Retire in style? Maybe not quite so soon. *The New York Times, 154*(53278) [Special Section 2], p. 2.

Hershey, D.A., Mowen, J.C., & Jacobs-Lawson, J.M. (2003, April). An experimental comparison of retirement planning intervention seminars. *Educational Gerontology, 29*(4), 339–359.

Howard, A., & Bray, D.W. (1988). *Managerial lives in transition: Advancing age and changing times.* New York: Guilford Press.

Jamieson, A., Shin, H.B., & Day, J. (2002, February). *Voting and registration in the election of November 2000.* Washington, DC: U.S. Census Bureau. Available at: http://www.census.gov/prod/2002pubs/p20-542.pdf

Johnson, R.W., & Penner, R.G. (2004, October). *Will health care costs erode retirement security?* (Issue in Brief, 23), Chestnut Hill, MA: Trustees of Boston College, Center for Retirement Research.

Kinder, G., & Galvan, S. (2005, April). EVOKE™: A life planning methodology for the coming revolution in client relationships. *FPA Journal of Financial Planning, 18*(4), 46–55.

Kolata, G. (2007, January 3). A surprising secret to a long life: Stay in school. *The New York Times, 156*(53813), pp. A1, A16.

Kossck, E.E., & Lee, M.D. (2005). *Making flexibility work: What managers have learned about implementing reduced-load work.* Summary of findings from Phase II of Alfred P. Sloan Grant #2002-6-11. East Lansing, MI: Michigan State University and McGill University.

Kotlikoff, L.J., & Burns, S. (2005). *The coming generational storm: What you need to know about America's economic future.* Cambridge, MA: The MIT Press.

Leonhardt, D. (2005, August 8). Acting like there's no tomorrow when there may be many tomorrows left. *The New York Times,* p. C5.

Lewis, N. (2006, February). Setting goals together. *Black Enterprise, 36*(7), 79–80.

Lohr, S. (2005, March 6). The late, great "golden years." *The New York Times, 154*(53145), pp. 1, 6.

Maurer, T.J., & Rafuse, N.E. (2001, November). Learning, not litigating: Managing employee development and avoiding claims of age discrimination. *Academy of Management Executive, 15*(4), 110–121.

McKinsey & Company. (2006). *Cracking the consumer retirement code.* New York: Author. This report is available online at: http://www.mckinsey.com/ clientservice/bankingsecurities/latestthinking/retirement.asp

Merrill Lunch. (2005, February 22). *The new retirement study from Merrill Lynch reveals how baby boomers will transform retirement.* New York: Author. Available at: http://www.ml.com/ ?id=7695_7696_8149_46028_46503_46635

Merrill Lynch. (2006). *The 2006 Merrill Lynch new retirement study: A perspective from individuals and employers.* New York: Author.

Miller, J., & Miller, M. (2005, November 28). Get a life! *Fortune, 152*(11), 108–124.

Montenegro, X., Fisher, L., & Remez, S. (2002). *Staying ahead of the curve: The AARP work and career study* [Executive summary]. Washington, DC: AARP.

Morton, L., Foster, L., & Sedlar, J. (2005). *Managing the mature workforce: Implications and best practices.* New York: The Conference Board.

Mullich, J. (2003, December). They don't retire them, they hire them. *Workforce Management, 82*(13), 49–54.

Muson, H. (2003). *Valuing experience: How to motivate and retain mature workers* [Research report R-1329-03-RR]. New York: The Conference Board.

Neikirk, W. (2006, August 17). Bill would boost 401(k) plans. *Chicago Tribune,* p. 4.

O'Neil, J. (2006, April 11). Want to retire early and hang a shingle? It'll cost you. *The New York Times, 155*(53546), p. E4.

Parkinson, D. (2002). *Voices of experience: Mature workers in the future workforce* [Research Report R-1319-02-RR]. New York: The Conference Board.

Pear, R. (2006, May 2). Finances of Social Security and Medicare deteriorate. *The New York Times, 155*(53567), p. A23.

Penner, R.G. (1998, June 18). *The economic impact of trends in retirement and expected life: Testimony life before the Senate Finance Committee.* A statement submitted to the Senate Finance Committee. Available at: http://www.urban.org/publications/900273.html

Penner, R.G., Perun, P., & Steuerle, C.E. (2002). *Legal and institutional impediments to partial retirement and part-time work by older workers.* Washington, DC: Urban Institute.

Peterson, P. (2006, August 15). The quad deficits: Why they matter and what to do about them. Presentation given during the *Business and Finance: America and the Fiscal Future* lecture theme week at Chautauqua Institution, Chautauqua, NY.

Peterson, S.J., & Spiker, B.K. (2005). Establishing the positive contributory value of older workers: A positive psychology perspective. *Organizational Dynamics, 34*(2), 153–167.

Pilzner, A.M. (2006, October/November). Pension Protection Act of 2006: Mandates and options for retirement plans. *Legal Report,* 1–5.

Rajnes, D. (2001, September). Phased retirement: Leaving the labor force. *EBRI Notes, 22*(9), 1–8.

Roberts, B.W., Walton, K.E., & Viechtbauer, W. (2006). Patterns of mean-level change in personality traits across the life course: A meta-analysis of longitudinal studies. *Psychological Bulletin, 132*(1), 1–25.

Rogers, R.W. (2005). *Realizing the promise of performance management* (Rev. ed.). Pittsburgh, PA: DDI Press.

Roper ASW. (2002, September). *Staying ahead of the curve: The AARP work and career study.* Washington, DC: AARP.

Rose, J., & Liebl, R. (2006, October). Pension Protection Act of 2006: Long-term implications for the PBGC. *Employee Benefit Plan Review, 61*(4), 7–10.

Samuelson, R. (2005, April 6). Economic death spiral. *The Washington Post,* p. A19.

Schramm, J. (2006). Women and work (issue). *Workplace Visions, 3,* 7.

Seburn, P.W. (1991, December). Evolution of employer-provided defined benefit pensions. *Monthly Labor Review, 114*(12), 16–23.

Shadovitz, D. (2006, May 2). Workers acknowledge move to defined contribution. *Human Resource Executive, 20*(6), 63.

Shore, L., & Goldberg, C. (2004). Age discrimination in the workplace. In R.L. Dipboye & A. Colella (Eds.), *Discrimination at work: The psychological and organizational bases* (pp. 203–225). Mahwah, NJ: Lawrence Erlbaum Associates.

Siems, T.F. (2001, January 23). Reengineering Social Security in the new economy. *The Cato Project on Social Security Privatization, 22.*

Sinar, E.F., & Byham, W.C. (2006). *Age effects on competency-based job performance.* Manuscript in preparation, Development Dimensions International.

Smith, A. (2006, October). EEOC approves targeting of older workers for recruitment. *HR Magazine, 51*(10), 29, 36.

Smith, N. (2006, July 2). Britons are living longer, but they face an unhealthy old age. *The Sunday Times,* News 5.

Social Security and Medicare Boards of Trustees. (2006, May 2). *Status of the Social Security and Medicare programs: A summary of the 2006 annual reports.* Baltimore, MD: Social Security Administration. Available at: http://www.ssa.gov/OACT/TRSUM/trsummary.html

Society for Human Resource Management & American Association of Retired Persons. (1998). *SHRM/AARP older workers survey.* Alexandria, VA: SHRM.

Szinovacz, M.E. (2003). Contexts and pathways: Retirement as institution, process, and experience. In G.A. Adams & T.A. Beehr (Eds.), *Retirement: Reasons, processes, and results* (pp. 6–52). New York: Springer Publishing.

Taylor, M.A., & Shore, L.M. (1995, March). Predictors of planned retirement age: An application of Beehr's model. *Psychology and Aging, 10*(1), 76–83.

Taylor, M.A., Shultz, K., & Doverspike, D. (2005). Recruiting and retaining older workers. In P.T. Beatty & R.M.S. Visser (Eds.), *Thriving on an aging workforce: Strategies for organizational and systemic change.* Melbourne, FL: Krieger Publishing.

Taylor-Carter, M.A., & Cook, K.A. (1995). Adaptation to retirement: Role changes and psychological resources. *Career Development Quarterly, 44*(1), 67–82.

Tierney, J. (2005, June 14). The old and the rested. *The New York Times,* *154*(53245), p. A23.

Toner, R., & Rosenbaum, D.E. (2005, June 12). In overhaul of Social Security, age is the elephant in the room. *The New York Times,* *154*(53243), Section 1, pp. 1, 37.

Trafford, A. (2003). *My time: Making the most of the rest of your life.* New York: Basic Books.

Trafford, A. (2004). *My time: Making the most of the bonus decades after 50.* New York: Basic Books.

Turning boomers into boomerangs. (2006, February 18). *The Economist,* *378*(8465), 65–67.

U.S. Census Bureau. (2006). 98—Expectation of life and expected deaths by race, sex, and age: 2002. Available from archived Statistical Abstract of the United States page on the U.S. Census Bureau's web site: http://www.census.gov/prod/2005pubs/06statab/vistat.pdf

U.S. Department of Labor, Bureau of Labor Statistics. (2005, December 7). *Civilian labor force participation rates by sex, age, race, and Hispanic origin.* Available at: http://www.bls.gov/emp/emplab05.htm

United States Government Accountability Office (GAO). (2005, April 27). *Redefining retirement: Options for older Americans* (GAO-05-620T). Washington, DC: Author.

University of Michigan Institute for Social Research. (2004). *Health and retirement study: A longitudinal study of health, retirement, and aging.* Ann Arbor, MI: Author.

Waggoner, J. (2005, October 26). To retire well, start saving yesterday. *USA Today,* pp. 1B–2B.

Wallace v. O.C. Tanner Recognition Company, et al, 299F.3d96, 100 (1st Cir. 2002).

Wallechinsky, D. (2006, April 25). Is the American dream still possible? *Parade,* April 23, p. 5.

Walsh, M.W. (2006, August 8). Court rules for I.B.M. on pension. *The New York Times, 155*(53665), pp. C1, C10.

Walsh, M.W. (2006, August 8). Public pension plans face billions in shortages. *The New York Times, 155*(53665), pp. A1, C10.

Watson Wyatt Worldwide. (2004). *Phased retirement: Aligning employer programs with worker preferences.* Washington, DC: Author.

Watson Wyatt Worldwide. (2004, April). Phased retirement: A retention strategy whose time has come. *Insider, 14*(4), 6. Available at: http://www.watsonwyatt.com/us/pubs/insider/pdfs/2004_04.pdf

Weckerle, J.R., & Shultz, K.S. (1999, September). Influences on the bridge employment decision among older USA workers. *Journal of Occupational and Organizational Psychology, 72*(3), 317–329.

Wellins, R.S., Byham, W.C., & Wilson, J.M. (1991). *Empowered teams: Creating self-directed work groups that improve quality, productivity, and participation.* San Francisco: Jossey-Bass.

Wellner, A.S. (2002, March). Tapping a silver mine: Older workers represent a wealth of talent—but may require increased flexibility from HR. *HR Magazine, 47*(3), 26–32.

Wiatrowski, W.J. (2001, April). Changing retirement age: Ups and downs. *Monthly Labor Review, 124*(4), 3–12.

Wingate, P.H., Thornton, G.C., III, McIntyre, K.S., & Flame, J.H. (2003, February). Organizational downsizing and age discrimination litigation: The influence of personnel policies and statistical evidence on the litigation outcomes. *Law and Human Behavior, 27*(1), 87–108.

DDI Research Design and Methodology

All Datasets

1. Individuals for all datasets (except the *Selection Forecast*) were classified into five age categories, and these categories were used for all analyses: 1) Less than 26 years old; 2) 26 to 35 years old; 3) 36 to 45 years old; 4) 46 to 55 years old; and 5) 56 years of age or older.

Performance by Age Group

2. For all analyses involving manager-provided job performance ratings (e.g., as represented in Figure 7.1), the total dataset included 8,615 individuals drawn from 39 DDI validation studies and 29 different client organizations (some organizations, such as a large retailing organization and a large bank, contributed several distinct studies). Sample sizes for individual performance criteria varied based on the frequency with which each performance criterion was present across individual validation studies.

3. The median validation study sample size was 141 and ranged up to 1,153. To ensure that results were not overly influenced by certain studies contributing large sample sizes, we conducted several preliminary analyses using a sub-sampling approach in which no more than 250 individuals were included from each study. These analyses produced very similar results to the full sample analyses. Therefore, we focused on the full sample for further performance analyses to maximize statistical power to detect effects.

4. Age category frequencies for the 7,348 individuals within this sample providing age information were as follows: 1) Less than 26 years old = 1,601 (21.8%); 2) 26 to 35 years old = 2,100 (28.6%); 3) 36 to 45 years old = 1,730 (23.5%); 4) 46 to 55 years old = 1,292 (17.6%); and 5) 56 years of age or older = 625 (8.5%).

5. Within this sample, 81.8% were team member-level (nonmanagement) employees, 3.2% were professional individual contributors, and 15.0% were leaders. Several of the analyses focused solely on either the team member or the combined individual contributor/leader subsamples.

6. This sample included employees from the following industries: aerospace (1.8%), banking (13.7%), consumer products manufacturing (4.7%), food and beverage (10.3%), government (1.2%), health care (2.8%), industrial manufacturing (9.0%), media (3.6%), metals and mining (0.9%), pharmaceuticals (0.4%), retail (46.2%), and telecommunications (5.5%).

7. All job performance data were gathered in the course of validation studies conducted by Development Dimensions International (DDI) between 1997 and 2006. These studies followed a uniform approach involving performance rating sessions and were preceded by detailed frame-of-reference and rater error training, in which supervisors rated employees using several behavioral statements for each of 8 to 10 competencies. Performance ratings were utilized for research purposes only and described to participants as such; ratings were not made available to the client organizations, and no administrative decisions were possible on the basis of the information. Employees also provided voluntary demographic information (e.g., birth date/age category) during the course of their study participation (e.g., completing predictor measures). Within each organization and sample, we standardized average ratings such that performance ratings reflected an employee's performance relative to others within his or her respective organization.

Employee Engagement (E3®) Scores by Age Group

8. For all analyses involving employee engagement, the total sample was a subset of the Performance by Age Group dataset described above. Employee engagement data were available from a total of 4,352 individuals from nine of the validation samples described above. Due to the smaller number of samples and to avoid excessive influence on the results by a small number of large samples, random subsets of no

more than 250 individuals per sample were selected for the analyses, for a total of 1,872—1,322 of whom were nonmanagement workers and 550 of whom were either individual contributors or leaders.

9. Individuals completed DDI's 17-item E3 employee engagement survey in the course of their participation in the validation studies described above.

10. Within each job level (nonmanagement or individual contributor/leader), we standardized employee engagement scores such that they reflected an employee's engagement level relative to others within that person's job level.

11. Age frequencies for the 1,322 nonmanagement individuals within this sample providing age information were as follows: 1) Less than 26 years old = 324 (24.5%); 2) 26 to 35 years old = 392 (29.7%); 3) 36 to 45 years old = 282 (21.3%); 4) 46 to 55 years old = 217 (16.4%); and 5) 56 years of age or older = 107 (8.1%).

12. Age category frequencies for the 550 individual contributor or leader individuals within this sample providing age information were as follows: 1) Less than 26 years old = 47 (8.5%); 2) 26 to 35 years old = 171 (31.1%); 3) 36 to 45 years old = 166 (30.2%); 4) 46 to 55 years old = 125 (22.7%); and 5) 56 years of age or older = 41 (7.5%).

Retention Likelihood Scores by Age Group

13. For all analyses involving retention likelihood, the total sample was a subset of the Performance by Age Group dataset described above. Retention likelihood data were available from a total of 4,072 individuals from 10 of the validation samples described above. Due to the smaller number of samples and to avoid excessive influence on the results by a small number of large samples, random subsets of no more than 250 individuals per sample were selected for the analyses, for a total of 1,645—1,178 of whom were nonmanagement workers and 467 of whom were either individual contributors or leaders.

14. Individuals completed four retention likelihood items in the course of their participation in the validation studies described above.

15. Within each job level (nonmanagement or individual contributor/leader), we standardized retention likelihood scores such that they reflected an employee's retention likelihood level relative to others within that person's job level.

16. Age frequencies for the 1,178 nonmanagement individuals within this sample providing age information were as follows: 1) Less than 26 years old = 287 (24.4%); 2) 26 to 35 years old = 351 (29.8%); 3) 36 to 45 years old = 256 (21.7%); 4) 46 to 55 years old = 184 (15.6%); and 5) 56 years of age or older = 100 (8.5%).

17. Age category frequencies for the 467 individual contributor or leader individuals within this sample providing age information were as follows: 1) Less than 26 years old = 44 (9.4%); 2) 26 to 35 years old = 151 (32.3%); 3) 36 to 45 years old = 141 (30.2%); 4) 46 to 55 years old = 101 (21.6%); and 5) 56 years of age or older = 30 (6.4%).

Personality Scores by Age Group

18. For all analyses involving personality scores, the total sample was a subset of the Performance by Age Group dataset described above, focusing specifically on nonmanagement employees. To avoid excessive influence on the results by a small number of large samples, random subsets of no more than 250 individuals per sample were selected for the analyses, for a total of 1,629.

19. Within each organization and sample, we standardized personality scores such that they reflected an employee's personality scores relative to others within that person's respective organization.

20. Age category frequencies for the 1,629 individuals within this sample providing age information varied by personality scale, with maximum values as follows: 1) Less than 26 years old = 326 (20.0%); 2) 26 to 35 years old = 623 (38.2%); 3) 36 to 45 years old = 392 (24.1%); 4) 46 to 55 years old = 239 (14.7%); and 5) 56 years of age or older = 49 (3.0%).

Situational Judgment and Analytical Problem-Solving Test Scores by Age Group—Supervisory Candidates

21. Job candidates (5,002) for supervisory positions completed Situational Judgment and Analytical Problem-Solving subtests contained within DDI selection instruments, as implemented by 14 organizations.

22. Within each organization, we standardized Situational Judgment and Analytical Problem-Solving scores such that they reflected a candidate's scores relative to other candidates in that person's respective organization.

23. To avoid excessive influence on the results by large samples, random subsets of no more than 1,500 candidates per sample were selected for the analyses.

24. Age category frequencies for supervisory candidates providing age information were as follows: 1) Less than 26 years old = 1,502 (30.0%); 2) 26 to 35 years old = 1,813 (36.2%); 3) 36 to 45 years old = 1,066 (21.3%); 4) 46 to 55 years old = 516 (10.3%); and 5) 56 years of age or older = 105 (2.1%).

Situational Judgment and Analytical Problem-Solving Test Scores by Age Group—Managerial Candidates

25. Job candidates (5,136) for management positions completed Situational Judgment and Analytical Problem-Solving subtests contained within DDI selection instruments.

26. Within each organization, we standardized Situational Judgment and Analytical Problem-Solving scores such that they reflected a candidate's scores relative to other candidates in that person's respective organization.

27. Age category frequencies for management candidates providing age information were as follows: 1) Less than 26 years old = 939 (18.3%); 2) 26 to 35 years old = 2,109 (41.1%); 3) 36 to 45 years old = 1,383 (26.9%); 4) 46 to 55 years old = 604 (11.8%); and 5) 56 years of age or older = 101 (2.0%).

Situational Judgment and Analytical Problem-Solving Test Scores by Age Group—Customer Service Candidates

28. Job candidates (3,346) for customer service positions completed Situational Judgment and Analytical Problem-Solving subtests contained within DDI selection instruments, as implemented by 6 organizations.

29. Within each organization, we standardized Situational Judgment and Analytical Problem-Solving scores such that they reflected a candidate's scores relative to other candidates in that person's respective organization.

30. To avoid excessive influence on the results by large samples, random subsets of no more than 1,500 candidates per sample were selected for the analyses.

31. Age category frequencies for customer service candidates providing age information were as follows: 1) Less than 26 years old = 1,519 (45.4%); 2) 26 to 35 years old = 998 (29.8%); 3) 36 to 45 years old = 509 (15.2%); 4) 46 to 55 years old = 259 (7.7%); and 5) 56 years of age or older = 61 (1.8%).

Selection Forecast Job Seeker Motivations by Age Group

32. Job seekers from the United States and Canada (1,183) answered questions from a 2006 DDI and Monster.com survey (*Selection Forecast*) about topics related to organizational selection.

33. Age category frequencies for job seekers were as follows: 1) Less than 20 years old = 66 (5.6%); 2) 21 to 30 years old = 338 (28.7%); 3) 31 to 40 years old = 275 (23.4%); 4) 41 to 50 years = 307 (26.1%); and 5) 51 years of age or older = 190 (16.2%). Seven job seekers did not provide their age.

34. Each job seeker responded to two questions about his or her motivations to take or leave a job: 1) Other than salary and benefits, what are the most important things you are looking for in a job? and 2) If you are thinking about changing jobs, or if you recently left a job, what were the main reason(s)?

35. In both questions, job seekers were asked to select all options that apply out of a list of 14 (Question 1) or 16 (Question 2).

36. For each question, answers were ranked based on the percentage of job seekers in each age category who answered "yes" to that answer option.

Acknowledgments

Getting a book from concept to the bookshelf always requires so much more than just the author's effort. Over the past 22 months, dozens of people have lent their considerable talents, ideas, support, expertise, and encouragement to launch *70: The New 50*. I deeply appreciate their efforts. They include:

Helen Wylie, my special assistant, who has worked with me on this project from its conception. Not only did she type and organize 13 iterations of the manuscript—often working from handwriting (mine) that was barely legible—but she also tracked source material and helped to coordinate the efforts of our research associate. She has an excellent memory to go with her considerable planning and organizing skills and, when called upon, could recall specific iterations in which a passage was changed or deleted. Helen's cheerful demeanor belied the long days and frequent weekends she spent working on the book. As with my previous book, *Grow Your Own Leaders,* Helen's dogged determination saw us through to completion. I could not have completed this book without her.

Bill Proudfoot, who served as chief editor, came on board midway into the fifth iteration of the manuscript and worked his way through another nine versions. As he did with *Grow Your Own Leaders,* Bill put in hundreds of hours editing, proofing, and polishing drafts before managing the final text through formatting and final proofing, and then working with our publisher. Bill also served as a sounding board and helped me ensure that the concepts presented would be clear to the reader. Saying thanks can't begin to express my appreciation for the work that Bill did.

Janet Wiard was our graphic designer on *70: The New 50*. Not only did she design the crisp, clean layout and graphics, but she also persevered through numerous last-minute revisions. Her attention to detail during that time was stellar, as was her dedication to getting the job done. Janet is quite the expert in the formatting software we used; without her skills, our book would still be a manuscript. Outstanding job, Janet!

Carla Fogle served as our research associate. She had the unenviable—and frequently frustrating—task of tracking down and then citing the reference material that much of this book was built upon. Carla logged many, many hours—often at her local library after DDI work hours—verifying references or searching for specific passages in print and online material. Carla, you did a great job!

Shawn Garry wore many hats during this project: proofreader, editor, reference checker, and "the audience." Shawn joined the team late in the manuscript process to lend his editorial eye to proofing and editing text before it was typeset. Then, once the document had been formatted, Shawn proofed it again. He also worked closely with Carla to confirm the dozens of references that appear in the End Notes section. Last, but not least, he compiled the comprehensive bibliography. Excellent work, Shawn!

Evan Sinar and **Ann Howard** were charged with searching through more than 50 DDI research studies to assemble the summaries reported in the book. **Doug Reynolds** and **Paul Bernthal** added their insights to interpreting the data and how they could be best presented. Evan, Ann, Doug, and Paul, all of your contributions were invaluable.

Early on, **Robin McLean** contributed to the content and direction of the book. She also interviewed people and lent valuable insights.

Dave Thomas, who served as our resident technical expert relative to benefit plans, read three iterations of the book and made sure it was accurate.

Joan Mancing helped me with topics dealing with legal issues and researched court and government documents that were pertinent to this book. Thank you, Joan.

I also want to acknowledge **Susan Ryan** for her cover design; **Stacy Infantozzi, Mike Lawley,** and **Lisa Weyandt** for their help with graphics and formatting; and **Tammy Pordash** for transcribing my dictation.

Many DDI associates volunteered their time to review various iterations of this book. Their feedback was of immense help in improving the content of *70: The New 50*. These reviewers included **Scott Erker, Ann Howard, Bill Koch, Sheryl Riddle, Bob Rogers,** and **Pete Weaver.**

I also want to thank **Maureen Van Dine** and **Michael Garrett,** two old and very dear friends, who read chapters and made excellent suggestions for content revisions.

Special Thanks

Proof that 70 is, indeed, the new 50 was **Ben Fischer,** labor movement activist and professor at Carnegie Mellon University (CMU), who died on November 12, 2006. At the time of his death, he was 92 years old and still very much active. During the final week of his life, the labor economist taught a class at CMU, wrote some of his autobiography, and worked on mediating a labor dispute, while also writing a prologue to this book. He will be missed!

About DDI

For more than 37 years, Development Dimensions International (DDI) has helped leading organizations worldwide create and execute talent strategies that enable them to hire, develop, and retain the best people. Retirement management is one of those strategies.

The three keys to a successful retirement management strategy are strong leaders with a clear understanding of their unique role, an accurate picture of the organization's future talent needs and possible retirements, and a working, defensible performance management system. DDI helps organizations achieve these keys to success by:

- Building Success Profile-based recruitment and selection systems that lead to better hiring and promotion decisions. Our expertise includes defining the four elements of a Success Profile, application of tests, simulations, and Targeted Selection®, the world's first and most widely used behaviorally based interviewing system.

- Developing retirement management leadership skills for frontline and middle managers. Our proven, competency-based curriculum of more than 55 leadership courses is available in multiple languages, delivery modalities, and leadership areas.

- Assuring a supply of the right senior leaders in the right jobs, at their peak performance. DDI can create a framework for identifying high potentials early, using executive acceleration centers and other tools to provide a complete picture of their strengths, derailers, and development priorities. To accelerate their development, we customize executive education tools that build critical strategic skills and self-awareness.

- Building and installing performance management systems that link company business strategies to clear accountabilities and that develop leaders' ability to better manage their employees' performance.

- Helping organizations plan and execute a retirement management strategy through consulting and skill development.

DDI is all about providing the kind of business impact our clients want. The work we do together is tied to our clients' strategies and becomes part of their business and culture. This leads to solutions with long-term sustainability.

For multinational clients, DDI has precisely the kind of global resources needed to implement their talent initiatives effectively and consistently worldwide, with more than 1,000 sales, consulting, and implementation associates working at 75 offices in 26 countries.

For more information about programs and services available from DDI, visit our web site at **www.ddiworld.com** or call us between 7:30 a.m. and 5:30 p.m. (Eastern Standard Time) at 1-800-933-4463 or 412-257-0600 in the United States or 1-800-668-7971 in Canada.

For more information about this book, visit our web site:
http://www.ddiworld.com/70thenew50/

About the Author

I had my 70th birthday on September 14th, 2006, somewhere over the Pacific Ocean on the way to Beijing. I have to admit that I hated the thought of being 70 and was secretly relieved that I was not going to be around my friends and family to help me "celebrate" this event. I was hoping just to keep it as quiet as possible. On reaching Beijing around midnight, I was taken to my hotel room to find that a birthday celebration had been laid out for me, featuring a special Chinese delicacy (a pastry that looks like a peach) served particularly for 70th birthdays.

Almost everywhere I went for the next nine days, I was congratulated on my birthday and had the same delicacy served to me. During that time, my attitude about being 70 changed from acceptance to pride that I was still contributing to society and to the success of my company, Development Dimensions International (DDI). Incidentally, following my stay in China, I flew to London, making speeches and attending meetings for another nine days.

This book, *70: The New 50,* is in no way an autobiography, although my life does illustrate many of the points made in it. After graduating from Ohio University and Purdue, I immediately went to work, and I've been working ever since. My first job as an industrial/organizational psychologist was with a large New York advertising agency, Kenyon & Eckhardt, followed by six years at J.C. Penney as that company's first industrial/organizational psychologist. During my early years in New York City, I was lucky enough to meet and make friends with Dr. Douglas Bray, a noted industrial psychologist at AT&T and the inventor of the modern assessment center. Doug had a major impact on my life, starting with helping me put in the first managerial assessment center in a retail organization. In 1970 I wrote the first popular article about the assessment center method for *Harvard Business Review,* drawing a lot of large organizations to the methodology. Seizing an entrepreneurial opportunity, Doug and I started DDI in 1970 to provide assessment center consulting and materials. I have been the CEO ever since—some 37 years.

Full retirement has never entered my mind because I enjoy my work so much and because I've been able to shift the focus of my activities over time very much in the manner of the transition-to-retirement jobs that I explore in this book. At 60, I gave up the day-to-day running of the organization to DDI's President, Bob Rogers, and have spent my time writing and speaking on areas of human resource management that interest me, particularly areas that typically yield poor returns on investment, such as selection, training, multirater (360°) instruments, and succession management. Too many companies implement programs that really don't materially benefit them.

All of my adult life, I've written books. *70: The New 50* is my 22nd book. It's a companion piece to *Grow Your Own Leaders,* a book I coauthored with two of my DDI colleagues. Both focus on what organizations should do to prepare themselves for the retirement of baby boomers.

As I go around the world talking about HR issues, I'm constantly asked when I'll retire, and I always answer, "When I'm no longer contributing to the organization." I'm not taking any chances that DDI will be disrupted by my retirement; we have a solid succession management program in place and an organization full of highly qualified people of all ages.

As I look back on my career, some professional highlights include:

- Cofounding, with Dr. Douglas Bray, Development Dimensions International in 1970.

- Championing the application of the assessment center method worldwide.

- Developing the first behavior-based interviewing system, Targeted Selection®, in 1970.

- Coauthoring *The Law and Personnel Testing*—the first book on the implications of Equal Employment Opportunity law and other legal constraints on personnel testing and selection.

- Codeveloping Interaction Management®, the first commercially available leadership training program using behavior modeling, in 1975.

- Authoring *Zapp!*® *The Lightning of Empowerment*, a seminal book about empowerment that has sold more than 4.5 million copies.

- Helping to make teams and teamwork successful in organizations throughout the world, including coauthoring three books on teams (i.e., *Empowered Teams: Creating Self-Directed Work Groups That Improve Quality, Productivity, and Participation; Leadership Trapeze: Strategies for Leadership in Team-Based Organizations;* and *Inside Teams: How 20 World-Class Organizations Are Winning Through Teamwork*).

- Encouraging the expansion of employee empowerment through writings, speeches, and programs, including my best-selling business book, *HeroZ™—Empower Yourself, Your Coworkers, Your Company.*

- Devising new methods of succession management that dramatically depart from conventional replacement planning techniques and coauthoring the book *Grow Your Own Leaders.*

- Making multirater (360°) feedback more effective in creating on-the-job behavior change through the development of training programs for feedback recipients and their managers and through the book, *What Now?*

I hope you enjoy reading this book and that those of you who are decision makers in your organization will use at least some of the ideas to retain or hire the highly skilled and motivated resources that are available to you as the baby boomers enter their 60s and 70s.

I welcome your comments about *70: The New 50.* Please feel free to write to me at:

Development Dimensions International
Attention: Bill Byham
1225 Washington Pike
Bridgeville, PA 15017

or via e-mail at Bill.Byham@ddiworld.com

Other Books from DDI

Empowered Teams: Creating Self-Directed Work Groups That Improve Quality, Productivity, and Participation by Richard S. Wellins, William C. Byham, and Jeanne M. Wilson (available in English, German, and Portuguese)

Grow Your Own Leaders by William C. Byham, Audrey B. Smith, and Matthew J. Paese (available in English, Chinese [Simplified], Japanese, Russian, and Portuguese)

HeroZ™—Empower Yourself, Your Coworkers, Your Company by William C. Byham and Jeff Cox (available in English, French, German, Spanish, Korean, Chinese, Arabic, and Portuguese)

Inside Teams: How 20 World-Class Organizations Are Winning Through Teamwork by Richard S. Wellins, William C. Byham, and George R. Dixon

Landing the Job You Want: How to Have the Best Job Interview of Your Life by William C. Byham with Debra Pickett

Leadership Trapeze: Strategies for Leadership in Team-Based Organizations by Jeanne M. Wilson, Jill George, and Richard S. Wellins, with William C. Byham (available in English, Korean, and Portuguese)

Organizational Change That Works: How to Merge Culture and Business Strategies for Maximum Results by Robert W. Rogers, John W. Hayden, and B. Jean Ferketish, with Robert Matzen

Realizing the Promise of Performance Management by Robert W. Rogers

The Selection Solution: Solving the Mystery of Matching People to Jobs by William C. Byham with Steven M. Krauzer

The Service Leaders Club by William C. Byham with Ray Crew and James H.S. Davis (available in English and Korean)

Shogun Management™: How North Americans Can Thrive in Japanese Companies by William C. Byham with George Dixon (available in English and Japanese)

Succeeding With Teams: 101 Tips That Really Work by Richard S. Wellins, Dick Schaaf, and Kathy Harper Shomo

Team Leader's Survival Guide by Jeanne M. Wilson and Jill A. George

Team Member's Survival Guide by Jill A. George and Jeanne M. Wilson

Zapp!® Empowerment in Health Care by William C. Byham with Jeff Cox and Greg Nelson

Zapp!® in Education by William C. Byham with Jeff Cox and Kathy Harper Shomo

Zapp!® The Lightning of Empowerment—revised edition by William C. Byham with Jeff Cox (original edition available in English, French, German, Japanese, Dutch, Chinese [Simplified], Korean, Thai, Portuguese, and Spanish); also available as a video

Index

F

G

training in retirement management
for leaders, 194–196
diversity training, 195–196
quick-check discussions,
127–128
retirement planning, 173
taking action with poor
performers, 123–124, 196

transition-to-retirement jobs, 27,
29, 43, 60, 139, 151, 201,
202, 213, 226
coaches, consultants, and
trainers, 49, 60–61, 120–121,
152
interview training for, 176
leaders helping older workers
implement, 129
legality issues, 36–37, 220
loss of power associated with
some, 47–48
other names for, 43

traveling with spouse/significant
other (inducement to
continue working), 50–51

Turner Broadcasting System (TBS),
75

Turner Temps (Turner
Broadcasting System), 75

TVA, 184–185

U

UAW (United Auto Workers)
and General Motors, health
care costs, 14

U.S. government and retirement
management, 213–221

USA Today, 23–24

V

Verizon, 12, 13

W

Wal-Mart, 92

war for talent, 217
labor shortage fueling, 19, 20

Welch, Jack, 49

what older workers want in a job,
43–52
legality of incentives, 62–63
new responsibilities and
challenges, 47–49

work habits of older workers,
82–83

work history (job challenges)
and Success Profile, 150

Y

YourEncore™, Inc. (Procter &
Gamble, Eli Lilly, Boeing), 74